Successful Project Management

Successful Project Management

A Step-By-Step Approach With Practical Examples

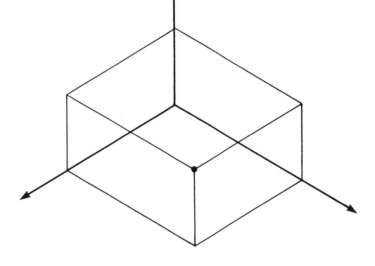

Milton D. Rosenau, Jr.

VNR VAN NOSTRAND REINHOLD
New York

Designer: Richard Kharibian
Content Editor: Sylvia Stein
Illustrator: John Foster

Printed in the United States of America

Published by Van Nostrand Reinhold
115 Fifth Avenue
New York, New York 10003

Van Nostrand Reinhold International Company Limited
11 New Fetter Lane
London EC4P 4EE, England

Van Nostrand Reinhold
480 La Trobe Street
Melbourne, Victoria 3000, Australia

Macmillan of Canada
Division of Canada Publishing Corporation
164 Commander Boulevard
Agincourt, Ontario M1S 3C7, Canada

10 9 8 7

Library of Congress Cataloging in Publication Data

Rosenau, Milton D. Jr.   1931–
  Successful project management.

  Includes bibliographies and index.
  1. Industrial project management. I. Title.
HD69.P75R67   658.4′04   80-24720
ISBN 0-534-97977-7

Preface

Who This Book Is For

This book is for you if you have been trained in a professional skill and now find yourself thrust into a position of project management, in which you've had very little or no direct experience. Now you must not only demonstrate your professional skill, but must also take responsibility for schedule and budget, using physical and human resources over which you may have little or no real control. You may be an engineer or scientist asked to take responsibility for a project; a computer programmer assigned lead responsibility on a computer system project; a civil engineer obliged to manage a construction project; or an office administrator charged with coordination of a facility relocation. No matter what your previous skill, if you're now responsible for getting something done by a specified date and with a limited budget, this book will help you grasp and master key practical skills for successful project management.

This Book's Approach to Project Management

While no treatment can or should make trivial a subject as complex as project management, this book is specifically designed to make it as simple as possible. SUCCESSFUL PROJECT MANAGEMENT provides a step-by-step approach which I have found effective in 25 years of industrial experience and in teaching hundreds of seminar students, working adults of all ages from a wide variety of industries. By taking you through the project management process in 18 steps, the book aims to equip you with detailed tools which you can immediately apply to your first (or next) project and which will help you overcome the pitfalls that typically bedevil the beginning project manager.

Useful and Unique Features of This Book

- While there are many books on single specialized aspects of project management (for instance, PERT and CPM) and several books on project management in specialized applications (for instance, the construction or aerospace industry), *this is the first book intended specifically for the beginner* who manages projects of any description.

- Each short chapter is devoted to a single topic and can be absorbed in one to three hours in the evening. Thus the entire book can be mastered in a single month of evening study, making it uniquely useful for the working adult.

- The book covers the subject matter chronologically, from a project's beginning to its end, and includes an *example project* which is developed step-by-step.

- Typical problems which may be encountered are highlighted in each chapter.

- Simple quiz material will allow you to test yourself on many important techniques, and an answer or discussion for each quiz is at the end of the book.

- Useful references in each chapter point you to other recent publications if you'd like to read more on any topic.

How This Book is Organized

The step-by-step approach divides the project management process into five phases, and emphasizes the importance of satisfying the three constraints of performance specifications, schedule and budgets. The following table summarizes how the subject matter is organized within this framework:

Chapter	Topic	Phase
1	The Concept of Project Management	
2	The Triple Constraint	
3	How To Acquire Winning Projects	Definition
4	Negotiations	
5	Planning—Why and How	
6	Planning the Performance Dimension	
7	Planning the Schedule Dimension	Planning
8	Planning the Cost Dimension	
9	Integrated Triple Constraint Planning	
10	Organizing the Project Team	
11	Organizing the Support Team	Implementation
12	The Role of the Project Manager	

Milton D. Rosenau, Jr.

Acknowledgments

In a sense, this book grew out of an invitation from the late Robert D. Gray to share my years of industrial experience with a group of undergraduate students at the Industrial Relations Center at California Institute of Technology. Over the next few years, that talk was followed by a series of management seminars there for working adults and more recently by a series of television lectures on project management broadcast over the University of Southern California's interactive television network. Network director Jack Munushian showed the notes for that television program to Lifetime Learning Publications, who agreed to publish this book. I am indebted to all these people.

I also wish to express my thanks to hundreds of seminar students, the various university and other sponsors of these seminars, some clients, and my many colleagues in industry who provided so many helpful suggestions and illustrative materials. I am also grateful to John and Yukiko Nichols of Nichols and Company and especially to Ward Speaker of Atlantic Software for providing computer printout examples illustrating some of the typical computer support programs available to the project manager.

It is a pleasure to acknowledge my deep appreciation to Kay Neves, who typed, retyped, and retyped still again the numerous drafts of this manuscript. Her efforts have been invariably cheerful and virtually faultless. Beyond this, she has made several constructive suggestions to clarify the material.

The editor, Sylvia E. Stein, has done an outstanding job of clarifying my material. She has found better, shorter, and more lucid ways to express much of what I wrote. I am sure that the readers of this book will benefit greatly because of her work. Whatever errors or confusion may still remain are obviously my responsibility.

Finally, my wife Ellen has read and critiqued much of the book in a most helpful and constructive way. Most important, she has been supportive of the time taken out of our lives together to permit this book to be written.

Contents

ABBREVIATIONS COMMONLY EMPLOYED
IN PROJECT MANAGEMENT

ACO	—	Administrative Contracting Officer
ACWP	—	Actual Cost of Work Performed
B & P	—	Bid and Proposal
BAC	—	Budget at Completion
BCWP	—	Budgeted Cost of Work Performed
BCWS	—	Budgeted Cost of Work Scheduled
CCDR	—	Contractor Cost Data Reporting
CCN	—	Contract Change Notice
CDR	—	Critical Design Review
CDRL	—	Contract Data Requirements List
CFE	—	Customer Furnished Equipment
CFSR	—	Contract Funds Status Report
CMO	—	Contract Management Office
CPFF	—	Cost Plus Fixed Fee
CPIF	—	Cost Plus Incentive Fee
CPM	—	Critical Path Method
C/SCSC	—	Cost/Schedule Control System Criteria
C/SSR	—	Cost/Schedule Status Report
CWBS	—	Contract Work Breakdown Structure
EAC	—	Estimate at Completion
ETC	—	Estimate to Complete
FFP	—	Firm Fixed Price
FP	—	Fixed Price
G & A	—	General and Administrative
GFE	—	Government Furnished Equipment
IR & D	—	Internal Research and Development
ODC	—	Other Direct Cost
PDR	—	Preliminary Design Review
PERT	—	Program Evaluation and Review Technique
PM	—	Project (or Program) Manager (or Management)
PO	—	Purchase Order
PR	—	Purchase Requisition
RFP	—	Request For Proposal
RFQ	—	Request For Quotation
SOW	—	Statement Of Work
T & M	—	Time and Material
WBS	—	Work Breakdown Structure
WO	—	Work Order

Successful Project Management

CHAPTER 1

The Concept of Project Management

This chapter differentiates project management from other managerial activity by examining how projects differ from other activities. It describes the process sequence that characterizes project management and discusses the requisite organizational arrangements for successful management.

Distinguishing Characteristics of Projects

Origin

Imagine you are a mechanical engineer and your boss has asked you to manage a materials study project. Or imagine you are a computer programmer who has been asked to set up a new financial report, a civil engineer asked to manage a construction project, or a facilities administrator asked to manage the relocation of a division into a new building. How would you go about it?

Before reading farther, consider this hypothetical situation. How does this activity differ from others in which you might engage? Is it similar to going to your work place each day? In what ways does it differ?

At this point, you probably want more information about the project. For instance, is it small or large? What do you mean by small or large—the quantity of materials to be studied, the deadline, or the budget? How does project magnitude alter your approach?

This hypothetical project illustrates some of the characteristics that distinguish projects from other activities. Projects originate because something not done before must be done. Although going to work on some mornings may seem to be a major undertaking, it is not usually considered a project. Going to work is an activity that repeats a prior activity, namely, going to work the day before. This aspect of the definition of a project is not clear-cut. If your project had been to build an amplifier circuit, at

Projects are one-of-a-kind undertakings that originate when something has to be done.

some point building a second or third or fourth amplifier circuit ceases to be a project and becomes a repetitive activity (for example, electronic assembly). As a general rule, if the amplifiers are different from one another, then each is a project. If each amplifier is virtually identical, we have a production line for amplifiers and are not engaged in a project per se.

Product

There are hardware and software projects.

There are many ways to characterize projects. "Hardware project" and "software project" are common terms, depending on whether the final result is a tangible product (hardware) or a report or some other form of documentation (software).

Thus, the product or end result of a project is a second characteristic. A project is not an ongoing activity but rather an undertaking that ends with a specified accomplishment. In the first hypothetical example, this would be the completion of the materials study project.

Marketplace

Projects can be categorized by their source or sponsorship, as shown in Table 1-1. If the customer is a governmental entity, there will probably be very formal procedures. If your company wishes to conduct a study of new materials for its own information, the process may be very informal.

For whom a project is done affects how it is done.

The nature of the competition is also important. The only materials laboratory in a region is in a favorable situation. A materials laboratory that is one of many in some small city is in a very different and less favorable competitive situation.

Once an organization or a project manager has successfully concluded a project, a company-sponsored software project, for instance, it will be

Table 1-1. Project Types.

Source	Project
Personal or family	Dig a ditch for roses Clean the garage Rake the leaves
Company sponsored—for the company itself	Set up a new computer Put a new plant into operation Commercialize a new product
Customer sponsored	Construct new shopping center Design and build mach 3 supersonic transport Produce pressure-sensitive postage stamps for the postal service
Government sponsored—done by a governmental entity	Issue new $1 coin Produce the surgeon general's report Redesign income tax forms

much easier to undertake a second project of that sort. Although there are similarities in managing all kinds of projects, successfully completing a company-sponsored software project is very different from successfully completing a customer-sponsored hardware project.

In general, projects are done by someone or some organization for someone else or for some other organization.

Project Size

"Program" is commonly used synonymously with "project." Thus, the expression "program management" is often used interchangeably with "project management." Some organizations use "task management" as well. Program management, project management, and task management are generally identical. But programs are usually larger than projects, and projects are usually larger than tasks. Thus, there is some connotation of size when terms other than project management are used. Nevertheless, the techniques and methodology are essentially the same, differing only in detail. I shall use "project" throughout the rest of this book.

The trans-Alaska pipeline and the manned lunar landing projects required many years and billions of dollars. The space shuttle project is also both long and very costly. Conversely, a computer programming project may be completed in a few hours or days. Hence, size or complexity does not distinguish a project from another activity. They do, however, affect project success.

Resources

Projects are accomplished by resources, namely, people and things. Many of the required resources are only marginally under the effective control of the project manager. For example, a required computer may be controlled by a data-processing group.

The project manager must organize these human and physical resources to deal with the constraints and emotional problems inherent in their use while trying to accomplish the project initiator's technical goals. I discuss organizational options and their influence on resource control and availability later in this chapter.

The Project Management Process

Projects require five steps, which may have some overlap.

Project management is a five-step process:

1. Define
2. Plan
3. Implement

4. Control

5. Complete

The first two steps are not necessarily separate and sequential except when the project initiator issues a firm, complete, and unambiguous statement of the desired project output, in which case the organization that will carry out the project may start to plan how to achieve it. It is more common to start with a proposed work definition, which is then jointly renegotiated after preliminary planning elucidates some consequences of the initially proposed work definition. In fact, the implementation phase often must be considered before planning can be finished. Similarly, as you will see in later chapters, replanning is almost always required, thus frequently causing some amendment to the negotiated definition.

Nevertheless, the five-step process covers each required action and is a useful conceptual sequence in which to consider project management. Thus, this book is organized according to it.

The Triple Constraint, an extremely important notion for project management, provides the defining parameters of a project. It consists of three dimensions:

1. performance specification

2. time or schedule

3. budget or money

Successful project management is the accomplishment of the performance specification (that is, objective or technical goals), on schedule, and within the budget.

All projects are defined and characterized by a Triple Constraint.

Quiz 1-1

What are the special characteristics of projects?

Organizational Forms

Projects have a finite life, from initiation to completion. Conversely, a company, government department, or other organization expects to exist indefinitely. This temporal difference makes it difficult to organize and manage a project within a larger organizational entity.

In addition, projects frequently require the part-time use of resources, whereas permanent organizations try to use resources full-time. Typical project requirements include the following: one hour of computer time each week; use of a backhoe next Tuesday for the afternoon; one-quarter of Jane Draftsperson's time this month and three-quarters of her time next month; use of Joe Technician full-time as soon as the project's circuit designer completes the design. No economically viable organization can afford to stockpile these resources to serve the project's needs instantly. Thus, it is important to organize for project work in adequately responsive ways, and it is important for project managers to recognize this is a compromise that is not fully responsive to project needs.

Organizational forms differ in response to projects.

There is a variety of ways companies or their divisions or governmental organizations can be organized and effectively manage projects. Some of the more common of these organizational forms are functional, project, matrix, venture, and task force.

Functional

Functional organizations (Figure 1-1) are common in companies dominated by marketing or manufacturing departments and exist in other kinds of companies as well. The person asked to manage a project in a company with functional organizations has generally been oriented and loyal to the functional group to which he or she belongs. Specialists are grouped by function, encouraging the sharing of experience and knowledge within the discipline. This favors a continuity and professional expertise in each functional area.

Because such an organization is dedicated to the existing functional organization, however, it can be difficult for a project to cross functional lines and obtain required resources. Absence of a project focal point may trouble a customer interested in understanding the project's status, and functional emphasis and loyalties may impede completion.

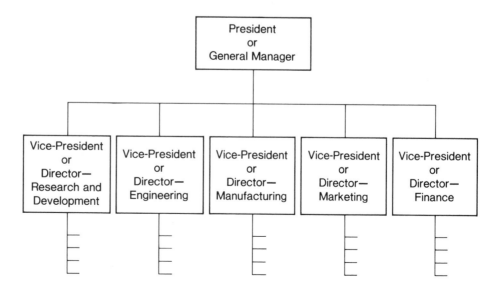

Figure 1-1. Typical organization chart of a functional organization.

Project

A project organization (Figure 1-2) emerges from a functional organization when the latter impedes project needs. The solution is to move many of the people working on the project from their functional group to the project manager. Line authority for the project is clearly designated, providing a single focal point for project management. All full-time personnel are formally assigned to the project, thus assuring continuity and expertise.

A major difficulty with this kind of organization is the uncertainty these people feel about where they will go when the project is completed. There is also a tendency to retain reassigned personnel too long. In addition, it is a rare project that has all the required resources assigned to it. Thus, such an organization still requires the project manager to negotiate with the remaining functional organization for much of the required support.

If the organization develops additional projects, managing them in this way leads to a splintering, with many separate project centers existing apart from the functional organization. Duplication of facilities and personnel can result. Managers within the functional organization may feel threatened as people are removed from their functional group. This produces another series of stressors. Project organization often inhibits the development of professional expertise in functional specialties and may not effectively utilize part-time assistance from them.

Matrix

The matrix organization (Figure 1-3) is a hybrid that may emerge in response to the pressures resulting from a functional or a project organization. It attempts to achieve the best of both worlds, recognizing the virtues of having functional groups but also recognizing the need to have a specific focal point and management function for each project. Line authority for the project is clearly designated, providing a single focal point. Specialists, including project managers, are grouped by function, encouraging the sharing of experience and knowledge within the discipline. This favors a continuity and professional expertise in each functional area. The matrix organization recognizes that both full-time and part-time assignment of personnel is required and simplifies allocation and shifting of project priorities in response to management needs.

The main drawback is matrix organization requires an extra management function, so it is usually too expensive for a small organization. It is even possible to have a matrix organization within a matrix organization (for example, the matrixed engineering department). In addition, the extra functional unit (that is, project management) can proliferate bureaucratic tendencies, and the balance of power between project management and functional units can exacerbate conflicts.

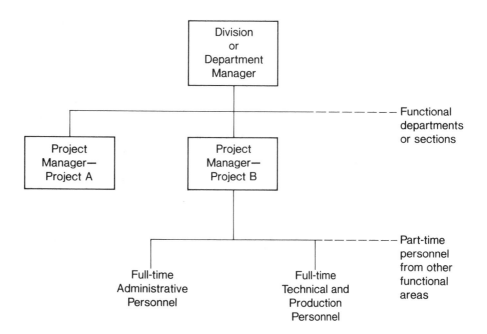

Figure 1-2. Typical organization chart of a project organization.

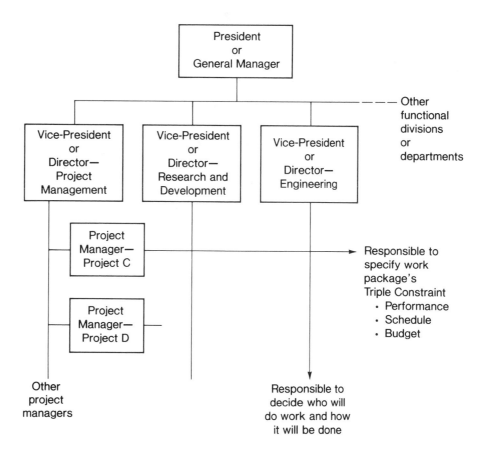

Figure 1-3. Typical organization chart of a matrix organization.

Venture

The venture organization, common in several very large commercially oriented companies, is especially appropriate for projects aimed at new product development. Basically, the goal is to set up a tiny functional organization within a giant corporation, thus achieving the advantages of compact size, flexibility, and the entrepreneurial spirit of the small company within and supported by the financial, physical, and human resources of the larger company. Where such a management organization exists, it is common to team up an engineer or researcher with a marketing person and a manufacturing person in the earliest phases of new product development. As the effort moves forward, the venture organization grows, ultimately becoming a functionally organized division within the parent company. Two practitioners of this managerial form are 3M and DuPont.

Task Force

Organizations frequently use a task force to cope with an unexpected project. Hence, this response is most commonly utilized by a functional organization because the other organizational forms are already able to deal with projects. A task force may be thought of as a rarely used one-project organization within the functional organization. It can be formed quickly, usually by a very senior officer.

Although the people selected to serve on the task force may be highly motivated by their selection, they frequently are not relieved of their usual duties and thus may not have sufficient time for the task force. If they are relieved of their normal duties, they may be anxious about their assignment when the task force has completed its job.

Although no organizational form is perfect, it is important to recognize the existence of projects when they are present. This means the organization must plan to accommodate this temporary disturbance and accept some disharmony.

Typical Problems

Failure to identify a project for what it truly is usually leads to missed specifications, late completion, and/or a budget overrun. The solution is to recognize there is a project when something must be done and then to organize to complete the project in the least disruptive way.

Materials Study Project

I shall use the project introduced here throughout the book to illustrate some of the issues discussed in each chapter. Imagine you are a mechanical engineer, Mel Chase, working for the Successful Project Management Company (SUPROMAC) (Figure 1-4). Your boss, Mike Miller, has asked you to act as project manager on a materials study project a customer (NERESCO or Need Results Corporation) wishes to have SUPROMAC perform. It is clear project management is going to be applicable.

Quiz 1-2

What organizational form are you going to be using?

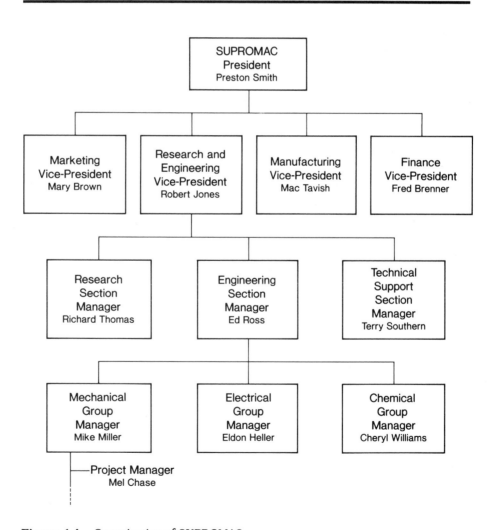

Figure 1-4.   Organization of SUPROMAC.

Highlights _____

- Projects are temporary undertakings with a specific objective that are accomplished by organized application of appropriate resources.
- Four distinguishing characteristics of projects are origin, product, marketplace, and resources.
- Size or complexity do not distinguish projects from other activities.
- Project management is the process of achieving project objectives in any organizational framework despite countervailing pressures.
- There are five steps to project management: definition, planning, implementation, control, and completion.
- The Triple Constraint defines a project: performance specification, time or schedule, and budget or money.
- Five common organizational forms for project management are functional, project, matrix, venture, and task force.

Further Reading _____

T. M. Adams. "Matrix Management—Panacea or Pandemonium?" *IEEE Engineering Management Review*, vol. 8, no. 1 (March 1980), pp. 55–64.) (Reprinted from *Personnel Psychology*, vol. 30, no. 1 [Spring 1977], pp. 55–64.)

This is a breezy article that compares functional, project, and matrix organization forms in terms of very practical issues.

R. D. Archibald. *Managing High-Technology Programs and Projects.* New York: Wiley-Interscience, 1976.

Chapter 2, section 3 is a good short discussion of the distinguishing characteristics of project management. Chapter 5, section 4 is a thorough discussion of organizational options with many examples.

S. M. Davis and P. R. Lawrence. "Problems of Matrix Organizations." *Harvard Business Review*, vol. 56, no. 3 (May–June 1978), pp. 131–142.

The article summarizes the main points in their book, providing a thorough treatment of the matrix form.

E. Jenett. "Guidelines for Successful Project Management." *Chemical Engineering* (July 9, 1973), pp. 70–82.

This is a really fine article with an excellent summary definition of projects. Although it treats the construction industry specifically, this is a valuable short article for all project managers.

H. E. Pywell. "Engineering Management in a Multiple- (Second- and Third-Level) Matrix Organization." *IEEE Transactions on Engineering Management*, vol. EM–26, no. 3 (August 1979), pp. 51–55.

This is a good discussion of matrix's value in large projects.

W. E. Souder. "Project Management: Past, Present, and Future—An Editorial Summary." *IEEE Transactions on Engineering Management*, vol. EM–26, no. 3 (August 1979), pp. 49–50.

This is an overview of matrix pros and cons.

R. Youker. "Organization Alternatives for Project Managers." *Management Review* (November 1977), pp. 46–53.

This is a succinct and graphic summary of organizational options.

Part ONE

Definition

2

The Triple Constraint

This chapter introduces the concept of the Triple Constraint as a project definition and identifies the obstacles to satisfying it. The consequences of various project outcomes are considered from the point of view of satisfying the Triple Constraint.

Obstacles to Satisfying the Triple Constraint

Three parameters, called the Triple Constraint, define projects: performance specification, time schedule, and money (or labor hour) budget.

Figure 2-1 illustrates the Triple Constraint, a very important notion I shall emphasize throughout the book. Successful project management means accomplishing the performance specification on or before the deadline and within the budgeted cost. Unfortunately, the Triple Constraint is very difficult to satisfy because most of what occurs during a project conspires to pull the performance below specification and to delay the project so it falls behind schedule, which makes it exceed the budget. The successful project manager is alert to these problems and satisfies the Triple Constraint.

Projects encounter a wide variety of problems. Some of the principal ones are enumerated in the following sections, organized by the dimension of the Triple Constraint most affected. Although Figure 2-1 shows these three dimensions to be orthogonal axes, hence mutually exclusive, project management is not that ideal. A late project, for example, will usually also overrun the budget. Thus, items listed as causes of time problems may also cause cost problems.

Performance Problems

There are many reasons the performance specification is difficult to achieve. I shall discuss three of them. First, there may have been poor communication between the contractor and the customer, that is, they have different perceptions of the specification or the wording is ambigu-

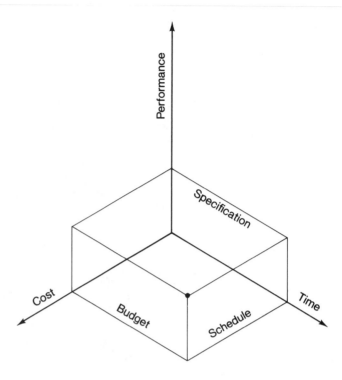

Figure 2-1.   The Triple Constraint.

It is essential to clarify unclear specifications.

ous. For instance, "gain" means different things to different people or in different contexts. To an engineer, it may mean amplification, to a thief, booty or spoil. An investor may define gain as increase in value. To a fencer, it may imply advancing the left heel toward the right heel.

A second problem arises because the contractor's or the customer's assumptions have been too optimistic. Their goals may have been too ambitious, which is not uncommon in advanced technology projects.

Third, the contractor may do a poor design job or make mistakes in executing contract performance. Unfortunately, workers (and managers) make errors occasionally, and these errors may cause a performance deficiency.

Time Problems

Schedule problems arise for several reasons, the most insidious being an overemphasis on the performance dimension at the expense of a balanced view of the Triple Constraint. For instance, scientists or engineers, who are commonly appointed project managers, tend to concentrate on the technology and to strive for technical innovations or breakthroughs. A computer programmer may emphasize work on a clever algorithm or use a new programming language rather than expeditiously completing the program with existing capabilities. Such striving is accomplished at the expense of the schedule, and it frequently has unfavorable cost repercussions. Even where a fascination with technology is not overwhelming, technically trained people tend to assume the performance specification is sacrosanct, whereas they consider it permissible to miss the schedule or budget objectives. Conversely, a customer might be satisfied to achieve 90 percent of the performance specification provided both the schedule and budget are met (for example, on a planetary exploration project, it is vital to be ready by the "launch window," a restricted range of dates, even if one of several instruments must be omitted).

A second source of difficulty in meeting the schedule arises because resources are not available when required. These resources may be either equipment (such as lathes or computer hours) or personnel (a well-qualified circuit designer, for example). This absence of planned resources forces the project manager to find substitutes, which may require a subcontract to get some programming work done or may mean using marginally qualified people who take longer to complete a circuit design than the well-qualified person previously assumed to be available.

Third, a project can get into schedule difficulty because those assigned to it are not interested in their tasks and choose to work on other things or work half-heartedly on the project.

The time schedule should change with the performance specification.

Fourth, schedule problems can arise because the performance specification is raised (increased efforts that lead to additional work are accepted). A common occurrence that illustrates this is a customer asking for a few extra control switches. The project manager may misperceive this as trivial because a control panel is already being provided. If he or she agrees to provide these extra switches, which were not part of the original proposal, the project manager is agreeing to do additional work without changing the schedule (or cost). There is, however, additional work called for to put in the switches, and it does not take many changes of this sort first to produce a one-day schedule slippage and then a one-week schedule slippage and so on until the project is in serious schedule difficulty.

Cost Problems

Cost problems arise for many reasons. When a project is in trouble on its time dimension, it will often be in trouble on its cost dimension as well because resources are not being used as efficiently as planned.

Do not "buy in" without a "get well" plan or a performance reduction.

A second cause is the "liars contest" that often occurs during contract negotiation. Imagine you have bid $10,000,000 to build a shopping center. During negotiations you were told that unless your price is lowered to $9,500,000, the contract will be awarded to another company. In your desire to obtain the work, you and your management agree to minor wording changes, which appear to reduce the scope of work a bit and permit you to justify a substantial cost reduction. When you make this kind of price reduction without fundamental work reductions, you have built in a cost overrun at the very beginning of the project. A professional, experienced project manager will never agree to this kind of negotiation unless he or she knows the money will be restored later in contract changes. This is a potential cost problem for which the less experienced project manager must be very alert.

A third source of cost difficulties arises because many of the initial cost estimates are simply too optimistic. They do not reflect the inefficiencies that will occur in scheduling resources to perform the work or the fact that less well qualified people may be assigned to do the work.

Occasionally, mistakes are made in the cost estimating. Like design mistakes, these are unfortunate, and careful scrutiny and review can minimize this occurrence.

A fifth reason for cost problems is simply an inadequate cost consciousness on the part of project management or a failure to have an adequate cost management system. This is never excusable.

Sixth, funding may not occur according to plan, and this may produce problems. Suppose your project is to run for three months and the customer originally proposes to fund you with $100,000 per month (that is, provide progress payments). The first month has gone according to plan and you have received your $100,000. At the start of the second month, your customer informs you they have only $50,000 available for that month but they will have $150,000 available the third month. You will still get $300,000, but you cannot apply the planned resources during the second month and must rush to catch up during the final month. Obviously, this would be a less efficient way to operate and means your costs will be higher than originally planned. When confronted with this sort of refunding proposal by a customer, therefore, the prudent project manager will insist on a budget increase if the performance specification and schedule are not to be changed.

Funding is required per plan.

Project Outcomes

A project may end anywhere in the three-dimensional space illustrated by the Triple Constraint. Whether a deviation from the Triple Constraint point is acceptable depends on the project. For example, a project might be late. If the project is to construct the grandstands for the presidential inauguration on January 20, lateness would be an intolerable outcome, regardless of grandstand quality or cost. As suggested earlier, schedule compliance is also the overriding concern for planetary launch projects, in which there is a restricted range of dates when the payload can be launched.

Project specifics determine the relative importance of each dimension of the Triple Constraint.

In other situations, the budget may be the most important issue. When a contractor accepts a fixed price contract to deliver a working piece of hardware, he or she will lose money if the budget is overrun. Conversely, on a cost reimbursable contract, the customer must pay for the overrun. In either situation, ability to pay is crucial.

Third, there are situations in which the performance specification may not be missed. Once again, the project specifics will determine whether this is crucial. In the early 1960s, before spacecraft could carry large instruments, the Stratoscope II project was undertaken. The goal was to carry a large telescope by balloon to twenty-five thousand meters, where it would be above almost all the earth's atmosphere, permitting the optical resolution of fine detail in distant nebulae. To accomplish this goal, the telescope's primary mirror had to be virtually perfect. Because the project could succeed only with such a mirror, there was no point in flying the balloon-borne telescope until this performance specification had been met. This required both more time than the original schedule and more money than the original budget.

Quiz 2-1

Why is the concept of the Triple Constraint important for project management?

Typical Problems

The project initiator's emphasis is almost always unclear initially, and project personnel tend to assume their own biases in ranking the relative importance of each dimension. This can easily lead to a disastrous outcome, which can be avoided by adequate discussions between the customer and the contractor at the project's inception.

The other major problem, mentioned earlier, is the myopic attention to the performance dimension by technical personnel. It can be overcome, or at least reduced, if the project manager clearly conveys the customer's emphasis and its rationale.

Materials Study Project

In discussions within SUPROMAC about the NERESCO materials study project, you realize there are easily half a dozen materials that might be relevant to their needs and that you might therefore reasonably examine. You feel this will require about one year and cost $1,000,000.

Discussions with NERESCO reveal they require the study results in six months and their budget cannot exceed $500,000.

Quiz 2-2

As Mel Chase at SUPROMAC, what might you do in this situation?

Highlights

- The Triple Constraint defines all projects.

- The Triple Constraint consists of performance specification, a time schedule, and a money or labor hour budget.

- Obstacles that prevent satisfying the Triple Constraint are not mutually exclusive.

- Project specifics determine the relative importance of each dimension of the Triple Constraint.

- Adequate and clear discussions among the customer, the project manager, and the technical personnel can help avoid many common problems.

Further Reading

R. D. Archibald. *Managing High-Technology Programs and Projects.* New York: Wiley-Interscience, 1976.

Chapter 1, section 5 has a brief discussion of some causes of poor project outcomes.

V. G. Hajek. *Management of Engineering Projects.* New York: McGraw-Hill, 1977.

Chapter 1, section 1 has a short discussion of some disciplines and functions needed to be successful with projects.

H. Kerzner. *Project Management: A Systems Approach to Planning, Scheduling and Controlling.* New York: Van Nostrand Reinhold, 1979.

Chapter 1, section 1 enumerates the social and environmental issues impacting project success.

CHAPTER 3

Acquiring Winning Projects

Proposals bridge the defining and planning phases of projects. This chapter examines the strategic issues that govern writing successful proposals. Project proposals constitute the definition embodied in the contract or work authorization. A good proposal includes a thorough plan for work performance that embodies the Triple Constraint. This chapter also discusses the proposal process in detail.

Strategic Issues

Framework

Figure 3-1 illustrates the strategic framework for obtaining winning projects. It does not matter whether the projects originate outside the organization by a customer or within the organization. However, many organizations dissipate their energies in preparing losing proposals, which

1. cannot win the competition

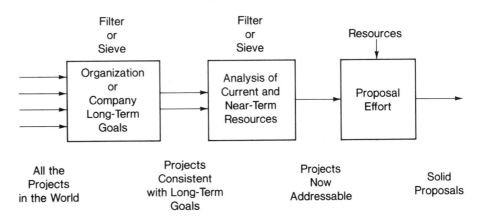

Figure 3-1. Strategy to obtain winning projects.

2. will have an unfavorable outcome with regard to the Triple Constraint

3. can be successful but are insignificant or irrelevant to the proposing organization

Concentrate on meaningful prospective winners.

Therefore, the basis of a successful strategy is to filter out losing projects. These include projects inconsistent with the organization's long-term goals or with the current and near-term resources within or otherwise available to the organization. Such filters might reject consumer project efforts in an industrial product company. Similarly, the filters could reject a fixed price contract for a technological development in a conservative company that will not normally undertake a fixed price contract for something not previously accomplished.

Filtering out the huge number of possible projects the organization might have addressed leaves a much smaller number of projects that are appropriate for the organization to consider. It can then address some of or perhaps all of these in proposal efforts to which it applies adequate and appropriate resources. The result of this process is an organization submits only very well founded proposals for consideration. This result is most likely to be achieved if the organization has a careful review process, often called the "bid/no bid" decision.

Bid/No Bid Decisions

Clear criteria are vital.

The decision whether to bid on a proposal opportunity, whether to an external organization or within the organization itself, must be taken within the context of the organization's strategic framework. This framework is of course specific to the organization at that particular time. The company that rejects consumer product projects today may have the interest and capability to undertake these projects five years from now. There are many issues involved in this decision, four of which I discuss.

The requirement.   The first issue is whether there is a real requirement. If a requirement exists, it is important to decide whether the funds are really available. It is possible there is a real requirement but no funds. For instance, many isolated rural villages in undeveloped nations could use an electric power generation system, but these villages and the nations of which they are a part cannot afford to pay for their installation. Contractors occasionally seek subcontractor proposals for "window dressing" to satisfy someone or otherwise justify an alternative approach they propose to take. Clearly, it is not worth responding to such requests for a proposal because the effort will not result in a winning project.

It is also important to examine the priority or importance of the proposed project. In this connection, the relationship of a particular proposal opportunity to present and future programs is also an important issue. Many small "paper study" projects, not attractive per se, actually are very attractive because they can lead in the future to large production programs.

Project value.   The project's social, ecological, and energy impacts might be highly significant to an organization in deciding whether or not to bid on a project. Presumably, a project to build the prototype of a device to clean up oil spills economically would be more attractive than a project to build a road through the last habitat of some endangered species. Similarly, a project that offers the opportunity to apply important new technology or otherwise enhance the organization's reputation might have high nonmonetary value. Conversely, the expected sales of a commercial new product project effort and the profits of such an effort would also be significant issues.

Finally, many projects are merely a hidden obligation for an organization to accept future financial commitments for new capital or facility investments. This must be discovered before any money is spent so as to be certain future major financial commitments are within the organization's resources and ability as well as being consistent with the project's prospective value.

The organization must have the ability.

Response ability.   The central issue here, also illustrated in Figure 3-1, is the organization's present capability first to prepare a winning proposal and second to perform the proposed work. If some capabilities are not actually present, there must be a viable plan to make them available when they are needed.

Winning the competition.   First an organization must ask whether there was advance information about the project available to it. This is particularly true about efforts arising from a customer organization and being presented to a contracting company as a request for a proposal (RFP), but it is also relevant for efforts within an organization. Lack of advance information often indicates someone else has a head start or the request was hastily created and lacks substance.

A second issue concerns the customer. Is it an individual (yourself, a friend, or someone else) or a commercial organization? If the latter, is it your organization or an external organization? If it is your own company, has your superior ordered you to carry out the project or must your project proposal compete with other project proposals management is considering for funding? If the customer is a governmental organization, a city, county, state, or federal (domestic or foreign) entity, there will probably be detailed specifications, formal quality standards, perhaps the necessity for surety bonds, and very often rigid and formalized inspection procedures. Who are the key personnel within the customer organization? Are they known to your organization? What history do you have with them or with their organization? Is your organization's reputation with the prospective customer favorable?

Your organization must have enough money to write the proposal and to sustain the postproposal selling and negotiating efforts. Therefore, you must know whether money to invest in this kind of activity is available. You must expect the project to earn more money than the proposal costs because you will not win every job on which you propose.

There are situations in which you will be the sole source recipient of an RFP, for instance, when your boss tells you to carry out a project within your organization. There is thus no competition, but how you perform the job is still important. It may be better to decline an effort when it is offered sole source if you are convinced the performance you can provide will be at best marginal.

Although you will not win every proposal, you must be willing and able to satisfy any commitments you propose to undertake.

All competition has to be analyzed. Some relevant issues are the competition's technical and managerial competence, its ability to produce the requested project output, an estimate of its interest in the particular type of project, its need (or degree of "hunger"), and its prior relationships with the customer or organization.

Quiz 3-1

What types of prospective projects should you avoid?

The Proposal Process _____

The proposal process entails more than writing the proposal. It includes the following:

1. authorization (which formally considers the issues previously discussed)

2. selection of a dominant theme

3. preparation of the statement of work

4. development of a plan to satisfy the Triple Constraint (an effort for which checklists may be helpful)

5. adjustment to remove inconsistencies and inadequacies

6. approval

7. submission

8. postsubmission follow-up, including presentations and contract negotiations

Authorization

The proposal process frequently starts before an RFP, in which case the effort is frequently called the preproposal effort. Regardless of when the proposal process is initiated, this activity must be authorized. A form such as that in Figure 3-2 can be used for this purpose. In preparing a proposal, an organization is going to commit a certain amount of effort and money to it. This investment should be made only when it seems the opportunity then available has a good chance of paying off and only if it is consistent with the organization's goals.

Consider, then begin.

Another point to consider at the time of proposal authorization is the individual who will manage it. Ideally, the proposal manager should be the intended project manager.

A proposal itself can be considered a project with a Triple Constraint, in which case the performance objective is submission of a winning proposal and price, in accordance with the required submission schedule, for a cost acceptable in view of the probable (financial) return to your organization.

Theme Fixation

Except in those very formal RFPs in which contact with the prospective customer is either prohibited or heavily constrained (for instance, some government RFPs), it is vital to spend time with your customer fixing the theme and central focus of your proposal effort. This includes clarifying which dimension(s) of the Triple Constraint should be emphasized.

There are several reasons theme fixation is important. In the first place, many customers are in fact organizations and "the customer" is comprised of people who view the contemplated undertaking in slightly different ways. It is necessary to understand these subtle differences and either harmonize them or deduce who has the most influence.

Decide what to emphasize.

In addition, the customer's statement of the problem in the RFP may be imperfect or incomplete. Working with the customer can correct this problem as well as demonstrate your organization's competence. In the course of this dialogue with your customer, you will have opportunities to launch trial balloons representing your initial approach to the proposal. You will learn your customer's preferences, which will permit you to adjust your thinking to produce a proposal more responsive to your customer's prejudices and predilections.

It is also important that everybody in your organization understands the chosen theme so their contributions are consistent with it. This theme will be used throughout your written proposal. It might be technical sophistication and elegance, early delivery, the fact that the unit you propose to furnish is a proven item, or that you have a team ready to put to work on the job. If everyone in your organization understands what the theme is, your proposal should be acceptable to your prospective customer.

PROPOSAL AUTHORIZATION	NUMBER	REVISION
TITLE		

	PERFORMANCE REQUIRED		
JOB	ESTIMATED STARTING DATE	ESTIMATED DURATION	
	ESTIMATED BID PRICE	ESTIMATED SUBCONTRACT TO OTHERS $ %	
	IS JOB FUNDED?	WHAT IS FOLLOW-ON POTENTIAL?	
	ESTIMATED NEED FOR CAPITAL AND FACILITY EXPENSE IF JOB IS OBTAINED		
	CUSTOMER ORGANIZATION		
	KEY CUSTOMER PERSONNEL		
	CONTRACT FORM	SPECIAL CONSIDERATIONS	SECURITY CLASS

COMPETITION	COMPETITORS
	COMPETITORS' STRENGTHS
	SIGNIFICANCE TO COMPETITORS IF THEY LOSE
	OTHER COMPETITOR WORK FOR CUSTOMER
	OUR UNIQUE ADVANTAGES

PROPOSAL

WHAT IS TO BE SUBMITTED?

DUE DATE	PROPOSAL COST (DETAIL BELOW)
PROPOSAL MANAGER	OTHER KEY PROPOSAL PERSONNEL

ACTIVITY \ EFFORT	PROJECT DEPT. (HOURS)	SUPPORT GROUP A (HOURS)	SUPPORT GROUP B (HOURS)	SUPPORT GROUP C (HOURS)	NONLABOR (DOLLARS)
PREPROPOSAL					
BIDDERS' CONFERENCE					
PROPOSAL PREPARATION					
CUSTOMER PRESENTATION					
CONTRACT NEGOTIATION					
OTHER					
TOTAL HOURS					X
TOTAL COST					

FUNDING NEEDED	JAN	FEB	MAR	APR	MAY	JUN	JUL	AUG	SEP	OCT	NOV	DEC
MONTHLY												
CUMULATIVE												

APPROVALS GROUP A DATE	MARKETING MANAGER DATE	VICE-PRESIDENT—FIN. DATE
GROUP B DATE	DIVISION CONTROLLER DATE	EXEC. VICE-PRESIDENT DATE
GROUP C DATE	DIVISION MANAGER DATE	PRESIDENT DATE
PROPOSAL MANAGER DATE	VICE-PRESIDENT—OPERAT. DATE	CHAIRPERSON OF BOARD DATE

Figure 3-2. Typical proposal authorization form.

Statement of Work

Content.   The statement of work (SOW) must describe the job to be done. It should designate any specifications that will be applied. It should identify measurable, tangible, and verifiable acceptance criteria so there is no uncertainty whether the final item is in fact acceptable.

When it is not possible to be this precise at the earliest phase of a job, because the final product is not assuredly realistic or clearly attainable, it is important to undertake a two-phase project effort. The first phase, perhaps extending to a customer review, is quoted completely, but the whole job is quoted only approximately, in a nonbinding fashion. The whole job quote represents the proposer's best estimate of project requirements. The first-phase quotation, however, is firm and includes sufficient effort to construct acceptance criteria for the rest of the job.

Make the SOW precise and measurable.

Clarification.   After it is drafted, the SOW should be reviewed with the customer prior to further work on the proposal itself. Ambiguous words should be avoided and it is desirable to be quantitative, using numbers and dimensions whenever possible.

A SOW such as "explore the continental shelf for oil" can be ambiguous. The contractor might interpret it as being satisfied by drilling one test well. The customer might expect a series of test wells to be drilled to a depth of ten thousand meters every two hundred meters over an area of many hectares.

Plan

A proposal is a bridging step in the overall project process, being involved in both the "define" and "plan" phases of a project. The proposal will contain a plan; additionally, the act of writing the proposal forces the organization to think through and attempt to simulate the entire project.

Simulation.   Simulation is used in many situations. Servomechanism engineers, for instance, will simulate on paper, and perhaps further using a digital or analog computer, the performance of a servomechanism before attempting to build even the breadboard. In doing this simulation, they are investigating how the servomechanism might perform if it is built according to certain specifications.

Simulation aids prediction.

Mechanical engineers will often examine the deformation of a building or a bridge to determine if it will have adequate strength if built according to the design drawings. Similar simulations occur in many other fields, such as aerodynamics, thermodynamics, and optical design. A major purpose of these simulations is to identify any potential problem areas in the prospective system before building it.

In the case of project planning, where the project plans are a simulation of how the project will be carried out, there are similar reasons for engaging in simulation. It is important to decide how to establish a price for the proposed work. A detailed simulation, that is, a plan, makes it more likely the price will be sufficient. If the plan has been thoroughly prepared, it will also convince the customer your organization understands the proposed job, which helps in negotiating your contract.

The Triple Constraint.   Because the Triple Constraint is so important to planning and planning is so important to the proposal process, Part Two is devoted to planning. But it is important to understand that the project plan devised during the proposal process and presented in the proposal is a plan to satisfy the Triple Constraint. You use the work breakdown structure (WBS) to describe your approach to the performance dimension. You use network diagram or in some cases a bar chart, in which each activity corresponds to a WBS element, to describe your approach to the time dimension. You use a complete cost breakdown for each activity to describe your approach to the money dimension and defend your price.

The plan has three dimensions.

These three planning elements are prepared in the order presented. First, the WBS is used to describe those things that will be undertaken to satisfy the performance specification. After that is complete, it is possible to prepare a network diagram for each of these designated elements in the WBS. Initially, each of these items should be estimated in a "natural" time frame; then these activities' logical relationship to each other can be established. If, as usually happens, this produces an unacceptably long program, it is then important to decide which activities will be scheduled to be completed in periods shorter than the "natural" time. That is, some of the project activities must be carried out faster than is desirable. After this has been done, prepare cost estimates for each activity. Note it is not desirable to prepare the cost estimates prior to determining the time to be allowed for a given activity. These issues will be treated in more detail in later chapters.

Checklists.   Checklists are designed to help assure nothing that will have to be dealt with during the course of the job has been forgotten or omitted from consideration in the proposal. A checklist should contain such items as design, prototype, assembly, test, shipment, consultants, computer time, equipment, leases, documentation, facility, supplies, travel, shift or overtime premium payments, and training aids. This list is not exhaustive and may not contain the most significant or most important items. It is meant to suggest the kind of items that might appear in a checklist.

Take advantage of experience.

The best way to develop a checklist is to create your own over a period of years. One way is simply to enter items on file cards whenever they occur to you during the course of project work. You may later sort out these cards alphabetically, by time phase, or by some other logical method. Having developed a checklist from your own experience, you will perform better on future projects because you will not forget items likely to be significant. Thus, you will consider their impact on a project during the proposal phase. They will not emerge as unexpected developments during performance of the project.

Quiz 3-2

Write down at least two dozen items to consider in preparing a proposal or planning a project.

Adjustments

Adjustments are often required after a proposal has been partially prepared. Perhaps someone discovers two departments contributing to the proposal have duplicated their efforts or have made differing assumptions about some significant item. Or perhaps someone discovers new information or corrects some oversight.

When an adjustment is required, all participants must join in deciding how to make it. The proposal manager should not assume this responsibility. Two benefits accrue from participants making the adjustment. First, the experts are considering the problem and presumably making the most sensible adjustment. Second, having contributed to the adjustment, other participants gain a sense of involvement in the decision and tend to perform the job better when the proposal has been converted into a project undertaking.

Approval

As with the initiation of the proposal effort, the conclusion of the proposal requires a managerial action within an organization. There will typically be a sign-off control sheet (Figure 3-3). Normally, each organization has a procedure that specifies the signature authority of given managerial levels, and such a procedure indicates which managers or officers must sign the control sheet signifying their approval for proposal submission. The sign-off control sheet must contain a brief description of the Triple Constraint contained in the proposal document being submitted. The sign-off control sheet is retained in the proposing organization's files and is not submitted to the customer.

Plan ahead for proposal approval.

It is important not to take the approval of senior managers for granted. Therefore, it is important to give these people timely briefings throughout the proposal preparation effort as to the scope of the proposal and the nature of the resources to be committed to the resulting project.

PROPOSAL SUBMISSION APPROVAL		COMPANY PRIVATE	
PROPOSAL TITLE		NUMBER	
CUSTOMER		CONTRACT FORM	
SUMMARY STATEMENT OF WORK			
SCHEDULE FOR JOB			
COST	FEE	TOTAL BID PRICE	
DOCUMENTS, REPORTS, MODELS, ETC., SUBMITTED			
SUMMARY OF OUR RISKS			
KEY PEOPLE PROMISED			
FINANCIAL COMMIITMENTS REQUIRED			
WARRANTY			
ACCEPTANCE CRITERIA			
REMARKS			
MARKETING MANAGER	DATE	VICE-PRESIDENT—FIN.	DATE
DIVISION CONTROLLER	DATE	EXEC. VICE-PRESIDENT	DATE
DIVISION MANAGER	DATE	PRESIDENT	DATE
VICE-PRESIDENT—OPERAT.	DATE	CHAIRPERSON	DATE

Figure 3-3.   Typical proposal submission approval form.

Although the proposal authorization document constitutes one such involvement of senior management, it alone will not suffice. The number and frequency of such briefings during proposal preparation depend on the organization, its rules and procedures, and the proposal manager's good judgment.

Submission

The time comes to submit the proposal to the designated recipient, who may require it bear a postmark by a certain date or be received at a given office and date stamped by a particular time. Such time standards are overriding and must be complied with.

Postsubmission

More work follows submission.

Mailing or delivering the proposal is not the end of a winning proposal effort. At the very least, the winning organization must negotiate a contract with the customer. Sometimes several proposing organizations are deemed qualified and negotiations are carried out with two or more of them prior to selecting the winning contractor.

In many proposal situations, the negotiation phase is preceded by a presentation to the customer. Such a presentation may be elaborate, requiring special graphics and models, and may entail extensive time and effort.

Quiz 3-3

(A) List the steps in the proposal process.
(B) Why does a proposal fit both the definition and planning phases of the project management process?

Typical Problems

The first problem encountered in proposing winning projects is attempting to do virtually the entire job during the proposal. That is, in trying to prepare a solid proposal, you spend too much time working through the plan for the project. You can overcome this by recognizing that risk must be balanced and planning only enough to reduce the project's uncertainty to an acceptable level. A related problem is inadequate project planning in the proposal. The solution here is to keep planning until it becomes too time-consuming. This is obviously a judgmental issue for which personal experience must provide guidance. Another problem is the last minute rush to complete the proposal in time to submit it. The solution to this problem is to have a schedule and adhere to it.

Materials Study Project

After being approached by NERESCO, you reviewed their project with SUPROMAC management. SUPROMAC has done prior work for NERESCO and the materials study project is deemed a lead to a still larger effort, so SUPROMAC is anxious to propose on the work, and a proposal is authorized. Your discussions with NERESCO about different initial perceptions of the desired Triple Constraint have led to an agreement to study only two materials, thus conforming to their wish for a six-month project and staying within their budget of $500,000. You have also agreed on which two materials will be studied. But they want a theoretical study included to reduce the risk resulting from omitting the study of the other four materials you felt should be studied.

Thus, you can now write the proposal. The SOW will name the two materials, the specific tests to be performed, and the kind and amount of data to be delivered. It will also contain a detailed schedule of work and cost breakdown.

Highlights

- Organizations must filter out losing projects.
- Winning projects arise from good proposals, thoughtfully initiated to be consistent with the organization's goals.
- Four issues involved in the decision to bid on a proposal opportunity are the nature of the requirement, the value of the project, the organization's response ability, and its ability to win.
- The proposal defines what the project will accomplish.
- The proposal process includes authorization, theme selection, SOW preparation, plan development, adjustment, approval, submission, and postsubmission follow-up.
- Project proposals describe the Triple Constraint with a work breakdown structure, activity network diagram or bar chart, and cost estimate for each activity, which then serve as a project plan.

Further Reading

V. G. Hajek. *Management of Engineering Projects.* New York: McGraw-Hill, 1977.

Chapter 4 contains a good description of the content of a proposal for an aerospace system project.

H. Kerzner. *Project Management: A Systems Approach to Planning, Scheduling and Controlling.* New York: Van Nostrand Reinhold, 1979.

This shows a typical proposal preparation and submission schedule on page 375 but has very little discussion.

Negotiations and Contracts

Negotiations between the customer and the contractor convert the final definition of work into a contract. This chapter emphasizes the importance of appropriate contract forms and the necessity to start the proposal process with attention to this issue. It also discusses the special case of projects involving a foreign customer.

Negotiating the Contract

Preproposal Negotiations

Make a proposal only if a contract seems possible.

Contract negotiation really begins in the preproposal phase because the expected contract form must be consistent with the job to be undertaken. If there is any reason to believe the customer will require a fixed price contract (Table 4-1), for instance, and the job calls for a major technological advance you are not certain you can achieve, it would not be prudent to continue in the preproposal and proposal effort. Hence, one objective of preproposal activity and discussions with a customer prior to major proposal expense is to assure the contract form they intend to issue is consistent with the contract form your company or organization is willing to negotiate considering the work to be undertaken. In addition, negotiations are designed further to improve the likelihood of the customer organization and contracting organization having the same perception of the job.

Customer and Contractor Perceptions

The perceptions of both contracting parties must be harmonious. It is always possible an RFP or the responding proposal will not be completely clear. If the preproposal process did not remove these potential mispercep-

Table 4-1. Common Contractual Forms.

Abbreviation	Definition
FFP	Firm fixed price—the price and fee are predetermined and do not depend on cost
FP	Fixed price—same as FFP
CPFF	Cost plus fixed fee—the customer agrees to reimburse the contractor's actual costs, regardless of amount, and pay a negotiated fixed fee independent of the actual costs
CPIF	Cost plus incentive fee—similar to CPFF except the fee is not preset or fixed but rather depends on some specified incentive
T AND M	Time and material—the customer agrees to pay the contractor for all time and material used on the project, including a fee as a percentage of all project costs

tions, the negotiation process offers the last opportunity to do so. Specifically, the final deliverables—software and/or hardware—must be well defined, and the criteria for measuring or judging acceptance and completion must be straightforward.

Contractual Forms

The contract form puts risk on either the customer or contractor.

At the simplest level, there are no contracts. This is typical of self-financed efforts such as a project to paint your own house. This situation also prevails in efforts supported by your own organization, such as a commercial new product development effort within a company.

When one organization enters into a contract with another organization, there is a variety of possible contractual forms (see Table 4-1). In the first of these, very common in commercial situations, the contract is a so-called fixed price (FP) or firm fixed price (FFP) contract. This has the lowest financial risk to the customer because the maximum financial obligation is specified; conversely, the FP form has the highest financial risk for the contracting organization but offers the highest potential reward if the estimated costs can be underrun. There are variations on this in which the price allows for escalation or redetermination due to some set of factors, such as inflation. Or there may be an FP contract with an incentive fee based on some performance aspect, perhaps early delivery.

Another class of contractual arrangements is those in some way cost reimbursable. Here the customer bears an obligation to reimburse the contractor for all costs incurred so the customer has a high financial risk and the contractor has a correspondingly low risk. Typical contracts of this sort are cost plus a fixed fee (CPFF) or cost plus an incentive fee (CPIF). Time and material (T and M) contracts are also a form of cost reimbursable contract.

Contracts entered into with the U.S. Department of Defense are governed by complex regulations. In the case of FP contracts, the government is never obligated to pay more than the specified amount. However, if the contractor performs very well and manages to underrun the cost budget substantially, the government has the right to reduce the amount paid to the contractor below the price specified in the contract. Thus, FP contracts are a one-way street to the government's advantage.

Quiz 4-1

Under what conditions would you prefer to use an FP contract?

Negotiations

Expect the negotiated contract price to be less than your proposed price.

In a typical negotiation, the customer attempts to increase the performance specification while reducing the schedule and budgeted cost. If it is a competitive solicitation, the customer will often play off one prospective contractor against another to try to maximize his or her apparent benefit. Therefore, one should expect the customer to behave in this way.

In addition, negotiators should understand clearly how far, if at all, their management is prepared to deviate from the terms and conditions offered in the submitted proposal it approved. Second, good planning aids negotiators in that there is a complete work breakdown structure, with an attendant activity schedule and cost estimate for each element of it. These help negotiators understand the job being negotiated and can usually help explain and/or defend it to the prospective customer.

In preparing for negotiations, it is frequently desirable for your organization to conduct a trial run with someone playing the customer. In short, be well prepared and know your minimum acceptable position. Also, because only one negotiating team member should talk at once, you can rehearse who will respond to particular issues if they are raised.

During actual negotiations, it is usually to your advantage first to define the job (the detailed statement of work, specifications, and test criteria) and the schedule. After that, you can negotiate the exact contract form, including any detailed terms and conditions, and the final price. The effective negotiator always "horse trades" and never makes a unilateral concession.

A negotiated change in one dimension of the Triple Constraint should be accompanied by a change in another dimension to compensate.

Nevertheless, there is often give and take in the negotiation process, and some changes may be agreed to. Whenever there is a change in one element of the Triple Constraint, there must be changes in other elements. For instance, a customer may offer to provide customer furnished equipment (CFE) to reduce the expected cost of some activity within the proposed project. In the case of the government, this is called government furnished equipment (GFE). When this occurs, language on the performance axis must be changed to indicate the performance specifications the CFE must meet and the schedule of CFE provision must be stipulated. When both these things have been accomplished, it is possible to agree to substitute the CFE for contractor procured items and offer a reduction in the proposed schedule or budget.

When the negotiations are concluded, the binding direction on the project is that specified in the contract. Only contract change notices suitably signed and agreed to by both parties can permit changes. Such changes should not occur outside the contracting mechanism, despite agreements reached by members of the contractor's and customer's support team, for instance, when two electronic engineers meet and agree that a new microcircuit would be a desirable item to include. Verbal redirection, which can easily occur because of the many individuals involved, is not binding until the contract is amended, as shown in Figure 4-1. Renegotiations such as these require the same amount of planning and preparation as the original negotiations. It is not uncommon to have several renegotiations during a long or complex project.

Quiz 4-2

How does the Triple Constraint enter into negotiations?

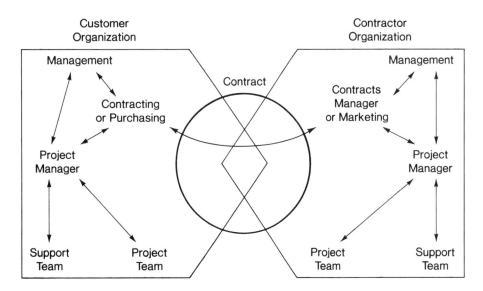

Figure 4-1. Interpretation of the Triple Constraint must be controlled through the contract.

Legal Aspects

There are a myriad of legal aspects in project contracts. This is not a law book and can merely suggest some of the issues that should be understood. Discussions with suitable people in your organization are often helpful.

In the case of U.S. government contracts, there is a host of special regulations. A typical government contract will include the following:

1. customer's name and address ⎱
2. contractor's name and address ⎰ authorized signatures
3. statement of supplies (items), services, and prices
4. description or specification of what is required (statement of work)
5. preservation, packaging, and packing instructions
6. delivery or performance period
7. inspection and acceptance terms
8. special provisions (funding limitations or customer furnished equipment)
9. contract administration data
10. general provisions (reference to armed services procurement regulations or overtime payment terms)
11. list of required documentation

Misrepresentation of costs is illegal and can produce serious consequences. In addition, in the case of fixed price contracts, failure to deliver can expose the contractor to very serious cost penalties far beyond absorbing the cost of his or her own effort. Such penalties may not only include termination but may obligate you to pay the costs of a substitute the government hires to deliver after you are in default.

Understand the legal implications.

If any patents are obtained in the course of the program, the government may own them. In addition, there are frequently highly proscribed procedures specifying how many of the actions throughout the project must be performed. Costs are frequently subject to audit when the job is completed, and the amount finally paid to the contractor is frequently reduced.

In the case of commercial contracts, restrictions are far less one-sided. Force majeure may permit a contractor to escape any penalty for failure to deliver on time. In addition, the suitably drawn contract will specify disputes are to be settled by arbitration rather than by the courts. This is far simpler, quicker, and less costly to both parties. Nevertheless, antitrust regulations and many other laws limit the kind of commercial arrangements into which two companies may enter.

International Projects

International projects are not fundamentally different from domestic projects. In practice, however, the travel lure of a remote and apparently salubrious destination seems to affect human judgment. International projects expose a contracting organization to special problems related to language, currency, and unfamiliar business practices.

Remoteness

Recognize the travel lure.

The other party in an international project is typically located in some remote area of the world. The far-off hills often look green. When two project opportunities are available to a company or organization at the same time, the one that originates in Zurich will receive far more attention than the one that originates in Cleveland, and this is independent of the intrinsic merits of the project opportunity. This is the "travel lure," and it is a problem you must recognize and identify for what it is.

There are occasions, however, when you should undertake a project involving a foreign customer or partner. When this is the case, it is often desirable to get more information about the foreign organization or the business in which it is engaged. If your organization has an office in the country, that is the best source of information. The foreign organization's country may have a chamber of commerce in the United States, which may be able to provide useful information. The United States embassy or trade centers in the foreign country may have information, as may the U.S. Department of Commerce or the World Bank.

Having gathered all the information you can without leaving the United States, you may then have to succumb to the travel lure and go to the foreign country to discuss the project or negotiate. It is generally prudent to go several days before the initial meeting to compensate for jet lag.

Business Practices

The business practices governing project performance as well as negotiations and discussions leading to the project will typically be those dictated by the customer's country. For instance, Japanese tend to discuss a project at great length to try to achieve consensus. When this has been done, a handshake or verbal agreement is binding.

Staffing requirements will frequently require some of the work be reserved for the customer's nationals. Sometimes nationals of a third country are stipulated, for a variety of reasons. Permits or "red tape" enter into business practices, and these will often absorb far more time than expected. In some cases, export or import controls can impose severe restrictions, so it is always important to understand these issues early.

Language

Be prepared for unfamiliar customs, language, and currency.

Usually, the customer's language will prevail, and the contract will be written in it. If you are using a translation, it is prudent to have several prepared because the original host language document is the controlling document and interpreters are likely to interpret it differently. If you find wording differences, you can explore their significance with a language expert.

Price

As with language, it is common for the customer's currency to be the stipulated media of financial settlement. Because currency rates fluctuate, it may be desirable to insure your company against these fluctuations. This is done with a hedge contract. Alternatively, you may use letters of credit to satisfy the future payment obligations. In any event, your price must allow for the extra expense of doing business at a great distance.

Typical Problems

The most common negotiation problem is deciding how to cope with the inevitable price squeeze the customer will try to inflict. Several things help:

1. a good plan, well explained
2. a clear understanding of where you have inserted negotiating "cushion" or "fat" (as distinct from contingency, which is discussed in a later chapter) and a negotiating plan on how to horse trade it
3. management guidance, or clearance, on how much you can give up
4. a reputation for having met prior commitments

Finally, if you are forced to surrender schedule or price, be sure to try to alter the performance specification or obtain CFE.

Materials Study Project

Preproposal discussions between SUPROMAC and NERESCO have narrowed the scope of negotiations considerably. Because SUPROMAC believes this project will lead to more work later, it is not interested in taking a tough and unbending negotiation posture. Nevertheless, SU-

PROMAC might first try to justify a price in excess of $500,000 because of the theoretical study NERESCO substituted for the four materials omitted from the study.

On the presumption that an FP contract is jointly agreed to, SU-PROMAC can attempt to gain favorable detailed terms and conditions. These might include progress payments and a degree of informality in the required reports.

Highlights

- A proposal should be made only if a reasonable contract can be negotiated.
- There are several contractual forms, including fixed price, firm fixed price, cost plus fixed fee, cost plus incentive fee, and time and material.
- Both parties must be prepared to make concessions during negotiations.
- Government contracts include numerous special regulations.
- International projects introduce special problems, such as unfamiliar business practices, language, and currency and distance.

Further Reading

R. H. Clough and G. A. Sears. *Construction Project Management*, 2nd ed. New York: Wiley-Interscience, 1979.

Chapter 1 discusses contracting and negotiating issues in the construction industry.

V. G. Hajek. *Management of Engineering Projects*. New York: McGraw-Hill, 1977.

Chapters 7–10 provide the best (extensive and thorough) treatment of contracts, negotiations, and legal issues.

V. Maieli. "Sowing the Seed of Project Cost Overruns." *Management Review* (August 1972), pp. 7–14.

This is a general discussion of the causes of cost overruns, with very useful pointers on traps to avoid during negotiations.

M. Silverman. *Project Management—A Short Course for Professionals*. New York: Wiley Professional Development Programs, 1976.

Chapter 4 provides a fairly extensive coverage of negotiations and contract forms.

Part TWO

Planning

5

Why and How to Plan

The planning phase of the project management process is crucial. Plans are the simulation of a project, comprising the written description of how the Triple Constraint will be satisfied. Therefore, project plans are really three plans: one for the performance axis (the work breakdown structure), one for the schedule axis (preferably a network diagram but occasionally a milestone listing or bar chart), and one for the cost axis (a financial estimate). This chapter reiterates the need for plans, describes how these three kinds of plans are made, reviews several planning issues, and discusses "the Plan," a document or series of documents embodying the project's planning agreements.

The Need for Plans

Plans aid coordination and communication, provide a basis for control, are often required to satisfy requirements, and help avoid problems.

Coordination and Communication

Let others plan their work.

Most projects involve more than one person. The project plan is a way to inform everyone on the project what is expected of them and what others will be doing. Plans are a vehicle to delegate portions of the Triple Constraint down to the lowest (task or subtask) reporting level. If these people also participate in making the plans, they will have an added impetus to adhere to them. A story illustrates this:

> Walter Piston, the great musician and composer at Harvard, tells of taking a rather back-roads route through Vermont from a concert at Tanglewood in the Berkshires to Hanover, New Hampshire, for an engagement at Hopkins Center and coming to a fork in the road that had signs pointing in both directions saying *White River Junction.*

"Does it make any difference," he inquired of an old-timer standing nearby, "which road I take to White River?" If not enlightened, Walter was duly impressed by the answer: "Not to me it don't."

(Quoted from *What the Old Timer Said* by Allen R. Foley, published by The Stephen Greene Press, 1971. Copyright © 1971 by Allen R. Foley. Reproduced by permission.)

Your project plans matter. Even if your project can be performed in your office, other people in the organization, for instance, your boss, will want to know where your project is headed, what you are doing, and for how long you will be doing it. Thus, project plans constitute an important communication and coordination document and may motivate people to perform better.

Basis for Control

Plans are also the basis of your project controls. Deviations from plan constitute your early warning signal during project performance that there are problems to be resolved.

When an airplane takes off from Los Angeles headed toward Honolulu, there is a planned course to be followed. During the flight, the navigator makes measurements of the plane's position, noting whether the path being followed has deviated from that planned. If there is a deviation, the pilot changes course after the navigator notes the deviation so the plane can get to Honolulu. If no flight path corrections are made, the plane might have to land in the middle of the Pacific Ocean, which would be as bad for the plane as a similar outcome would be for a project that deviated too far from its intended Triple Constraint point.

Plans are a detailed description, formulated before the project is carried out, for accomplishing its various aspects. Deviations may indicate the project will not reach its intended destination.

There are plans for all three dimensions of the Triple Constraint.

Figure 5-1 illustrates how all the techniques covered in Part Two are related. The work breakdown structure leads to a network diagram. The network is then time-phased and checked for resource allocation to be certain it is consistent. When this is done, it is possible to construct a schedule bar chart indicating the time frame for each subactivity or subtask of the entire project. The costs for these subtasks are then estimated and, when work is being performed on them, costs are reported back by a specific subtask in each of the expense categories. Part Four discusses how this detailed variance information can be used to help manage the project.

Requirement Satisfaction

Plans are sometimes created merely to satisfy requirements imposed by others, perhaps a customer or your boss. In such a situation, plans are

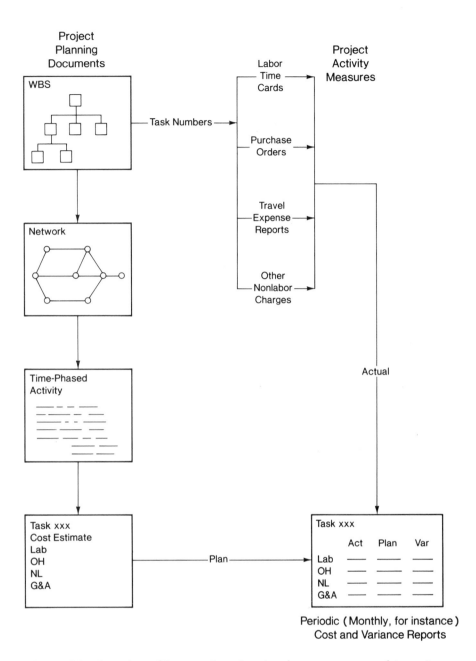

Figure 5-1. Overview of how project planning documents are used in project control phase.

often created under duress rather than because they are perceived to be valuable, even essential, in achieving project objectives.

Plans so created are frequently not followed. All too often they are generated and then discarded because they were prepared only to meet the requirement to prepare a plan. When there is such a requirement and the plans are prepared slavishly rather than thoughtfully, it is a waste of time for the preparer and those who read them.

Problem Avoidance

Project management is frequently a race with disaster. All too often the last crisis has scarcely been resolved before the current one begins, and then the project manager is too busy to anticipate and try to head off the next one.

A good plan helps you avoid problems during project performance. Consider the following example of a schedule and cost problem. Your project requires a final report. You assume it will be sixty pages with twenty figures, and the technical documentation group, which will prepare the report, agrees to do it in one week for $1,200. When you later ask them to prepare a one hundred twenty-page report with forty figures, you will be told you will get it two weeks later and it will cost $2,400. Obviously, you cannot "plan" for a two hundred-page report with one hundred figures because the price in your proposal may be too high for you to win the job. You must make the best plans and estimates you possibly can and then try to adhere to them. For instance, as you get to the final phase of the project and must prepare the report, assign writing to the participants in such a way that they all clearly understand the planning goal. Constrain the writing efforts to adhere to plans. If you do this, the report should be approximately sixty pages and twenty figures.

Planning is crucial; a good plan is essential.

Planning Issues

Plans relate to future events. That is, your plans are a simulation of how things will occur in the future. Clearly, however, plans can be no better than your present understanding. Because assumptions are involved in your planning, it is important to include contingencies, which will be discussed in Chapter 9. Good plans are quantitative rather than qualitative and as precise as possible.

A Choice Between Options

In preparing plans, as in carrying out project work, you are frequently confronted with options. Your plan may be considered the record of your choice between these options. Figure 5-2 illustrates this kind of choice. It shows two possible activity sequences. Which you choose depends on what is most important to you, in this case, a short schedule (option 2) or the higher assurance of instrument accuracy (option 1).

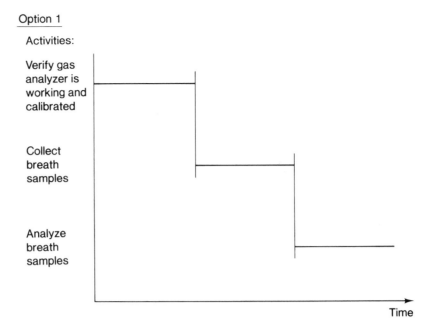

Option 1

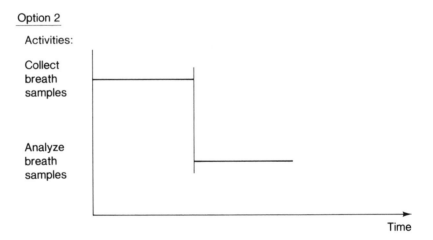

Option 2

Figure 5-2. Two possible schedule sequences.

Quiz 5-1

Can you identify a third option (for Figure 5-2) that has both a short schedule and higher assurance of instrument accuracy?

Frequently, participants in your project will present a plan that seems absurd to you. It may in fact be absurd. But perhaps the person who prepared it is simply emphasizing activities you are not stressing.

A common project activity, ordering required materials, illustrates this problem. Sensible choices are to order these materials as early as possible (to be certain they are available when required) or as late as possible (to reduce the possibility of having to change selection or to help your organization's cash flow). It is very important to discuss the perceptions of everyone involved in the undertaking.

Or imagine your boss asks you at 9 A.M. to join her on a 5 P.M. transcontinental flight to attend an important meeting. You agree and advise her you will meet her at the airport. This arrangement allows you to drive past your house en route to the airport and pack your suitcase. Your plan might be as shown in Figure 5-3. In this case, the sequence of activities A, B, and C may seem not to matter. And it does not in terms of your time. But it is desirable to start your secretary's assignment as early as possible so he can perform activity D while you do activities B and C. Thus, you should perform activity A first.

Quiz 5-2

Why plan?

Hazards

Planning their work motivates people.

There are innumerable hazards in preparing project plans. One follows from the preceding discussion. In an attempt to gain time in the early phases of a project or because you are addicted to your own ideas, you may tend to do much of the planning yourself. You should avoid doing so for the same reason you do not like to be told to carry out somebody else's plan: It is demotivating. In fact, it is important to involve the people who will actually be doing the work so they plan as much of their work as possible.

In addition, poor planning frequently occurs. Other than sheer laziness, the basis of almost all poor planning is a misunderstanding of the Triple Constraint point. Taking the time to create plans allows you to identify your perception of the Triple Constraint point and shows if and where it differs from somebody else's.

Occasionally, a tool commonly called a planning matrix is used. It lists activities to be carried out along one side of a piece of paper and designates involved personnel along the perpendicular side. Where these rows and columns intersect at a check mark, the designated personnel are involved in the designated activity. This kind of document may be helpful to some managers, but it is a misnomer to call it a planning matrix rather

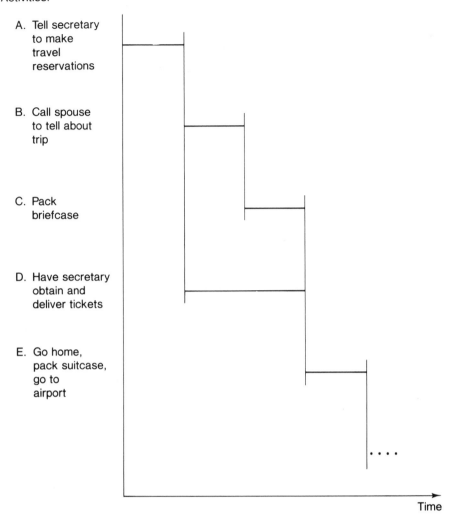

Activities:

A. Tell secretary to make travel reservations

B. Call spouse to tell about trip

C. Pack briefcase

D. Have secretary obtain and deliver tickets

E. Go home, pack suitcase, go to airport

Time

Figure 5-3.   Option for trip preparation.

than an involvement matrix. To put it another way, a planning matrix may be a helpful document, but it is not a plan.

Currentness

Keep everyone current on revisions.

Once you have decided to plan your project and have issued the plans, people should take them seriously. They can do so only if they know the plans are current. Therefore, it is very important to know who has copies of them. When you revise plans, be absolutely certain to provide revisions to all people who have copies of previous plans. When you do this conscientiously, everyone involved in your project will know you take planning seriously. They will know the plans they have reliably indicate the project intention.

"The Plan"

In many projects, there is a book called "the Plan" or "the Project Plan." It may be one or a series of thick notebooks.

Issues Addressed

"The Plan" addresses many topics. It frequently describes what is to be delivered as a result of the project and any specifications for those items. If there will be acceptance tests, it will describe them in detail. In general, the purpose of this kind of plan is to describe what is to be done, by when, and for how much, in other words, to expand upon the Triple Constraint.

Topics Covered

Typically, "the Plan" will cover many of the following topics:

1. project summary
2. project requirements
3. milestones
4. work breakdown structure
5. network diagram of the activities with schedule dates
6. budget for all activities
7. project management and organization charts
8. interface definitions, including facility support
9. logistic support
10. acceptance plan
11. standards for property control and security
12. customer organization contact points, if relevant
13. nature of project reviews

Implementation

Project plans require implementation. First, obtain whatever higher level approvals are required, including those of the customer. Second, disseminate "the Plan" to all involved personnel. In very large projects, dissemination may require a chart room in which the walls are covered with charts displaying the plans for and status of various activities, including financial progress and resource allocation. Chart rooms are not required for smaller projects.

Project plans may vary from fairly simple one-page statements to records with overwhelmingly intricate levels of detail. There is an appropriate level for each project undertaking. There is no magic formula that establishes the right level of detail; in general, never spend more time planning than it would take to correct any problems encountered because planning had not been undertaken. That is, a basic purpose of planning is to avoid problems.

Spend no more time planning than you would spend correcting errors resulting from having no plan.

Quiz 5-3

How does the Triple Constraint apply to planning?

Typical Problems

There are two pervasive problems with planning. First, taking enough time to plan is costly. There is an old saying about this: "We don't have enough time to plan now; but we'll have lots of time to fix it up later." In fact, a little inexpensive planning early usually avoids a lot of very costly fixing later. It is difficult to decide how much planning is appropriate, but the inexperienced project manager usually does far too little.

Second, plans are frequently ignored because they are perceived as an irrelevant requirement of management. The solution is obvious: Write meaningful plans you intend to follow and keep current, and be sure everyone understands you have done so.

Materials Study Project

As project manager for the SUPROMAC materials study project, you have to decide what kind of planning to do. The next three chapters illustrate the work breakdown structure, schedule, and task cost estimates you should create and use. Because it is not a complex project, you can reasonably omit "the Plan" document and a chart room.

Highlights

- Plans delegate portions of the Triple Constraint to the lowest reporting level.

- Plans keep projects on course.

- If formulated only to meet someone's requirement for them, plans are virtually useless.

- Everyone involved must receive every plan revision.

- Planning notebooks, a series of planning notebooks, or a chart room may be needed.

- Never spend more time on a plan than would be required to correct mistakes resulting from lack of a plan.

Further Reading

R. D. Archibald. *Managing High-Technology Programs and Projects.* New York: Wiley-Interscience, 1976.

Chapter 7, sections 1–4 briefly cover many of the issues in this chapter and contain a complete enumeration of applicable techniques.

D. I. Cleland and W. R. King. *Systems Analysis and Project Management*, 2nd ed. New York: McGraw-Hill, 1975.

Chapter 15 provides a quick summary of the material in this and the next three chapters, set in the context of organizational planning.

P. W. Metzger. *Managing a Programming Project.* Englewood Cliffs, N.J.: Prentice-Hall, 1973.

The portion of Chapter 2 on project planning is especially useful for computer projects but has general utility as well.

CHAPTER **6**

Planning the Performance Dimension

The goal of a performance dimension plan is to be sure everything required to satisfy the performance specification is done. This chapter deals with planning for the performance dimension of the Triple Constraint. The statement of work is a useful aid, but the principal tool discussed is the work breakdown structure.

Statement of Work

The statement of work (SOW) is that portion of the contract that explicitly enumerates what the contracting organization will do for and deliver to the customer. In projects within your organization, the SOW may be contained in a memo or task authorization rather than in a contract. The SOW must always be accompanied by a project schedule and budget to be meaningful. Thus, a plan for the performance dimension of the Triple Constraint is primarily a listing of every activity that must be performed and every result that must be obtained. The SOW frequently contains explicit acceptance criteria and test specifications.

Work Breakdown Structure

Purpose

The work breakdown structure (WBS) is a convenient method for dividing a project into small work packages, tasks, or activities. A WBS reduces the likelihood of something dropping through the crack. To put it another way, it assures all the required activities are logically identified and related.

A WBS identifies all work required to complete a project.

Figure 6-1 is a WBS, in this case, for a photovoltaic power system. There is no magic formula for constructing a WBS. Project logic will dictate the kind of detail that appears. Figure 6-1 shows two levels of detail, but there is no standard number of levels to use. In general, probably at least three or four should be shown, but it might sometimes be appropriate to show five or ten or even more. The breakdown might occur using earlier or later activities, particular organizational involvements, or almost anything that makes reasonable sense. In general, it is best to structure the WBS on tangible, deliverable items, both software and hardware. Figure 6-2 shows another WBS.

The WBS must be tied to time and money plans.

The WBS defines the *work* packages and will be tied to attendant schedules and budgets for the work performers. Thus, it is desirable for the lowest-level packages to correspond to small work increments and short time periods (for example, three to nine months).

Quiz 6-1

What appears to be missing from the WBS in Figure 6-1?

Helpful Hints

In preparing a WBS, do not forget software tasks such as reports, reviews, and coordination activities. In fact, displaying them on a WBS is a good

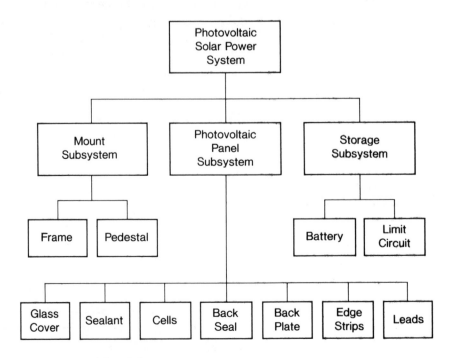

Figure 6-1. Work breakdown structure.

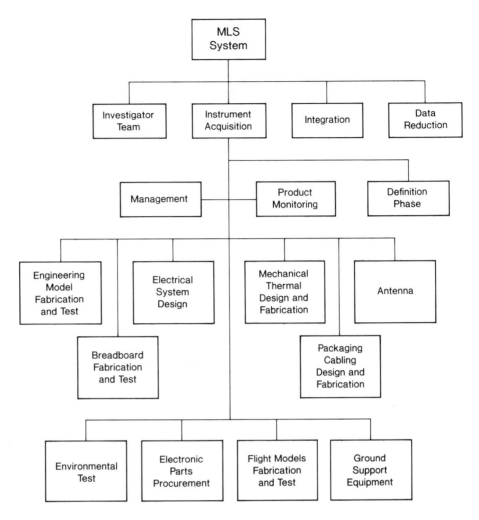

Figure 6-2. WBS for "MLS" system. (Provided through the courtesy of the National Aeronautics and Space Administration, Jet Propulsion Laboratory, California Institute of Technology.)

way to highlight that they are necessary and that resources must be devoted to them.

Fortunately, when a WBS is prepared, it tends to stress hardware integration activities. That is, junctions on the WBS frequently imply a hardware assembly or a test activity that must occur when these things are joined. Thus, a WBS again is useful for identifying an activity to which resources must be devoted.

Figure 6-3 shows a slightly different way to create a WBS. It is a "costed WBS," and the dollar volume attached to each branch of the total project is also included at the major headings. This kind of additional information, assuming large amounts of money are associated with large amounts of activity, will direct the manager's attention to those portions of the project that represent the most activity.

If you can afford the time, it is desirable to have another person make a WBS for your project, independent of yours, at least down to the third or fourth level. This will take only an hour or so and will highlight any discrepancies or oversights. You will have to repay the favor on later proj-

Others can help assure your WBS is complete.

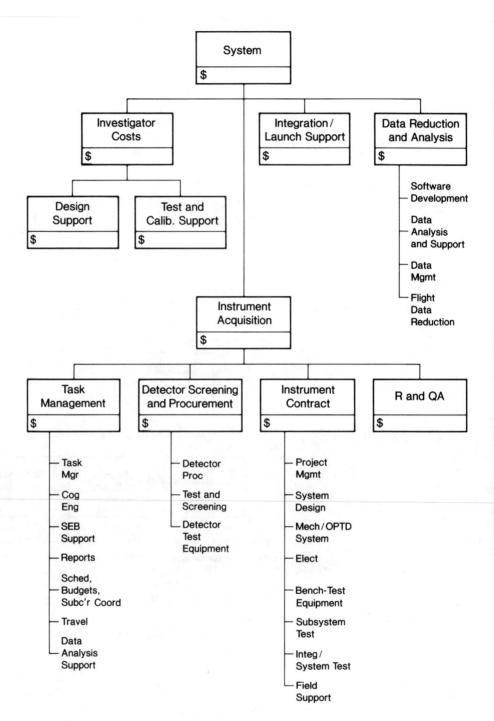

Figure 6-3. WBS with cost summary (dollars omitted). (Provided through the courtesy of the National Aeronautics and Space Administration, Jet Propulsion Laboratory, California Institute of Technology.)

ects, but that should help your organization by reducing problems on projects. In fact, some organizations require two or more people independently prepare a WBS for a given project before it can be approved.

After the initial WBS has been made, schedule planning can commence. The schedule planning may identify further items to add to the WBS. The same may occur as cost planning is done.

Quiz 6-2

Make a WBS for the breath analysis project of Figure 5-2 and Quiz 5-1.

Typical Problems

Vagueness in the SOW is a crucial problem in planning the performance dimension. For instance, it may state that "appropriate tests will be performed." Who decides, and when, what is appropriate? The solution is to write a specific and detailed SOW.

Another problem is the blind copying of a prior project's WBS for a new project. When this occurs, we have not a WBS but a waste of everybody's time—the people who prepared the WBS and the people who must read it. A project's WBS should be prepared thoughtfully, not by rote, to increase the odds of project success.

Materials Study Project

The materials study project calls for experimental work, theoretical work, and a final report. To do the experimental work, materials have to be tested in an apparatus. The WBS might be as illustrated in Figure 6-4.

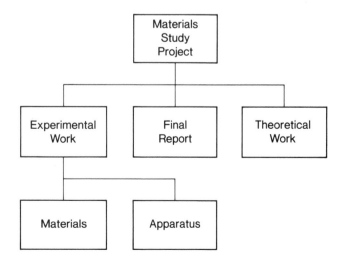

Figure 6-4. WBS for materials study project.

Highlights

- A work breakdown structure identifies all work required on a project.

- A coworker's independently produced WBS for your project will point out omissions on your WBS.

- The statement of work specifies what the customer will receive and when delivery will occur.

Further Reading

B. N. Abramson and R. D. Kennedy. *Managing Small Projects.* Redondo Beach, Calif.: TRW Systems Group, 1975.

Pages 12–17 of this breezy, short booklet give a graphic treatment of a WBS.

R. D. Archibald. *Managing High-Technology Programs and Projects.* New York: Wiley-Interscience, 1976.

Chapter 7, section 5 is a good treatment of a WBS, which Archibald calls the project breakdown structure.

J. A. Maciariello. *Program-Management Control Systems.* New York: Wiley-Interscience, 1978.

Chapters 4 and 7 provide a good treatment of the WBS, including the costed WBS.

Work Breakdown Structures for Defense Materiel Items. Military Standard 881A, Department of Defense, Washington, D.C. (25 April 1975).

This is a detailed, thorough manual on the WBS for military equipment.

Planning the Schedule Dimension

This chapter deals with the second dimension of the Triple Constraint. The plan for the schedule dimension orders activities so you can identify the logical relationship between them. In general, there are three approaches to scheduling: bar charts, milestones, and network diagrams. I discuss each but stress network diagram usage.

Bar Charts

Bar charts, often called Gantt charts after H. L. Gantt, an industrial engineer who popularized them during World War I, are frequently used for scheduling. Figure 7-1 is a bar chart. The project is divided into five activities with a planned duration of twelve months. When the bar chart was constructed, five open bars were drawn to represent the planned time span for each activity. The figure shows project status at the end of the sixth month. The shaded bars represent the forecasted span of the activities as of the end of the sixth month. Activity A was completed early. Activity B is forecast to be finished half a month late. Activity C is forecast to end approximately a month and half early. The percentage of completion for each activity in process is also illustrated. Activity A has been completed; B is 80 percent complete; and C is 30 percent complete.

Bar charts are simple to construct and easy to understand and change. They show graphically which activities are ahead of or behind schedule.

Offsetting these favorable features are some weaknesses, the most serious of which is that bar charts are essentially useless. Knowing the status of project activities gives no information at all about overall project status because one activity's dependence on another and the entire project's dependence upon any particular activity is not apparent. In addition, the no-

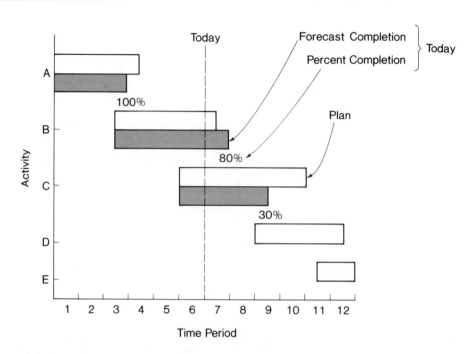

Figure 7-1. Typical bar chart, illustrating a project with five activities at the six-month review.

tion of a percentage completion is difficult. Does it refer to the performance dimension, the schedule dimension, or the cost dimension of the job? Unless an activity is linearly measurable, for instance, drilling a hundred holes in a steel plate, it is impossible to judge what percentage of it is complete. Therefore, percentage completion becomes highly subjective or is frequently taken merely as the percentage of cost expended compared to total projected cost. In neither situation is percentage completion a useful number. Bar charts are much more useful as an indication of what has happened than as a planning tool to aid the project manager in making things happen properly in the future.

A schedule that does not show task or activity interdependencies is useless by itself for planning.

Milestones

A milestone schedule notes a few key events, called milestones, on a calendar or bar chart. Milestones have been defined in various ways, but they probably are best defined as events clearly verifiable by other people or requiring approval before proceeding further. If milestones are so defined, projects will not have so many that the conclusion of each activity itself becomes a milestone.

When milestones have been defined, for instance, in the customer's request for a proposal or in your proposal document, listing them often helps in preparing your project plan. Having such milestones with attendant schedule and budget measures also adds extra emphasis to a few key points of a project. But, in common with bar charts, milestone schedules do not clarify activity or task interdependencies. Thus, they must be used with other tools if they are used at all.

Network Diagrams

Networks indicate crucial interdependencies.

There are many forms of network diagrams, but the Program Evaluation and Review Technique (PERT) and the Critical Path Method (CPM) are the most common. "Network diagram" is a generic term for PERT and CPM diagrams, arrow diagrams, bubble diagrams, and precedence networks. (It is not uncommon to have any network diagram designated a PERT chart, whether or not it truly is.) Network diagrams are the recommended approaches to planning the schedule dimension. They identify the precedence conditions and the sequential constraints for each activity.

PERT and CPM

PERT and CPM emerged in different ways in the late 1950s. PERT is event oriented (that is, the labels go in the nodes of the diagram) and has typically been used for aerospace and research and development (R and D) projects for which the time for each activity is uncertain. CPM is activity oriented (that is, the activity label is placed on the arrow) and has been applied to the construction industry, in which there is typically a controllable time for each activity. There are now many hybrid forms of network diagrams that provide the best features of PERT and CPM. The network purist undoubtedly cares about the distinctions between these two, but in reality they are not very important.

Arrows designate activities or tasks.

Conventions.   Figure 7-2 shows how an amplifier building project would be illustrated in PERT and CPM diagrams, and Figure 7-3 provides the symbolic conventions common to both. Activities are always shown as arrows with the start being the tail of the arrow and the completion being the barb. Events are shown as circles (or squares, ovals, or any other convenient closed figure). The event number is placed inside the closed figure. Event numbers are required in computer programs, which are sometimes used to facilitate network information manipulation. In such cases, a higher number activity always follows a lower number activity. In computer programs, activities are not labeled by their name (that is, "build amplifier" is not called "build amplifier") but rather by the start and end numbers (that is, 5–10 is build amplifier, if 5 is the number of the start node and 10 is the number of the finish node). It is also conventional to

PERT (Events Labeled)

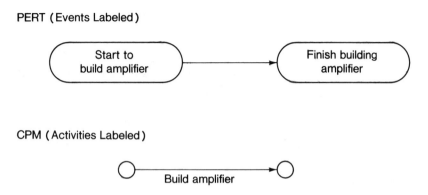

CPM (Activities Labeled)

Figure 7-2. Examples of PERT and CPM.

place early and late date numbers or other information such as slack time within the nodes. Whenever node numbers are used, there should be a legend explaining which number is which. Using these conventions, a network diagram consists of a series of nodes and arrows connected to show the order of activities.

The upper drawing of Figure 7-4 depicts a schedule plan in which activity R must be complete before activity S can commence and in which activity T must be complete before activity U can commence. The middle drawing shows a schedule plan in which both activities R and T must be complete before either S or U can commence. The bottom drawing introduces the concept of a dummy activity, which is a "no-activity" activity, that is, a precedence condition. It thus depicts a plan in which both activities R and T must be complete before activity S can commence and in

A dummy activity is a precedence condition.

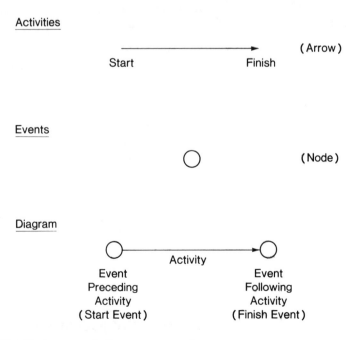

Figure 7-3. Basic network diagram conventions.

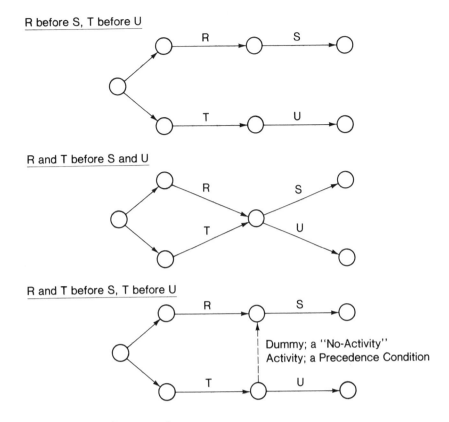

R before S, T before U

R and T before S and U

R and T before S, T before U

Dummy; a "No-Activity"
Activity; a Precedence Condition

Figure 7-4. Precedence requirements.

which activity T must be complete before activity U can commence. Activity U does not depend on activity R because the dummy arrow points in the other direction.

Network terms. Figure 7-5 illustrates three terms in network diagram usage. A burst node is a node or an event at which two or more activities can be initiated after completion of a preceding activity. A merge node or event is one in which two or more activities must be completed prior to initiation of the subsequent activity.

A dummy activity represents a dependency between two activities for which no work is specifically required. Dummies are also used to deal with an ambiguity that arises in computer-based network diagrams, also illustrated in Figure 7-5. As mentioned, in computer-based network diagram programs, the activity label is not the activity name but rather the number of the two nodes preceding and following it. Thus, is 6–7 G or H in Figure 7-5? Using a dummy task, one can make 6–7 activity G and 6–8 activity H. There is thus a dummy activity, 7–8, also required to remove the previous ambiguity.

Illustrative relationships. Consider the situation illustrated in Figure 7-6. You are the project manager for a project with six activities or

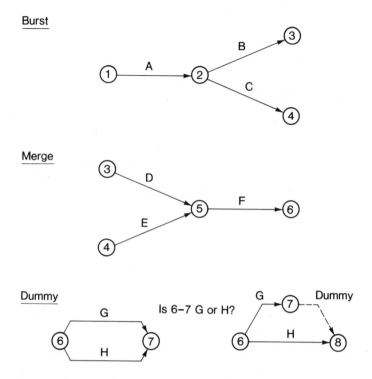

Figure 7-5. Common network terms.

tasks. At the end of eight months, you are conducting a project review (denoted by the small inverted triangle). Task managers provide status reports showing tasks A and C are two months late (denoted by the small triangles) and B and D are on schedule. The impact of these delays on the entire project's completion is not clear. (For simplicity in this example, assume task status is precisely measurable by counting the number of holes

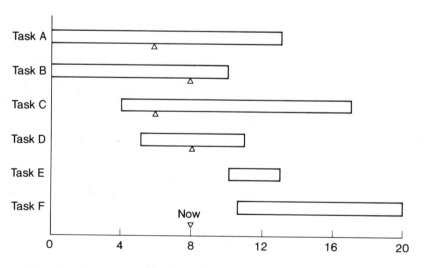

Figure 7-6. Bar chart showing tasks A and C to be two months late at eight-month project review.

drilled or drawings completed.) Your chief concern at this point is whether the entire project is late.

First you might break the tasks into their subtasks or subactivities, as in Figure 7-7. This provides additional information but still does not tell us whether the project will be late.

Networks have more information than bar charts.

At this point, a network diagram for the project can be examined (Figure 7-8). This contains more information than the bar charts because it shows the interrelationship (precedence) between different tasks. I have labeled each event in its node with the completion of the designated subtask. Thus, at the top of the diagram, you can see activity D must be com-

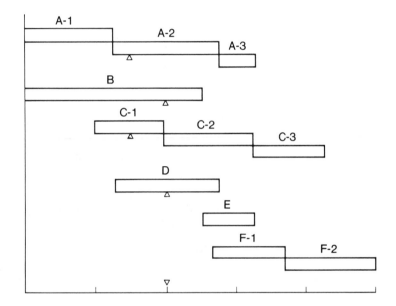

Figure 7-7.   Bar chart with subtask breakdown.

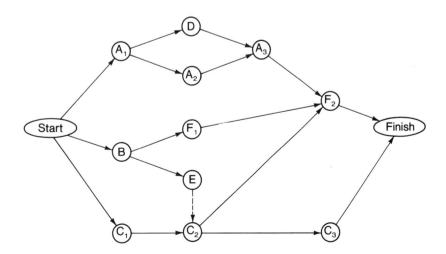

Figure 7-8.   PERT network diagram.

pleted before activity A_3. It also shows a dummy activity, indicating activity E must be completed before activity C_2.

Figure 7-8 also shows the problem with a PERT network: The activities per se are not illustrated, that is, there is no arrow uniquely associated with activity A_3 or F_2. This will always be the case where two or more arrows come to a single node, that is, at all merge nodes. This is not a problem for a skilled PERT practitioner, but it does seem to present an unnecessary conceptual difficulty, namely, when the activities are not explicitly shown on a diagram, it is more difficult for a project manager to visualize them and their relationship. A project manager's ability to influence the course of his or her project depends on his or her ability to influence the work of a given activity. The lack of its explicit visibility in a PERT diagram may therefore be troubling.

One resolution to this problem is constructing a hybrid diagram (Figure 7-9), which shows the specific task or subtask activity on each arrow. In addition, each node shows the completion of that activity. To accomplish this, however, a large number of dummy activities have been added to Figure 7-8. There is nothing wrong with this, but it adds a lot of lines that are not strictly required.

These extra lines can be eliminated if we go to a CPM network (Figure 7-10), which shows all activities by labels on the arrows. It clearly indicates the precedences. But in this representation, the nodes are ambiguous or redundant. For instance, the node to which D and A_2 arrows come would now have to be designated the completion of both D and A_2. The requirement of dummy activity P, a "no-activity" activity, is to indicate that the completion of activities E and C_2 (as well as activities A and F_1) must precede the start of activity F_2.

Figure 7-11 illustrates the next step in using the CPM diagram: redrawing it to a time scale in which the horizontal projection of each arrow is

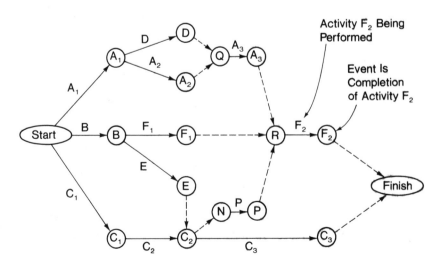

Figure 7-9. Hybrid PERT/CPM network.

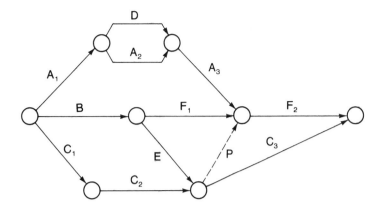

Figure 7-10. CPM network with each subtask activity.

proportional to the amount of time required for its activity. Doing this reveals one path (B, F_1, F_2) is longer than any other. This is called the critical path. It may also be identified as the path that contains no slack time (amount of time available on a path that is the difference between that required on the critical path and that required on the particular activity path with slack time).

Figure 7-11 begins to provide direct information as to the implications of the delay on activities A and C. Figure 7-12 is a redrawn version of Figure 7-11 in which the project manager has taken advantage of the slack time. That is, activities A, D, and C are drawn at the latest possible time they can be completed. Because of the dummy activity, P, note activity C_2 must be completed at the end of the fifteenth month rather than the sixteenth, which would be governed by C_3. In this case, there is still enough time before the fifteenth month to complete the work on activity A_2 (and

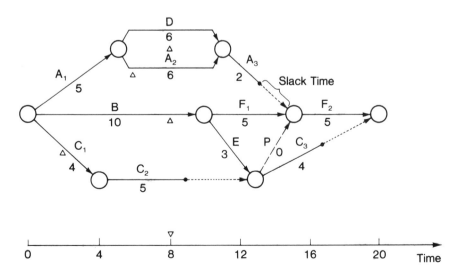

Figure 7-11. Time-oriented CPM network, drawn on assumption each subtask activity will commence at earliest possible time.

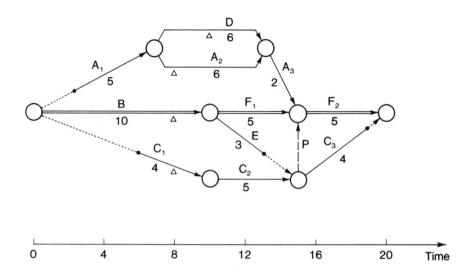

Figure 7-12. Redrawn time-oriented CPM network.

A_3) and also on C_1 (and C_2). Thus, although activities A and C are in fact later than planned, the project has not yet suffered any irretrievable schedule slippage. But the project now has three critical paths whereas it previously had only one. That is, there is no longer any slack in the upper branch (A_2 and A_3) or the lower branch (C_1 and C_2). Activity D is somewhat ahead of schedule; perhaps some of the resources allocated to it might be redeployed to one of the other critical path activities. But it is difficult enough to complete a project with one critical path. It is vastly more difficult to complete a project with more than one, and it is unlikely this project would be completed on schedule, although it is not yet irretrievably lost.

Example. Figures 7-13 and 7-14 are a CPM diagram and two versions of bar charts for a house-painting project. The network diagram clearly contains far more information than either of the bar charts, for instance, the dependency of D_1 and D_2 on A_3.

Include every element in the WBS in the network diagram.

Helpful hints. One frequently asked question is, "How do I start a network diagram?" One answer is, "With lots of scrap paper." But the best way to start is with the work breakdown structure. From the WBS, you can start the network diagram from either the beginning or the end of the project. There are frequently somewhat obvious large subnets you can quickly put down on a piece of scrap paper. As a general rule, it is probably best to start from each end with scrap paper and sort out the connectedness in the diagram where there are activities in progress simultaneously. You can then transfer the entire diagram to a clean piece of paper. It is probably helpful to do this with a time base and with the presumption that each activity starts at the earliest possible time.

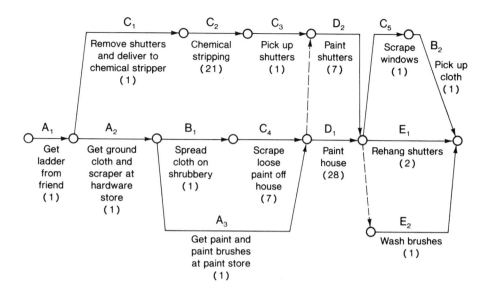

Figure 7-13. CPM network for house-painting project, with activity duration in days.

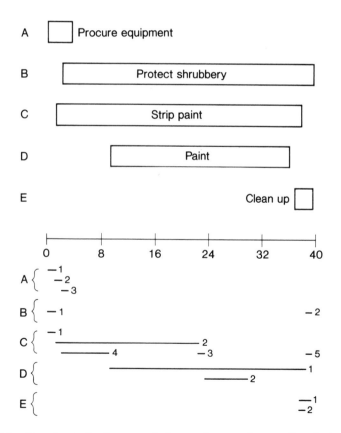

Figure 7-14. Bar charts for house-painting project, again revealing lack of task interdependency information.

This raises the question of how much time is required for each scheduled activity. Later in this chapter I describe PERT time estimating in more detail. Here I recommend you get the people who will be responsible for each activity to estimate how long it will take to carry it out on a normal work basis. When you put these time estimates onto the network diagram, it may become apparent that the entire project will take too long. At this point, you can identify particular activities for time compression, that is, planning to do them faster than is ideal.

As shown in Figure 7-15, network diagrams may require crossovers of lines. This is to be expected. Although some diagram rearrangement may get rid of crossovers, it may also distort the logical relationship of groups of activities, for instance, all those being carried out by one department being within a general band of the diagram. If activities A, B, C, D, E, F, and G in the figure are performed by one section, the upper diagram, which has two crossover intersections, would be preferable to the lower one. Thus, there are cases in which crossovers should be permitted.

The project manager should construct a network diagram of perhaps three dozen activities or up to five dozen if required. Such a diagram can normally be drawn in less than two hours and will fit onto a forty-three-by-fifty-six-centimeter sheet of paper. If some activity in this network is very large, its activity manager can make a network diagram for it. In this way, with a few hand-drawn networks of a few dozen activities each, large projects can be handled without the use of a computer-based network system.

Very large projects, however, will require a computer-based system,

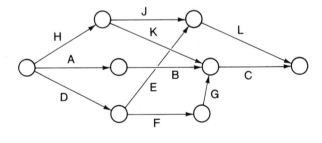

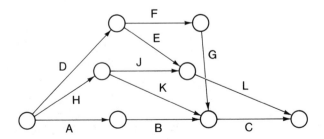

Figure 7-15. CPM network diagram with "crossovers."

Always use a network diagram to plan the schedule dimension, even if you do not show it to your management or customer.

and many are available. But you usually lose the "hands on" feel you can get by drawing your own network diagram. In general, avoid the computer until you are forced to use it. The time required to redraw a network periodically to keep it current is usually less than what you would spend correcting incorrect data entry into the computer.

Quiz 7-1

Construct a network diagram, preferably of the CPM form, to satisfy the following requirements (note the duration of each activity is designated by a bracketed number. You may wish to use the adjacent bracketed letter to label the activity's arrow):

ARROW DIAGRAMING EXERCISE

(Copyright © 1965 by the President and Fellows of Harvard College. Reproduced by permission. This case was prepared by William K. Holstein and Walter H. Warrick.)

A major firm in the field of industrial machinery fabrication is planning to launch a massive campaign to push the sale of a recently developed item of industrial hardware. You are asked to prepare the arrow diagram from which schedules for the campaign preparation can be developed. You have available the information listed in the following paragraphs. The number in parentheses following the description of each activity indicates the estimated time required for its accomplishment.

In general, the project may be broken down into three major categories:

A) the training of sales personnel
B) consultation with and training of marketing personnel
C) preparation of the necessary advertising and instruction material for the campaign

Sales
In order to save time on the sales side, it has been decided to: prepare phase #1 of the training program for salesmen. (8)(A)

At the same time sales managers are selecting sales personnel who are to be trained. (2)(B)

Both the above activities will therefore begin at the start of the project.

Following their selection, the chosen sales personnel must be relieved of their responsibilities in their areas and sent to the company's training center in the home office. (4)(C)

Obviously it would be foolish for the salesmen to arrive before phase #1 of the training program is ready for them. When phase #1 of the program is prepared, the salesmen will be trained in this part of the program. (10)(D)

While the salesmen are being trained in phase #1 of the program, phase #2 will be prepared. (9)(E)

As soon as the salesmen's training in the first phase is completed and phase #2 of the program has been completed and approved (approval cannot be given until the General Marketing Approach, see "marketing" section, has been determined), sales training in the second phase can commence. The second part of the program will take (12)(F).

At the conclusion of the two major phases of their training, the sales personnel will be issued "Customers Instruction Manuals" on the new machine and will spend a short time at the home office becoming familiar with them. (5)(G)

When the salesmen are familiar with the manuals, they will return to their respective territories ready to begin their effort simultaneously with the national advertising campaign. Getting back to their territories should take (1)(H).

MARKETING

I. Personnel
The first step in the project for the marketing side will be the determination of the general marketing approach. (10)(I)

When this has been arranged, the necessary marketing personnel will be selected (4)(J) and brought into the home office. (2)(K)

Following the determination of the general marketing approach, and while the marketing trainees are being selected and brought in, specific training plans for the marketing personnel will be consolidated. (2)(L)

After these plans are consolidated, a familiarization course for these personnel will be designed. (8)(M)

When personnel and course are ready, the training of marketing personnel will proceed. It is estimated to take (8)(N).

II. Advertising
Immediately after the general marketing approach has been determined, advertising plans must be consolidated. ("Firmed up" in the jargon of the trade.) (6)(O)

When this consolidation is complete, a paper is to be *prepared*, (6)(P) and *printed* in a professional journal. (8)(Q)

Also immediately following the consolidation of advertising plans, national advertising must be prepared, (10)(R) approved, (4)(S) and distributed to the proper media. (2)(T)

Not until the *marketing* people are trained, the professional paper published, and the advertising distributed will the national advertising be released and carried by the media involved. The release and preparation to carry the national advertising will take about (2)(U)

It is not planned to proceed further with the national advertising campaign until the salesmen have returned to their territories.

III. Printing
As soon as the advertising plans are consolidated, (the first step under "Advertising" above) a general brochure will be drafted and approved. (4)(V)

Following the approval of the brochure, a *layout* must be designed (5)(W) and the brochure *printed*. (3)(X)

As soon as the brochure is approved, a "Customers Instruction Manual" will be prepared. (3)(Y)

The "Instruction Manual" in its turn must be approved (1)(Z) and printed. (2)(α)

Copies of the "Instruction Manual" alone will be sent to the training center (1)(β) where the "Manual" will be utilized in completing the training of the salesmen.

As soon as both the brochure and manual are printed, they will be packaged together and delivered to marketing for general distribution. The packaging and delivery together should take about (8)(γ).

Actual implementation of the campaign (which may be regarded as the termination of this project) cannot begin until the salesmen are in their territories, the national advertising campaign released, and the proper brochures and manuals have been received by marketing.

Required:
Prepare the arrow diagram for this project and select the critical path or paths. You will probably show from 30 to 35 activities (including dummies) and from 20 to 25 events.

Earliest and Latest Start and Finish Times

The entire project is always assumed to start at time zero. Thus, the start of each activity that emerges from the start node has zero as its earliest start time. The earliest finish time for each of these initial activities is the duration of the activity itself (see Figure 7-16). Earliest start and finish

The difference between earliest and latest times at a node indicates the amount of slack.

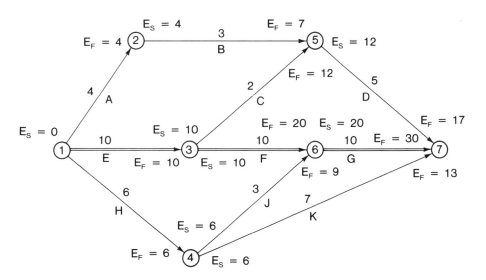

Figure 7-16. Earliest start (E_S) and earliest finish (E_F) calculation.

times are calculated by proceeding from the start node to the finish node. In Figure 7-16, activity duration is shown by the number above the middle of the activity arrow. The earliest finish of an activity is equal to the activity duration plus the earliest start. At a merge node, the earliest start of the following activity is the higher of the earliest finishes for the preceding activities. On the critical path, the earliest finish at the finish node is both the minimum project duration and the latest finish for that activity.

Figure 7-17 shows how to calculate latest finish and latest start times for each activity. Calculation commences at the finish node and proceeds backward to the start node. In Figure 7-17, on the critical path, the latest and earliest times are equal. The latest start of an activity equals the latest finish of that activity minus the activity duration. At a burst node, the latest finish of the preceding activity is the lower of the latest starts for the following activities.

Figure 7-18 shows the kinds of data provided by a typical computer printout for the project illustrated in Figures 7-16 and 7-17. Although less graphic, these data reveal the same information.

Quiz 7-2

Determine the critical path for the CPM diagram in Figure 7-19. For each activity, determine:
1. earliest start
2. earliest finish
3. latest start
4. latest finish

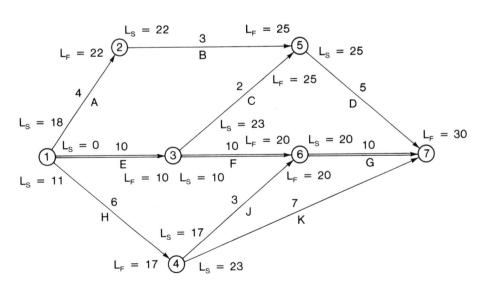

Figure 7-17.   Latest start (L_S) and latest finish (L_F) calculation.

Event				Start		Finish		
Start	Finish	Description	Duration	E	L	E	L	Slack
1	2	Activity A	4	0	18	4	22	18
1	3	Activity E	10	0	0	10	10	0
1	4	Activity H	6	0	11	6	17	11
2	5	Activity B	3	4	22	7	25	18
3	5	Activity C	2	10	23	12	25	13
3	6	Activity F	10	10	10	20	20	0
4	6	Activity J	3	6	17	9	20	11
4	7	Acitivty K	7	6	23	13	30	17
5	7	Activity D	5	12	25	17	30	13
6	7	Activity G	10	20	20	30	30	0

Figure 7-18. Typical data provided in a computer printout for computer-based network reporting. (Use with Figures 7-16 and 7-17.)

PERT Time Estimating

PERT networks originated in projects characterized by uncertain times for activities. This problem was dealt with by requiring three time estimates for each activity:

1. the most probable activity time (T_m)

2. the optimistic activity time, namely, the shortest time that might be achieved 1 percent of the time such an activity was carried out (T_o)

3. the pessimistic activity time, namely, the time that would be exceeded only 1 percent of the time such an activity was carried out (T_p)

As Figure 7-20 shows, this permits calculation of the expected time for the activity (T_e). The basis for this calculation is unproven and unprovable,

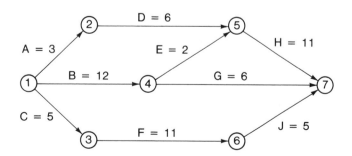

Figure 7-19. CPM diagram for Quiz 7-2.

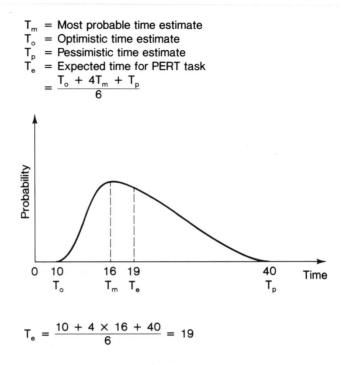

T_m = Most probable time estimate
T_o = Optimistic time estimate
T_p = Pessimistic time estimate
T_e = Expected time for PERT task
$\quad = \dfrac{T_o + 4T_m + T_p}{6}$

$$T_e = \frac{10 + 4 \times 16 + 40}{6} = 19$$

Figure 7-20.   PERT time estimating.

PERT time estimating is useful when time schedule is critical.

but it is the rule applied in PERT networks. You can also calculate the uncertainty of that time, which is called the standard deviation (σ). The calculation is illustrated in Figure 7-21.

Figure 7-22 shows how to figure the expected time for a path and the standard deviation of the path's expected time. The significance of the calculated standard deviation is the same as with the normal (Gaussian) probability distribution: Two-thirds of the time, the work will be completed within plus or minus one standard deviation of the expected time; 95 percent of the time, it will be completed within two standard deviations; and 99 percent of the time, it will be completed within three standard deviations. This kind of calculation can be important and helpful if there will be a cost penalty for lateness because you can estimate the likelihood of being late.

T_o = 2
T_m = 5
T_p = 14

$$T_e = \frac{(1 \times 2) + (4 \times 5) + (1 \times 14)}{6} = 6$$

$$\sigma = \frac{1}{6}(T_p - T_o) = 2$$

Figure 7-21.   PERT time uncertainty (σ-standard deviation) for a single event.

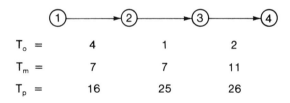

Figure 7-22. PERT expected time and uncertainty for a path.

Because it requires a lot of effort to make three time estimates and even more to calculate the expected time and standard deviation, you would normally do this work only with a PERT network that was being put on a computer. Nevertheless, it is important to appreciate the technique and apply it where warranted.

Quiz 7-3

Figure 7-23 illustrates a path with three time estimates for each activity on it. Calculate the expected time and standard deviation for the path (without a calculator, please). Next determine the likelihood that completion will require more than thirty-five days.

①	②	③	④
$T_o =$	4	1	2
$T_m =$	7	7	11
$T_p =$	16	25	26

Figure 7-23. Path with three time estimates for each activity.

Bar Chart Formats of Network Diagrams

Although it is often said network diagrams are difficult to use during project reviews and management briefings because of their apparent complexity, many organizations insist they be used for these purposes. There are at least two ways to make management personnel attending such reviews comfortable with network diagram presentations. First, activities can be displayed in a bar chart, indicating their planned time and the earliest start and latest finish, as shown in Figure 7-24. A second approach is to use vertical connections between activities that are dependent on one another to illustrate that dependency (Figure 7-25).

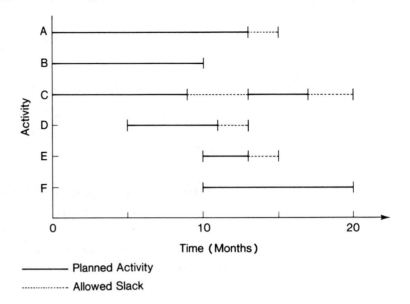

Figure 7-24. Bar chart representation of network diagram from Figure 7-11.

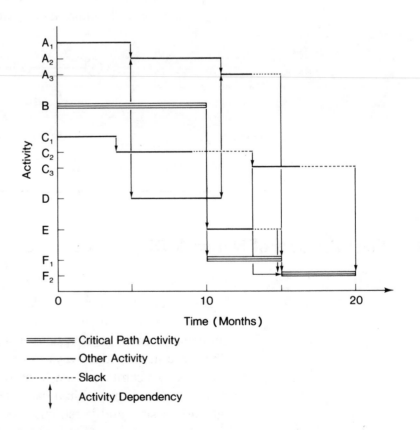

Figure 7-25. Bar chart representation of network diagram from Figure 7-11, with task dependency illustrated.

Typical Problems

In many ways, the worst schedule dimension planning problem is to avoid the indicated scheduling problems. For instance, the completed network diagram may show required materials will not arrive early enough. This conflict is often avoided or dismissed by saying this can be adjusted later. Maybe it can, but that is hoping for luck to save your project schedule. The solution is to admit the problem exists and revise the schedule to overcome it—now, not when there is no longer time to correct the problem and maintain your schedule.

It is also difficult to obtain accurate time estimates for things not done before. As suggested earlier, getting a few people together, including especially those who will be responsible for the activity, and pooling judgments is the best solution to this problem.

Materials Study Project

For the materials study project, in terms of the schedule, assume the following:

- experimental task

  1. materials

     A. select (three weeks)

     B. obtain (six weeks)

  2. apparatus

     C. build (twelve weeks)

     D. debug (two weeks)

     E. use to conduct the experiment (eleven weeks)

     F. document the design (six weeks)

- theoretical task

     G. review the literature (six weeks)

     H. theoretical study (ten weeks)

     J. report of theoretical results (five weeks)

- final report task

     K. final report (one week)

This can be presented in a bar chart (Figure 7-26). It could also be shown in a network diagram (Figure 7-27).

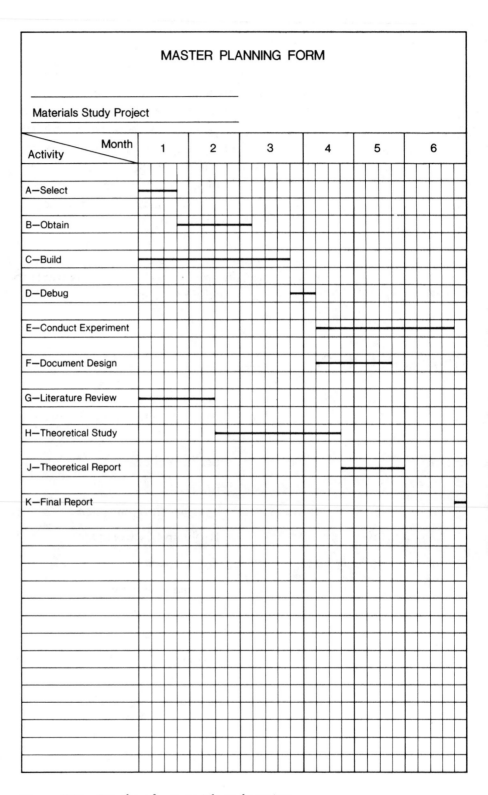

Figure 7-26. Bar chart for materials study project.

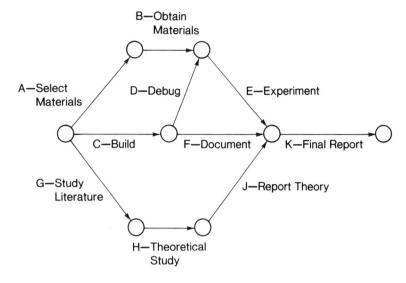

Figure 7-27.   Network diagram for materials study project.

Quiz 7-4

For the materials study project, construct a bar chart with dependencies similar to that shown in Figure 7-25.

Highlights

- Although easy to make and understand, bar charts and milestones alone are inadequate for schedule planning because they do not show how one activity depends on another.
- Network diagrams show activity interdependencies.
- The most common network diagram forms are PERT and CPM.
- Always use a network diagram, which must include every element in the WBS, to plan the schedule dimension of the Triple Constraint.

Further Reading

J. Gido. *An Introduction to Project Planning.* Schenectady, N.Y.: General Electric, 1974.

This is a simple, concise treatment of network diagrams.

D. W. Lang. *Critical Path Analysis*, 2nd ed. London: Hodder and Stoughton Paperbacks, 1977.

This is a good book on networks.

J. Mulvaney. *Analysis Bar Charting—A Simplified Critical Path Analysis Technique*, U.S. ed. Washington, D.C.: Management Planning and Control Systems, 1977.

This is a simple, concise treatment of precedence diagrams.

J. J. O'Brien, ed. *Scheduling Handbook*. New York: McGraw-Hill, 1969.

Chapters 1–5 provide a thorough and extensive treatment of network diagrams (although PERT is mislabeled).

J. D. Wiest and F. K. Levy. *A Management Guide to PERT/CPM*, 2nd ed. Englewood Cliffs, N.J.: Prentice-Hall, 1977.

This is the best book on PERT and CPM. It is clear and complete.

CHAPTER 8

Planning the Cost Dimension

Having a cost plan can help you avoid a situation where actual project cost overruns the estimate or you fail to get the job because you overestimated costs during the proposal and negotiation phase. This chapter tells you how to estimate costs and describes several of the most commonly used cost systems.

Cost Estimating

Costs may be stated only in terms of the number of labor hours required, a situation not uncommon in a programming group in which a certain number of program hours have been allocated to a particular project. Cost is more commonly stated in dollars (or yen or marks), however, which entails converting labor hours into dollars. Different hourly rates typically prevail for different seniority levels, and the cost of nonlabor elements (purchases or travel, for instance) is also included. Figure 8-1 shows one way to summarize and total time-phased labor and nonlabor estimates for a task.

Plan costs to the level of detail to which they will be reported to you.

Cost is of course necessary for planning, both to sell and manage the job. In general, do not plan costs in detail greater than what you will receive in accounting cost reports. There is no point making cost plans out on a daily basis if the organization's cost reports are furnished biweekly or monthly. Cost plans, regardless of how they are arrived at, should typically be summarized in monthly periods corresponding to expense reporting. In counting such things as travel cost or computing hours, however, one works with hours or days of travel in estimating and sorts these into monthly periods.

PROJECT _Materials Study_____ TASK _B - Obtain Materials_ DEPARTMENT _Mechanical_

COST ELEMENT			HOURS EACH MONTH						TOTALS	
			1	2	3	4	5	6	HOURS	DOLLARS
LABOR	SR. PROF.	$25/hr.	8	4	2				14	350
	JR. PROF.	$20/hr.		40					40	800
	SR. TECH.	$15/hr.								
	JR. TECH.	$10/hr.								
			DOLLARS EACH MONTH							
DOLLARS	LABOR COST									1150
	OVERHEAD	100%								1150
	DIRECT NONLABOR		200							200
	PRIME COSTS									2500
	G & A	15%								375
	TOTAL COSTS									2875
	PROFIT	20%								
	TOTAL BILLING									

ASSUMPTIONS _____

_____

PREPARED BY _____ DATE _____ APPROVED BY _____

Figure 8-1. Typical task cost estimate.

Just as with the schedule dimension plans, there are inaccuracies inherent in cost estimates, and these must be expected and tolerated. But tolerating such inaccuracies does not mean encouraging them. The goal is to be as accurate as possible and to recognize that perfection is impossible.

Techniques

"Forecasting" and "estimating" are frequently used interchangeably to refer to preparing a plan for the cost dimension. Actually, the dictionary definitions of these words are somewhat different. In project management, we are talking about the amount of money required to complete a piece of work.

If you were asked to estimate *pi*, you could do so as accurately as you wish because *pi* is a known quantity (3.14159 . . .). If, however, you were asked how long an untelevised football game will take, you would probably reply two and a half hours. You are now estimating a future event's duration based on similar previous events. You might have made this estimate by looking up the time for the longest and shortest football games ever played and by noting the times of all other football games for which durations were recorded. You would have learned that the vast majority of football games took between two and a quarter and two and three-quarter hours; therefore, two and a half hours was a reasonable estimate.

Actually, the football game you will see will not take two and a half hours. The probability of your estimate being correct is essentially nil. The fact that you are not going to be right means you should become accustomed to being wrong and should not be afraid of it. But it does not imply you should not try to be accurate. Despite these hazards, the goal in estimating is to have a meaningful plan for your project, one you can use to sell the project proposal to your customer, explain your actions to your boss, and provide enough resources to do the job successfully.

Schedule first; estimate second.

There is no point in attempting to estimate a budget for an activity until you have established its duration. In addition, you should understand the preceding and following activities in order to define better the activity you are estimating. Such understanding may clarify that a following activity is farther downstream than it first appears. If so, the activity you are estimating probably is longer, and therefore costs more, than you first thought.

Estimate the cost of each task.

You go about this by breaking the project into tasks and activities, using the WBS and network diagrams. The budget of any large activity is the sum of the smaller tasks that compose it, as shown in Figure 8-2. In general, use as much detail as possible. Every task in the WBS should probably have an individual task estimate prepared by the responsible task manager.

Shortcuts

There is a variety of means to prepare cost estimates. Using as much detail as possible is commonly called the "bottom up" method. The major project is divided into work packages small enough to allow accurate estimation. The project estimate is the sum of the estimates for all the individual work packages.

There are shortcuts to estimating some of the small work packages. You can use similarities to and differences from other tasks to shortcut a complete level of detail for a second task. Or you can use ratios or standards to relate one small task to another.

Whenever you use the bottom up technique, judge it against a "top down" estimate. The best method is to use both, one against the other, and the best sequence is bottom up, then top down. For instance, assume the bottom up estimate comes to $10 million. You may think the job should not exceed $5 million. Go back and look at each individual work package to find out where the excess costs arise. Examine each package to discover to what extent there has been an incorrect assumption as to the amount of work called for. Or you may think the total job should cost $20 million. Explore the details to find out what has been overlooked or what unwarranted simplifying assumptions were made.

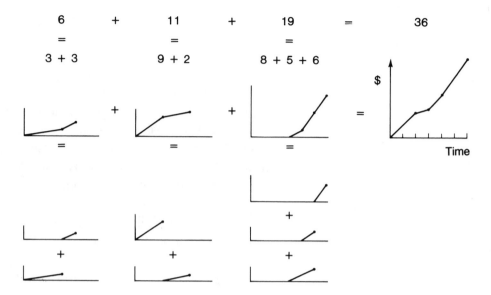

Figure 8-2. A project's cost is the summation of costs for all project tasks.

Cautions

There is a danger signal project managers must be alert to when receiving cost estimates: the person-month dimension to describe the labor requirement. This is a danger signal because it frequently indicates a snap judgment on the part of the estimator (and not because it is an inappropriate measure, although hours seem preferable). The person who can do the task in two months may not be available when he or she is needed. Or a task that can be done by one person in three months (three person-months) may require four people if it must be completed in one month (four person-months).

On lengthy projects, have an inflation hedge.

To make a project cost estimate, add detailed task estimates for each work department and adjust them if the overall summation seems unreasonable.

A pertinent question today is how to plan for inflation. Such planning can be done only with great difficulty and caution. Unfortunately, there are no guarantees in dealing with the future, so some method of coping must be adopted. Make the best estimate of labor hours regardless of when the activity will occur. Then, estimate the rates for these labor hours and the dollar amounts for nonlabor ingredients in current dollars. You can then apply inflation factors for future years to these numbers by consulting with your organization's financial planners.

Project Cost System

To use project cost reports, you must have a project cost accounting system, which is a means to accumulate costs by project and project activity or task detail. The elements of such a system are

- labor

own people

other people in company

- overhead burden

- nonlabor

purchases

subcontracts

travel

computer charges

- general and administrative burden

There are many variations in detail for project cost systems, some of which are shown in Table 8-1. I am making the simplifying assumption that the organization has three projects (A, B, and C), which all start at the beginning and will end at the close of the fiscal year. It does not matter whether the work is for the company or an outside client or whether it is to be accomplished by the sale of goods or contract billing. The point is there has to be some way of allocating the cost of these three projects to different customers or product lines. The table illustrates four methods of allocating these costs to the three projects. In method 1, the direct labor and direct nonlabor are allocated to the project and these are summed to provide a direct total. All the burden and overhead accounts are then lumped and apportioned to each project in proportion to the direct total expenses. In method 1, these are equal and the billings to each of the three projects would also be equal.

In method 2, the direct labor and direct nonlabor are treated as before but the overhead portion is allocated to each project in accordance with the amount of direct labor it requires. Nevertheless, the general and administrative (G and A) expenses are allocated to the projects in accordance with the direct total, as in method 1. In this case, the billings to the projects are not equal. Project A is more than B, which is more than C.

Method 3 and variants of it are the most common project cost systems.

In method 3, the overhead is treated as in method 2 and the direct nonlabor is treated as in both methods 1 and 2. But in this case, all these items and direct labor are joined to come up with a prime cost, and the G and A burden is allocated in proportion to that. In this case, we arrive at a still higher amount of billing for project A.

Method 4 is one of many common variations of method 3. Direct labor and overhead are treated as in method 3 but purchases are subject to a material handling charge. (In method 3, this material handling charge is included in G and A; in method 4, it is pulled out of G and A and assigned to the projects in proportion to their required purchases.) But other direct nonlabor, in this case, travel, is not allocated a handling fee as illustrated in project C. This results in a still different prime cost. Finally, the G and A

Table 8-1. Four common project cost systems, illustrated for three projects.

	Project A	Project B	Project C		
Direct Labor	50	30	10	Labor / Purchases / Travel	150
Direct Nonlabor	0	20	40		
Overhead on DL		90			270
General & Admin.		30		Fringes / DL Indirect / Indir. Labor / Facility / Gen. Supplies / Publications	120

Method 1	*A*	*B*	*C*			
DL	50	30	10			
DNL	0	20	40			
Direct Total	50	50	50	= 150		
Burden on Direct Total	40	40	40	= 120		
Total Costs	90	90	90			= 270
Method 2	*A*	*B*	*C*			
DL	50	30	10			
DNL	0	20	40			
Direct Total	50	50	50	= 150		
OH on DL	50	30	10	= 90	= 120	
G & A on Direct Total	10	10	10	= 30		
Total Costs	110	90	70			= 270
Method 3	*A*	*B*	*C*			
DL	50	30	10			
OH on DL	50	30	10	= 90		
DNL	0	20	40			
"Prime" Cost	100	80	60			
G & A on "Prime"	12.5	10	7.5	= 30		
Total Costs	112.5	90	67.5			= 270
Method 4	*A*	*B*	*C*			
DL	50	30	10			
OH on DL	50	30	10	= 90		
DNL—Purchases	0	20	20			
Material Handling	0	5	5	= 10	= 30	
DNL—Other	0	0	20			
"Prime" Cost	100	85	65			
G & A on "Prime"	8	6.8	5.2	= 20		
Total Costs	108	91.8	70.2			= 270

expenses are again distributed and a still different billing arrangement is arrived at.

All these methods, and others as well, are used. The project manager must understand his or her company's method in order to know when to use subcontract help and when to use in-house direct labor.

It is also important to understand any subcontractor's cost accounting system. If you are placing a labor intensive contract with a subcontractor, you should not use a subcontractor who practices method 3 as opposed to method 1.

Quiz 8-1

Use cost method 3 from Table 8-1 and the labor hour and burden rates from Figure 8-1 to estimate the total cost of the three-task project shown in Table 8-2.

Table 8-2.   Project for Quiz 8-1.

Task	Weeks	Project Department	Technical Support Department
A	1–4	Sr. Prof. 40 hr./wk. Travel $1,000 in week 3	
B	5–6	Sr. Prof. 20 hr./wk. Jr. Prof. 40 hr./wk.	Sr. Tech. 40 hr./wk. Jr. Tech. 80 hr./wk. Purchases $2,000 in week 5
C	7–10	Sr. Prof. 30 hr./wk. Jr. Prof. 40 hr./wk.	

Typical Problems _____

There are three important problems in planning the cost dimension of the Triple Constraint. First, many project groups or project managers have a deplorable tendency to make cost estimates for support group work. This forecloses the possibility of benefiting from support group expertise. This is easily solved by requiring every department to approve the estimate for the work it will do.

A second problem is dealing with inflated estimates by support groups. Here the project manager can first try discussion and negotiation. If that does not produce a satisfactory agreement, the project manager could alter the nature of the requested support work. Two other possible solutions are to subcontract the support work to another company or appeal to higher management.

Higher management, if they decide to "buy in," often cause a third problem. If you are convinced buying in is disaster, you can request someone else assume project management. Or you can record your objections in a memo and try to accomplish the promised work within the budget. Finally, you can undertake the job and work actively to sell your customer on changes of scope that provide an opportunity for more funding.

Materials Study Project

Each department should estimate its work on each task.

The materials study project consists of ten tasks divided among five departments. Having identified the tasks by the work breakdown structure (Figure 6-4) and the involved departments by reference to the logical work elements and the organizational arrangement (Figure 1-4), it is then possible to identify which tasks have to be estimated as to cost and schedule by which departments. This is summarized in Figures 8-3 and 8-4. Figure 8-3 shows the twenty-five estimates to be made and how computers can summarize them. The estimates and the summaries are illustrated in Figures 8-5 through 8-11 and are identified in Figure 8-4.

TASK \ SECTION	PROJECT (MECH.)	CHEM.	ELEC.	RESEARCH	TECH. SUPPORT	ALL
A	E	E				S
B	E	E				S
C	E		E		E	S
D	E		E		E	S
E	E	E	E		E	S
F	E				E	S
G	E			E		S
H	E			E		S
J				E		I
K	E	E	E		E	S
ALL	S	S	S	S	S	S

E = ESTIMATE MADE BY INDICATED DEPARTMENT FOR INDICATED TASK

S = SUM OF COLUMN OR ROW PREPARED BY COMPUTER OR ADMINISTRATIVE AIDE

I = SUM OF COLUMN OR ROW IS IDENTICAL TO ONLY ENTRY IN COLUMN OR ROW

S = SUM OF ENTIRE PROJECT, PREPARED BY COMPUTER OR ADMINISTRATIVE AIDE

Figure 8-3. Estimation of the materials study project is accomplished by making twenty-five individual estimates.

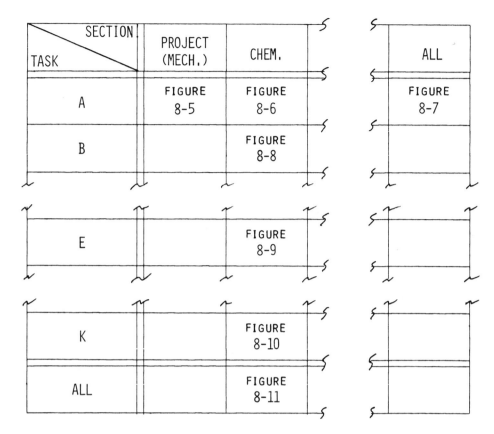

Figure 8-4. Guide to examples of estimates and summaries.

The computer can simplify planning by quickly summarizing large amounts of numerical data. For very small projects, this can easily be done by hand and is not sufficient justification for using a computer. Figure 8-7 illustrates the summation for task A and Figure 8-11, for the chemical group.

Once all the cost estimates are summed by task, it is possible to complete a costed WBS (Figure 8-12) should this be desired.

Highlights _____

- Cost estimates are usually made in dollars
- Cost estimates can be made "bottom up" or "top down," but the best method is to do both, in that order.
- The elements of a project cost accounting system, a means to tally costs by project and project task, are labor, overhead burden, nonlabor, and general and administrative burden.

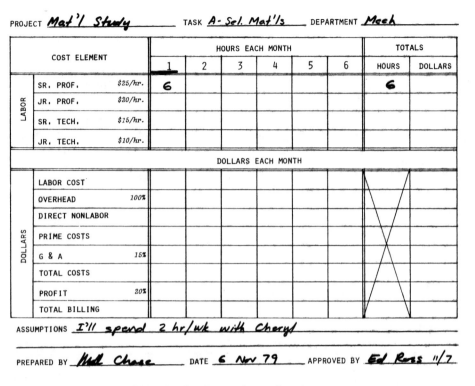

PROJECT _Mat'l Study_   TASK _A - Sel. Mat'ls_   DEPARTMENT _Mech_

	COST ELEMENT		HOURS EACH MONTH						TOTALS	
			1	2	3	4	5	6	HOURS	DOLLARS
LABOR	SR. PROF.	$25/hr.	6						6	
	JR. PROF.	$20/hr.								
	SR. TECH.	$15/hr.								
	JR. TECH.	$10/hr.								
			DOLLARS EACH MONTH							
DOLLARS	LABOR COST									
	OVERHEAD	100%								
	DIRECT NONLABOR									
	PRIME COSTS									
	G & A	15%								
	TOTAL COSTS									
	PROFIT	20%								
	TOTAL BILLING									

ASSUMPTIONS _I'll spend 2 hr/wk with Cheryl_

PREPARED BY _Mel Chase_   DATE _6 Nov 79_   APPROVED BY _Ed Ross 11/7_

Figure 8-5.   Estimate for task A by the mechanical engineering group.

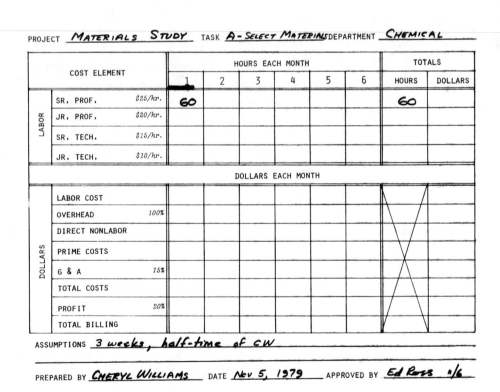

PROJECT _MATERIALS STUDY_   TASK _A - SELECT MATERIALS_ DEPARTMENT _CHEMICAL_

	COST ELEMENT		HOURS EACH MONTH						TOTALS	
			1	2	3	4	5	6	HOURS	DOLLARS
LABOR	SR. PROF.	$25/hr.	60						60	
	JR. PROF.	$20/hr.								
	SR. TECH.	$15/hr.								
	JR. TECH.	$10/hr.								
			DOLLARS EACH MONTH							
DOLLARS	LABOR COST									
	OVERHEAD	100%								
	DIRECT NONLABOR									
	PRIME COSTS									
	G & A	15%								
	TOTAL COSTS									
	PROFIT	20%								
	TOTAL BILLING									

ASSUMPTIONS _3 weeks, half-time of CW_

PREPARED BY _CHERYL WILLIAMS_   DATE _Nov 5, 1979_   APPROVED BY _Ed Ross 11/6_

Figure 8-6.   Estimate for task A by the chemical group.

PROJECT___ MATERIALS STUDY _____ TASK _A-SELECT MATERIALS_ DEPARTMENT ___ ENGINEERING ____

COST ELEMENT			HOURS EACH MONTH						TOTALS	
			1	2	3	4	5	6	HOURS	DOLLARS
LABOR	SR. PROF.	$25/hr.	66						66	1,650
	JR. PROF.	$20/hr.								
	SR. TECH.	$15/hr.								
	JR. TECH.	$10/hr.								
			DOLLARS EACH MONTH							
DOLLARS	LABOR COST		1,650							1,650
	OVERHEAD	100%	1,650							1,650
	DIRECT NONLABOR		0							0
	PRIME COSTS		3,300							3,300
	G & A	15%	495							495
	TOTAL COSTS		3,795							3,795
	PROFIT	20%	759							759
	TOTAL BILLING		4,554							4,554

ASSUMPTIONS _____

PREPARED BY _____ DATE ___19 NOV 79___ APPROVED BY_____

Figure 8-7. Summary of task A work in the engineering section (sum of mechanical engineering and chemical group efforts), prepared by computer or an administrator.

PROJECT _MATERIALS STUDY_____ TASK _B-OBTAIN MATERIALS_ DEPARTMENT _CHEMICAL_____

COST ELEMENT			HOURS EACH MONTH						TOTALS	
			1	2	3	4	5	6	HOURS	DOLLARS
LABOR	SR. PROF.	$25/hr.	40	4	2				46	
	JR. PROF.	$20/hr.								
	SR. TECH.	$15/hr.								
	JR. TECH.	$10/hr.								
			DOLLARS EACH MONTH							
DOLLARS	LABOR COST									
	OVERHEAD	100%								
	DIRECT NONLABOR		4,400							4,400
	PRIME COSTS									
	G & A	15%								
	TOTAL COSTS									
	PROFIT	20%								
	TOTAL BILLING									

ASSUMPTIONS _CW full-time at supplier during first week + $400 travel + $4,000 sub-contract; 1 hr/wk during next 4 wks to answer questions; 2 hr last week._

PREPARED BY_Cheryl Williams_____ DATE _Nov 5, 1979_ APPROVED BY _Ed Ross 11/6_

Figure 8-8. Estimate for task B by the chemical group.

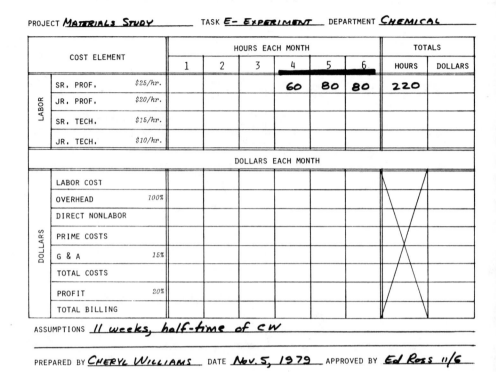

PROJECT _MATERIALS STUDY_ TASK _E- EXPERIMENT_ DEPARTMENT _CHEMICAL_

COST ELEMENT		HOURS EACH MONTH						TOTALS	
		1	2	3	4	5	6	HOURS	DOLLARS
LABOR	SR. PROF. $25/hr.				60	80	80	220	
	JR. PROF. $20/hr.								
	SR. TECH. $15/hr.								
	JR. TECH. $10/hr.								
		DOLLARS EACH MONTH							
DOLLARS	LABOR COST								
	OVERHEAD 100%								
	DIRECT NONLABOR								
	PRIME COSTS								
	G & A 15%								
	TOTAL COSTS								
	PROFIT 20%								
	TOTAL BILLING								

ASSUMPTIONS _11 weeks, half-time of CW_

PREPARED BY _CHERYL WILLIAMS_ DATE _Nov. 5, 1979_ APPROVED BY _Ed Ross 11/6_

Figure 8-9. Estimate for task E by the chemical group.

PROJECT **MATERIALS STUDY** TASK **K- FINAL REPORT** DEPARTMENT **CHEMICAL**

COST ELEMENT		HOURS EACH MONTH						TOTALS	
		1	2	3	4	5	6	HOURS	DOLLARS
LABOR	SR. PROF. $25/hr.						20	20	
	JR. PROF. $20/hr.								
	SR. TECH. $15/hr.								
	JR. TECH. $10/hr.								
		DOLLARS EACH MONTH							
DOLLARS	LABOR COST								
	OVERHEAD 100%								
	DIRECT NONLABOR								
	PRIME COSTS								
	G & A 15%								
	TOTAL COSTS								
	PROFIT 20%								
	TOTAL BILLING								

ASSUMPTIONS _1 week, half-time of CW_

PREPARED BY _CHERYL WILLIAMS_ DATE _Nov. 5, 1979_ APPROVED BY _Ed Ross 11/6_

Figure 8-10. Estimate for task K by the chemical group.

PROJECT ___MATERIALS STUDY___ TASK ___ALL___ DEPARTMENT ___CHEMICAL___

COST ELEMENT		HOURS EACH MONTH						TOTALS	
		1	2	3	4	5	6	HOURS	DOLLARS
LABOR	SR. PROF. $25/hr.	100	4	2	60	80	100	346	8,650
	JR. PROF. $20/hr.								
	SR. TECH. $15/hr.								
	JR. TECH. $10/hr.								
		DOLLARS EACH MONTH							
DOLLARS	LABOR COST	2,500	100	50	1,500	2,000	2,500		8,650
	OVERHEAD 100%	2,500	100	50	1,500	2,000	2,500		8,650
	DIRECT NONLABOR	4,400							4,400
	PRIME COSTS	9,400	200	100	3,000	4,000	5,000		21,700
	G & A 15%	1,410	30	15	450	600	750		3,255
	TOTAL COSTS	10,810	230	115	3,450	4,600	5,750		24,955
	PROFIT 20%	2,162	46	23	690	920	1,150		4,991
	TOTAL BILLING	12,972	276	138	4,140	5,520	6,900		29,946

ASSUMPTIONS _____

PREPARED BY _____ DATE ___19 NOV 79___ APPROVED BY _____

Figure 8-11. Summary for entire materials study of work to be done by the chemical group, prepared by computer or administrator.

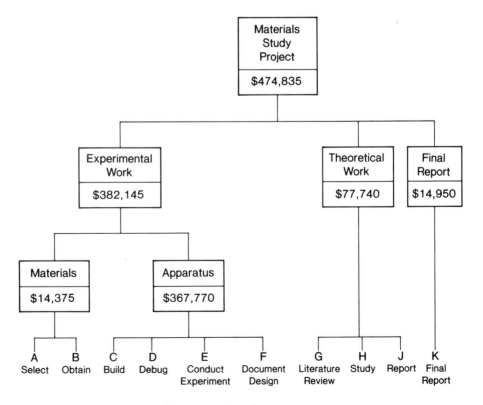

Figure 8-12. Costed WBS for materials study project.

Further Reading

R. H. Clough and G. A. Sears. *Construction Project Management*, 2nd ed. New York: Wiley-Interscience, 1979.

Chapter 3, although specific to the construction industry, is a thorough treatment of estimating.

V. G. Hajek. *Management of Engineering Projects.* New York: McGraw-Hill, 1977.

Chapter 6 has a brief discussion of cost estimating pitfalls.

J. A. Maciariello. *Program-Management Control Systems.* New York: Wiley-Interscience, 1978.

Chapter 7 is a brief treatment of project cost accounting systems.

CHAPTER 9

Integrated Triple Constraint Planning

This chapter treats several topics that typically involve two or three dimensions of the Triple Constraint. The first is resource allocation. Then, I present the techniques that allow analysis of schedule and budget trade-offs. Following that, I review methods to provide vitally important schedule and cost contingency. Next, I cover ways to use computers to assist planning. Finally, I discuss a hybrid system, C/SCSC, used in large Department of Defense contracts.

Resource Allocation

Resources are either people or things. Human resources may include everyone in a particular unit or those with a specific skill (typing, design engineering, or computer programming, for example). Things include any kind of equipment, for instance, lathe availability or computer time as well as floor space to house the equipment and the people. Money may also be considered a nonhuman resource.

There are three reasons to consider resource allocation in a project management environment. First, projected use of some key resource (for instance, circuit designers) may indicate there will be surplus personnel at some future period. This information should warn the appropriate managers either to obtain new business to utilize the surplus talent or to plan to reassign the involved personnel.

Surplus resources waste money and talent.

Another reason for resource allocation is to avoid inherent inconsistencies, for instance, using a particular resource (Jane Draftsperson, for example) on two tasks at the same time. Preparing a network diagram to a time base emphasizes resource allocation and reveals latent conflicts.

A network diagram can show what resources are required and when, which may reveal more of some resource will be needed than will be available at some time. When you discover this, you must adjust the network diagram to shift the overloaded resource requirement to some other time. If you fail to do this, slippage will occur. Figure 9-1 illustrates resource allocation. In this case, the resource is the personnel headcount. Tasks A and B, each of eight weeks duration, require three and five personnel, respectively. Tasks C, D, and E are not on the critical path, and examination of the earliest and latest times for them shows they can be commenced immediately or as late as the eleventh week. If the company performing this project employs only six people, task D would have to start early enough to be completed before the end of the eighth week, when task B is scheduled to start.

A third use of this kind of analysis occurs in a large company. Imagine tasks C, D, and E are performed by a particular support department, for instance, the design and drafting section. If the design and drafting section was provided with resource allocation information for all projects, as shown in Figure 9-1, they could identify the earliest and latest dates at which the support, in this case, C, D, and E, would have to be applied. Doing the same for all projects would allow the support group to even out its work load and to identify in each case the impact of any slippage.

Resource allocation can be done by manual inspection of predicted resource use. Computers can also do resource leveling and work load prediction and are not prone to making arithmetical mistakes (assuming, of course, they have been programmed correctly and the data have been loaded accurately). Figures 9-2, 9-3, and 9-4 show how computers can assist with resource allocation.

A network diagram is not merely a schedule dimension plan; it also clarifies resource allocation.

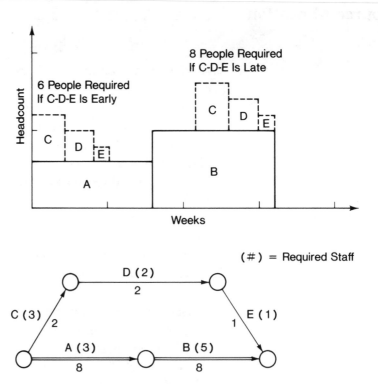

Figure 9-1.   Resource allocation.

DECEMBER 28, 1979   ATLANTIC SOFTWARE   COPY 1 PAGE   2

P C / 7 0   P R O J E C T   P L A N N I N G   R E P O R T

SCHEDULED TO AVAILABILITY

C O N D	PR TY	TASK	RESC	....DESCRIPTION....	START CURRENT	CALC/ ACTUAL	TARGET CURRENT	CALC/ COMPLETE	TASK PREC	AL GO	P L A N	PASG HDAY DURA DAY	PLAN HRS	DEC 31 79	JAN 28 80	FEB 25 80	MAR 24 80	APR 21 80	MAY 19 80	JUN 16 80	JUL 14 80	AUG 11 80	SEP 08 80
10		B3	MEL	PROVIDE ASSISTANCE	01/28/0	01/28/0	02/18/0	02/18/0	B1	A		1H MDAY	4		4								
10		B4	CHER	WRAP-UP	02/29/0	02/29/0	02/29/0	02/29/0	B3	A			2			2							
10		B4	MEL	WRAP-UP	02/29/0	02/29/0	02/29/0	02/29/0	B3	A			2			2							
20		C0	ENGR	BUILD APPARATUS	12/31/9	12/31/9	03/20/0	03/20/0		A		81D											
20		C1	MEL	PLAN & SUPERVISE	12/31/9	12/31/9	03/21/0	03/21/0		A			409	122	141	146							
20		C2	MARV	DESIGN	12/31/9	12/31/9	03/21/0	03/21/0		A			480	160	160	160							
20		C2	MOIR	DESIGN	12/31/9	12/31/9	03/21/0	03/21/0		A			480	160	160	160							
20		C3	ELDN	FABRICATE PARTS	01/21/0	01/21/0	03/21/0	03/21/0		A			360	40	160	160							
20		C3	TSPR	FABRICATE PARTS	01/21/0	01/21/0	03/21/0	03/21/0		A			360	40	160	160							
20		C3	TSSR	FABRICATE PARTS	01/28/0	01/28/0	03/07/0	03/07/0		A		16H	480		320	160							
20		C4	ED M	INSPECT & FIT	02/11/0	02/11/0	03/21/0	03/21/0		A			240		80	160							
20		C4	TSSR	INSPECT & FIT	01/21/0	01/21/0	03/21/0	03/21/0		A		8H	360	40	160	160							
20		C5	TSJR	SUB-ASSEMBLY	02/11/0	02/11/0	03/21/0	03/21/0		A		16H	480		160	320							
20		C6	TSJR	FINAL ASSEMBLY	02/11/0	02/11/0	03/21/0	03/21/0		A		16H	480		160	320							
20		D0	ED M	DEBUG	03/24/0	03/24/0	04/04/0	04/04/0	C6	A			80				80						
20		D0	ELDN	DEBUG	03/24/0	03/24/0	04/04/0	04/04/0	C6	A			80				80						
20		D0	MARV	DEBUG	03/24/0	03/24/0	04/04/0	04/04/0	C6	A			80				80						
20		D0	MEL	DEBUG	03/24/0	03/24/0	04/04/0	04/04/0	C6	A			74				74						
20		D0	MOIR	DEBUG	03/24/0	03/24/0	04/04/0	04/04/0	C6	A			80				80						
20		D0	TSJR	DEBUG	03/21/0	03/21/0	04/03/0	04/03/0	C6	A		16H	160			16	144						
20		D0	TSPR	DEBUG	03/24/0	03/24/0	04/04/0	04/04/0	C6	A			80				80						
20		D0	TSSR	DEBUG	03/24/0	03/24/0	04/04/0	04/04/0	C6	A		16H	160				160						
25		E0	ENGR	EXPERIMENT	04/07/0	04/07/0	06/19/0	06/19/0	B4 D0	A		74D											
20		E1	CHER	PLAN & SUPERVISE	04/07/0	04/07/0	06/20/0	06/20/0	B4 D0	A		50F	220				40	80	80	20			
20		E1	ELDN	PLAN & SUPERVISE	04/07/0	04/07/0	06/20/0	06/20/0	B4 D0	A		1H	55				10	20	20	5			
20		E1	MEL	PLAN & SUPERVISE	04/07/0	04/07/0	06/20/0	06/20/0	B4 D0	A			430				77	160	160	33			
20		E2	TSJR	SET UP EQUIPMENT	04/14/0	04/14/0	04/25/0	04/25/0	B4 D0	A		24H	240				120	120					
20		E2	TSSR	SET UP EQUIPMENT	04/14/0	04/14/0	04/25/0	04/25/0	B4 D0	A		16H	160				80	80					
20		E3	ED M	CONDUCT TESTS	04/07/0	04/07/0	06/20/0	06/20/0	B4 D0	A			440				80	160	160	40			

COND-CONDITION CODE   L=CALCULATED START OR TARGET DATE IS LATER THAN YOUR PLAN
                      E=CALCULATED TARGET DATE IS EARLIER THAN YOUR PLAN
                      O=RESOURCE IS OVERSCHEDULED
                      U=SIMULATION MODE, UPDATE THE PC/70 MASTER FILE
                      D=SIMULATION MODE, DO NOT RETAIN DATA ON PC/70 MASTER FILE

Figure 9-2. Person project work load report showing task and subtask labor distribution. (This computer-generated report is furnished courtesy of Atlantic Software, Inc. [ASI]. It is a sample output from Project Control/70 [PC/70], the proprietary project planning and control system that is the exclusive property of ASI. All rights are reserved.)

Time Versus Cost Trade-Off

CPM has historically been associated with network diagrams in which there is considered to be a controllable time for each activity. This implies activities can be accelerated by devoting more resources to them. Thus, there is a time versus cost trade-off for each activity and consequently for a path or the entire project.

Figure 9-5 shows this kind of situation. If you are trying to accelerate a project, you should accelerate the critical path. Of all the activities on the critical path, the most economical to accelerate are those with the lowest cost per amount of time gained.

Figure 9-6 shows another aspect of this. The direct cost curve depicts

PERSON PROJECT	JAN06	13	20	27	FEB03	10	17	24	MAR02	09	16	23	30
CHERYL WILLIAMS (CW)													
100 MATERIALS STUDY PROJECT	12.0	20.0	20.0	32.0	16.0	1.0	1.0	1.0	1.0	1.0	1.0		
PERSON AVAILABILITY	28.0	20.0	20.0	8.0	24.0	39.0	39.0	39.0	39.0	39.0	39.0	40.0	40.0
ELDON MILLER (EM)													
100 MATERIALS STUDY PROJECT	6.0	10.0	10.0	10.0	34.0	40.0	40.0	40.0	40.0	40.0	40.0	40.0	34.0
PERSON AVAILABILITY	34.0	30.0	30.0	30.0	6.0								6.0
MEL CHASE (MC)													
100 MATERIALS STUDY PROJECT	24.0	40.0	40.0	40.0	40.0	40.0	40.0	40.0	40.0	40.0	40.0	40.0	33.0
PERSON AVAILABILITY	16.0												7.0
TOM RICHARDS (TOM)													
100 MATERIALS STUDY PROJECT	18.0	30.0	30.0	30.0	38.0	40.0	14.0	8.0	40.0	40.0	40.0	40.0	40.0
PERSON AVAILABILITY	22.0	10.0	10.0	10.0	2.0		26.0	32.0					
JOB AVAILABILITY	100.0	60.0	60.0	48.0	32.0	39.0	65.0	71.0	39.0	39.0	39.0	40.0	53.0

30DEC79   FOR MECH   MEL CHASE   RPT 05 --RESOURCE ALLOCATION--- PAGE 3 JOB SR PROF   WEEKLY HOURS
TIME STAMP 01/22/80 101005

Figure 9-3. Person project work load and time still available report. (Computer printout furnished courtesy of Nichols & Company, Culver City, California.)

those costs associated with carrying out the project that are time dependent and for which there is a cost premium associated with shortening the program. In addition, there might very well be continuing costs associated with the program, for instance, the rental of standby power generators or other such facilities. In this kind of situation, there will be a time that leads to the lowest cost for the project.

Quiz 9-1

Use the network diagram in Figure 7-19. Assume all times are in weeks. To carry out this project, you must rent a standby generator for the entire duration of the project (however long it is) at a cost of $1,000 per week. Your purchasing department has told you the subcontractor performing activity B has offered to shorten its perfor-

PERSON	WEEK	PROJECT	TASK	PRTY	WEEK	MON	TUE	WED	THU	FRI	SAT	SUN
MEL CHASE	(MC)	(CONTINUED)										
	2MAR80 100	MATERIALS STUDY PROJECT	0410 OBTAIN MATERIALS	5	1.0	1.0						
			0730 THEORETICAL STUDY	5	4.0		1.0	1.0	1.0	1.0		
			AVAILABLE TIME									
	9MAR80 100	MATERIALS STUDY PROJECT	0230 BUILD	5	35.0	7.0	7.0	7.0	7.0	7.0		
			0410 OBTAIN MATERIALS	5	1.0	1.0						
			0730 THEORETICAL STUDY	5	4.0		1.0	1.0	1.0	1.0		
			AVAILABLE TIME									
	16MAR80 100	MATERIALS STUDY PROJECT	0230 BUILD	5	35.0	7.0	7.0	7.0	7.0	7.0		
			0730 THEORETICAL STUDY	5	5.0	1.0	1.0	1.0	1.0	1.0		
			AVAILABLE TIME									
	23MAR80 100	MATERIALS STUDY PROJECT	0230 BUILD	5	35.0	7.0	7.0	7.0	7.0	7.0		
			0730 THEORETICAL STUDY	5	5.0	1.0	1.0	1.0	1.0	1.0		
			AVAILABLE TIME									
	30MAR80 100	MATERIALS STUDY PROJECT	0230 BUILD	5	7.0	7.0						
			0510 DEBUG	5	24.0			8.0	8.0	8.0		
			0730 THEORETICAL STUDY	5	2.0	1.0	1.0					
			AVAILABLE TIME		7.0		7.0					
	6APR80 100	MATERIALS STUDY PROJECT	0510 DEBUG	5	40.0	8.0	8.0	8.0	8.0	8.0		
			AVAILABLE TIME									
	13APR80 100	MATERIALS STUDY PROJECT	0510 DEBUG	5	16.0	8.0	8.0					
			0730 THEORETICAL STUDY	5	3.0			1.0	1.0	1.0		
			0810 CONDUCT EXPERIMENT	5	21.0			7.0	7.0	7.0		
			AVAILABLE TIME									
	20APR80 100	MATERIALS STUDY PROJECT	0730 THEORETICAL STUDY	5	5.0	1.0	1.0	1.0	1.0	1.0		
			0810 CONDUCT EXPERIMENT	5	35.0	7.0	7.0	7.0	7.0	7.0		
			AVAILABLE TIME									
	27APR80 100	MATERIALS STUDY PROJECT	0730 THEORETICAL STUDY	5	1.0	1.0						
			0810 CONDUCT EXPERIMENT	5	39.0	7.0	8.0	8.0	8.0	8.0		
			AVAILABLE TIME									
	4MAY80 100	MATERIALS STUDY PROJECT	0810 CONDUCT EXPERIMENT	5	40.0	8.0	8.0	8.0	8.0	8.0		
			AVAILABLE TIME									
	11MAY80 100	MATERIALS STUDY PROJECT	0810 CONDUCT EXPERIMENT	5	40.0	8.0	8.0	8.0	8.0	8.0		
			AVAILABLE TIME									
	18MAY80 100	MATERIALS STUDY PROJECT	0810 CONDUCT EXPERIMENT	5	40.0	8.0	8.0	8.0	8.0	8.0		
			AVAILABLE TIME									
	25MAY80 100	MATERIALS STUDY PROJECT	0810 CONDUCT EXPERIMENT	5	40.0	8.0	8.0	8.0	8.0	8.0		
			AVAILABLE TIME									
	1JUN80 100	MATERIALS STUDY PROJECT	0810 CONDUCT EXPERIMENT	5	32.0		8.0	8.0	8.0	8.0		
			AVAILABLE TIME									

30DEC79   FOR MECH   MEL CHASE   RPT 04 -RESOURCE AVAILABILITY-- PAGE 14   JOB (SP) SR PROF   HOURS
TIME STAMP 01/22/80 100516

Figure 9-4. Weekly work schedule plan for individual resource. (Computer printout furnished courtesy of Nichols & Company, Culver City, California.)

mance time by as much as five weeks (that is, to seven weeks) but will charge $800 per week for every week less than the original twelve (that is, a premium charge of $800 for eleven weeks delivery, $1,600 for ten weeks delivery, . . . or $4,000 for seven weeks delivery). Should you accept this offer? Why or why not?

Contingency

Plans represent the future. Because nobody has a crystal ball, plans must include contingency. In fact, this contingency should be placed on each of the three-dimension plans of the Triple Constraint.

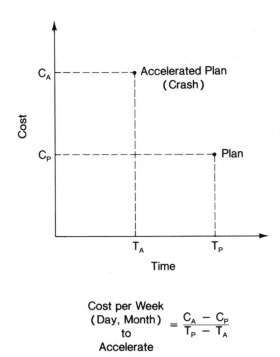

$$\text{Cost per Week} \atop \text{(Day, Month)} \atop \text{to} \atop \text{Accelerate} = \frac{C_A - C_P}{T_P - T_A}$$

Figure 9-5.   CPM time versus cost trade-off.

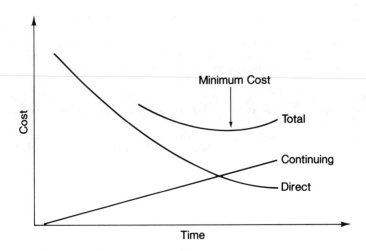

Figure 9-6.   Finding the lowest cost.

On the performance axis, it is important the contingency not take the form of gold plating. Where appropriate, include a small design margin. For instance, if the goal is to have a new car's weight be only a thousand kilograms, it might be appropriate to try to design the car to weigh nine hundred eighty kilograms. However, never carry this to an extreme (targeting the car's weight at seven hundred kilograms, for example).

All project plans must contain contingency.

Contingency is most often associated with the schedule and cost axes because projects will inevitably encounter difficulties there. Many things that occur simply require more time and money than planners think. For instance, whenever you must interact with other people, obtaining your boss' approval, perhaps, their schedules constrain you. You will not have instant access, and a delay will occur. Customer-furnished items frequently do not arrive when expected or in the condition promised. Work done at remote locations often takes longer than work done in your own organization's facilities because things like copying machines or other support resources are simply not as conveniently available. If your project involves hiring people, it takes time to train them and make them effective workers on the job. Similarly, there will be illnesses and vacations pulling people away from the job. These and other reasons, some of which are included in the following list, make it important to build in schedule and cost contingency.

- interface with others
- get approvals
- get support from other groups
- make mistakes
- train people
- replace sick and vacationing personnel
- obtain security clearances
- place major subcontracts and purchase orders
- obtain customer furnished equipment
- work at remote locations
- cope with travel delays
- handle customs duty clearance
- adjust for labor strikes
- comply with customer procedures
- advance the state-of-the-art

There are several ways to do this. The first is to have everybody who provides an estimate make his or her own time and cost contingency estimate. The problem with this approach is contingency gets applied on top of contingency, which is then applied on top of other contingencies, and so on. It does not take many multiplications of 110 or 120 percent before the price of the entire project exceeds the customer's reach, and it does not take many extra hours, days, weeks, or months before the schedule becomes unreasonable.

The second method to insert schedule and cost contingency is to put a small amount of contingency, 5 or 10 percent, on each activity in the network. This method is fine, but it misses the point that some activities can be accurately estimated and some others cannot. A variation of this technique, which is far better, is to explain to everyone providing estimates that they should be as accurate as possible. Then the entire group can discuss how much schedule and cost contingency should be put on which activities. There might be some highly uncertain activities that receive a contingency of 50 or more percent. Conversely, a final report might be assigned no or only a small percentage contingency.

A third method to add contingency is to add an unplanned, and hopefully unrequired, activity. For instance, adding a system management task is really a variation of the second method but provides only cost contingency. A given level of cost contingency, the amount of the system management task, is attached to the entire project. A weakness of this method is it does not inherently provide a time cushion as well.

The method I prefer is to add additional tasks near the end of the project, as shown in Figure 9-7. This has the effect of pushing activities forward from the project's scheduled completion, in this case, shipment, to the earliest possible point. These extra tasks thus have the effect of providing schedule contingency. Because money is also devoted to them, they also supply a cost contingency.

Plan

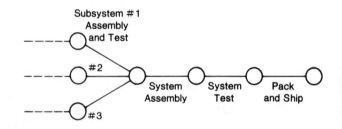

Plan with Contingency

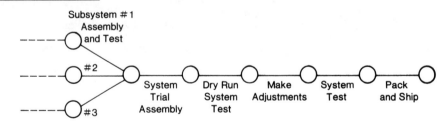

Figure 9-7. A way to insert schedule and cost contingency.

Other Computer Uses for Planning

Figures 9-8 and 9-9 are computer-generated bar chart displays. Some computer programs can control graphic output terminals to produce network diagrams. Computers can also furnish summary information for several projects, as shown in Figure 9-10, which reports on the materials study project, the ink development project, and the quill development project.

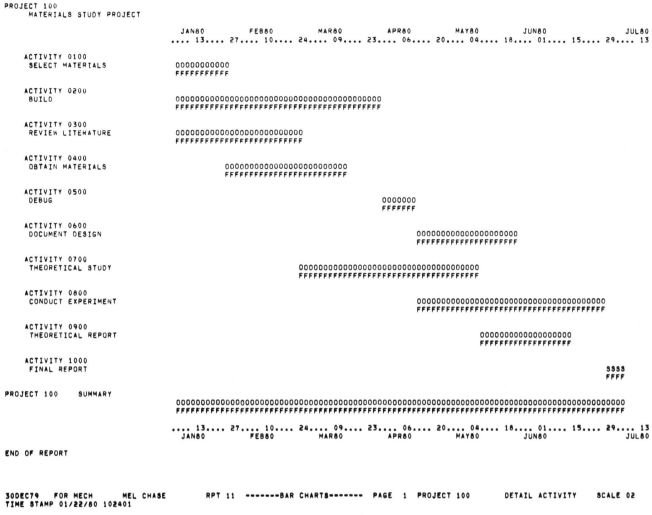

Figure 9-8. Bar chart printout indicating original and forecast schedules for tasks and project. (Computer printout furnished courtesy of Nichols & Company, Culver City, California.)

Computers are often useful for project planning.

Computers can easily provide a wide variety of other planning detail to the project manager, support group managers, and task leaders. Figures 9-11 and 9-12 show two forms in which such information can easily be furnished.

Cost/Schedule Control System Criteria

The Cost/Schedule Control System Criteria (C/SCSC) was devised by the U.S. Department of Defense to predict cost overruns earlier in major military procurement projects. On many projects, the actual cost being reported conformed closely to the initial planned cost, but this concealed the

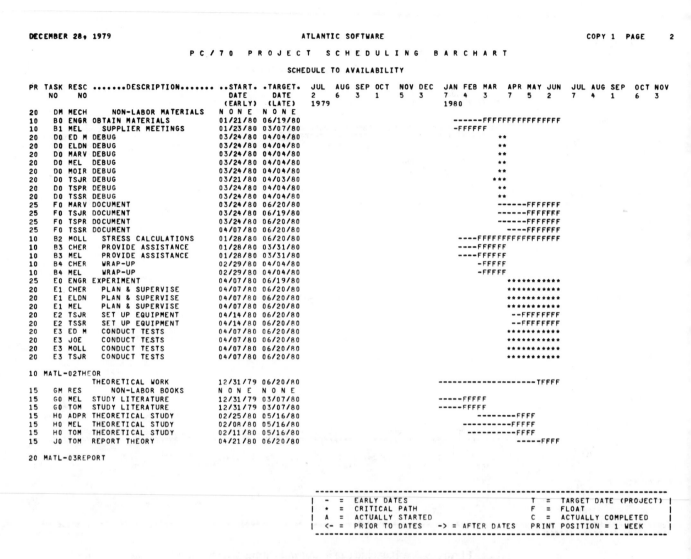

Figure 9-9. Bar chart printout with legend. (This computer-generated report is furnished courtesy of Atlantic Software, Inc. [ASI]. It is a sample output from Project Control/70 [PC/70], the proprietary project planning and control system that is the exclusive property of ASI. All rights are reserved.)

fact that actual work accomplishments were lagging behind plan. Consequently, the total project cost for the work performed exceeded planned cost for the work accomplished. Thus, when projects were far advanced and major commitments had been made to them, it became apparent there were going to be major cost overrun problems at the end.

As with many things done by the military, this is a very formal, rigid system. It provides a standard terminology and approach, which clearly are helpful, but it saddles both the military and its contractors with a highly detailed system. C/SCSC must be initiated in the planning phase, but it is really more useful as a control tool than as a planning device.

To work with this system, you must deal with three quantities, shown in Figure 9-13. The budgeted cost of work scheduled (BCWS) is compared with the budgeted cost of work performed (BCWP) in a given period. The

C/SCSC is used on major military projects.

```
DECEMBER 28, 1979                      ATLANTIC SOFTWARE                          COPY 1  PAGE    1
                              P C / 7 0   E X E C U T I V E   S U M M A R Y

PR PROJECT NUMBER AND DESCRIPTION   ...........DATE...........  ........DOLLARS........  ............HOURS............ PCT HOURS
TY                                  STARTED    TARGET  COMPLETE CURRENT TO/DATE CURRENT THIS   CURRENT TOTAL    TO     CPT VARI-
                                                                BUDGET          FORECAST WEEK   BUDGET  T/D   FINISH       ANCE

20 INK -01
            INK DEVELOPMENT PROJECT 01/14/80 05/13/80             14950           14950          260            260
*TOTAL INK  PROJECT                 01/14/80 05/13/80           $14950          $14950          260            260

10 MATL     MATERIALS STUDY                  06/29/80          $500000                         10500

        ********************************************
        *THE PROJECT CONSISTS OF 3 PARTS :        *
        * EXPERIMENTAL; THEORETICAL; AND REPORT.  *
        ********************************************

15 MATL-01EXPER
            EXPERIMENTAL WORK       12/31/79 06/20/80            370231          370231         8484           8484

        ********************************************
        *THIS PROJECT PART CONSISTS OF 2 PHASES :  *
        * SELECTING MATERIALS; BUILDING THE APPARATUS *
        ********************************************

10 MATL-02THEOR
            THEORETICAL WORK        12/31/79 05/23/80             79890           79890         1500           1500

        ********************************************
        *THE THEORETICAL PART OF THE PROJECT WILL GO  *
        * ON IN PARALLEL WITH THE EXPERIMENTAL PART.  *
        ********************************************

20 MATL-03REPORT
            FINAL REPORT            06/23/80 06/27/80            14950           14950           380            380
*TOTAL MATL MATERIALS STUDY         12/31/79 06/27/80          $465071         $465071         10364          10364

30 QUIL-01
            QUILL DEVELOPMENT PROJECT 04/07/80 06/13/80           6900            6900           120            120
*TOTAL QUIL PROJECT                 04/07/80 06/13/80            $6900           $6900           120            120
```

Figure 9-10. Summary report covering several projects. (This computer-generated report is furnished courtesy of Atlantic Software, Inc. [ASI]. It is a sample output from Project Control/70 [PC/70], the proprietary project planning and control system that is the exclusive property of ASI. All rights are reserved.)

difference between these is a measure of schedule variance. In addition, the actual cost of work performed (ACWP) is compared to the budgeted cost of the work performed and the difference, if any, is a cost variance. The details of the C/SCSC system are far too intricate to explain here and are of only limited interest. If you must use it, seek specialized training.

Typical Problems

When computers are used to assist with planning (or anything, for that matter), there is always the danger of entering incorrect data or making programming errors. With standard project control software, such as illustrated in this book, the software is proven, but there can still be incorrect data entry. Figure 9-14 shows a project budget for the materials study project in which the total ($472,266) does not agree with that previously shown in the costed WBS ($474,835, in Figure 8-12). To avoid this kind of problem, verify data entry or run manual spot checks of output. Never blindly accept any computer output as gospel.

```
           PROJECT INFORMATION                    PROJ LDR MEL CHASE                    PRTY IS 5      INDP START  1JAN80   ACTV THRU 0999
MATERIALS STUDY PROJECT                           BY DEPT  RESERCH & ENG                PROJ IS        ORIG START  2JAN80   OPTIONS
                                                  FOR DEPT RESERCH & ENG        100%    STATUS  WAIT   RVSD START  2JAN80   REQUEST
                                                  FOR DEPT                        0%    % DAYS   100   FCST START  2JAN80   CONTRACT
                                                  FOR DEPT                        0%    % COST   100   FCST COMPL  2JUL80   PRODUCT
                                                  PROJ DEPENDENT ON PROJ (TASK) -


                       ---- RESOURCES ----    ---- COST ---   ------- SCHEDULE --------   -------- DEPENDENCY --------- OPTIONS ERR
TASK  FUNC  DETAIL     DAILY     TOTAL    %    TOTAL      %    START   FINISH   DAYS   %   DATE        PROJECTS/TASKS

 ***  ACTIVITY   0100  TOTAL LABOR ***
      SELECT MATERIALS

      ORIG PLAN         66.0            1,650        2JAN80  22JAN80   21
      FORECAST          66.0   100      1,650  100   2JAN80  22JAN80   21   100
      VARIANCE                                                         0

 ***  ACTIVITY   0100  TOTAL MONEY ***
      SELECT MATERIALS

      ORIG PLAN        2,145           2,145        2JAN80  16JAN80   15
      FORECAST         2,145   100     2,145  100   2JAN80  16JAN80   15   100
      VARIANCE                                                        0

 ***  ACTIVITY   0100  TOTAL VALUE ***
      SELECT MATERIALS

      ORIG PLAN                        3,795        2JAN80  22JAN80   21
      FORECAST                         3,795  100   2JAN80  22JAN80   21   100
      VARIANCE                                                        0

**************************************************************************************************************************************

 ***  ACTIVITY   0200  TOTAL LABOR ***
      BUILD

      ORIG PLAN       4,130.0         72,650        2JAN80  25MAR80   84
      FORECAST        4,130.0  100    72,650  100   2JAN80  25MAR80   84   100
      VARIANCE                                                        0

 ***  ACTIVITY   0200  TOTAL MONEY ***
      BUILD

      ORIG PLAN      122,045         122,045        2JAN80  21MAR80   80
      FORECAST       122,045  100    122,045  100   2JAN80  21MAR80   80   100
      VARIANCE                                                        0

 ***  ACTIVITY   0200  TOTAL VALUE ***
      BUILD

      ORIG PLAN                      194,695        2JAN80  25MAR80   84
      FORECAST                       194,695  100   2JAN80  25MAR80   84   100
      VARIANCE                                                        0

**************************************************************************************************************************************

30DEC79   FOR MECH     MEL CHASE      RPT 06  ----PROJECT ANALYSIS----  PAGE 1  PROJ 100    PRTY 5  NEED  30JUN80  DETAIL 3
TIME STAMP 01/22/80 101251
```

Figure 9-11.   Detailed task labor, schedule, and money report. (Computer printout furnished courtesy of Nichols & Company, Culver City, California.)

Materials Study Project

The materials study project can be used to illustrate a resource allocation problem. Cheryl Williams is slated to work on three projects and also plans to attend a society meeting. A manual work load forecast (Figure 9-15) would show the conflict, and once it is identified, corrective action could be initiated (such as plan overtime work, cancel her society participation, or find some other chemist to work on the quill development project).

In more complex situations, where there are many projects, holidays, and vacations to be considered, a computer is usually better able to handle the data, as shown in Figure 9-16. Project control software often includes priority scheduling in which low priority projects are rescheduled so as

DECEMBER 28, 1979   ATLANTIC SOFTWARE   COPY 1 PAGE   2

P C / 7 0   P R O J E C T   S T A T U S   R E P O R T

PR TY	TASK NUM-BER	RES NUM-BER	......DESCRIPTION......	STARTED	TARGET COMPLETE	CURRENT BUDGET	TO/DATE	CURRENT FORECAST	THIS WEEK	CURRENT BUDGET	TOTAL T/D	TO FINISH	PCT CPT	HOURS VARI-ANCE
10	B4	MEL	WRAP-UP	02/29/80	02/29/80	115		115		2.0		2.0		
*TOTAL 11			MATERIALS PHASE			11385		11385		126		126		
20	CM	ELEC	NON-LABOR MATERIALS			9000		9000						NOBGT
20	CM	MECH	NON-LABOR MATERIALS			15000		15000						NOBGT
20	C0	ENGR	BUILD APPARATUS	12/31/79	03/20/80									NOBGT
20	C1	MEL	PLAN & SUPERVISE	12/31/79	03/21/80	23518		23518		409.0		409.0		
20	C2	MARV	DESIGN	12/31/79	03/21/80	22080		22080		480.0		480.0		
20	C2	MOIR	DESIGN	12/31/79	03/21/80	22080		22080		480.0		480.0		
20	C3	ELDN	FABRICATE PARTS	01/21/80	03/21/80	20700		20700		360.0		360.0		
20	C3	TSPR	FABRICATE PARTS	01/21/80	03/21/80	16560		16560		360.0		360.0		
20	C3	TSSR	FABRICATE PARTS	01/28/80	03/07/80	16560		16560		480.0		480.0		
20	C4	ED M	INSPECT & FIT	02/11/80	03/21/80	11040		11040		240.0		240.0		
20	C4	TSSR	INSPECT & FIT	01/21/80	03/21/80	12420		12420		360.0		360.0		
20	C5	TSJR	SUB-ASSEMBLY	02/11/80	03/21/80	11040		11040		480.0		480.0		
20	C6	TSJR	FINAL ASSEMBLY	02/11/80	03/21/80	11040		11040		480.0		480.0		
*TOTAL 12			APPARATUS PHASE			191038		191038		4129		4129		
20	DM	MECH	NON-LABOR MATERIALS			1000		1000						NOBGT
20	D0	ED M	DEBUG	03/24/80	04/04/80	3680		3680		80.0		80.0		
20	D0	ELDN	DEBUG	03/24/80	04/04/80	4600		4600		80.0		80.0		
20	D0	MARV	DEBUG	03/24/80	04/04/80	3680		3680		80.0		80.0		
20	D0	MEL	DEBUG	03/24/80	04/04/80	4255		4255		74.0		74.0		
20	D0	MOIR	DEBUG	03/24/80	04/04/80	3680		3680		80.0		80.0		
20	D0	TSJR	DEBUG	03/21/80	04/03/80	3680		3680		160.0		160.0		
20	D0	TSPR	DEBUG	03/24/80	04/04/80	3680		3680		80.0		80.0		
20	D0	TSSR	DEBUG	03/24/80	04/04/80	5520		5520		160.0		160.0		
25	E0	ENGR	EXPERIMENT	04/07/80	06/19/80									NOBGT
20	E1	CHER	PLAN & SUPERVISE	04/07/80	06/20/80	12650		12650		220.0		220.0		
20	E1	ELDN	PLAN & SUPERVISE	04/07/80	06/20/80	3163		3163		55.0		55.0		
20	E1	MEL	PLAN & SUPERVISE	04/07/80	06/20/80	24725		24725		430.0		430.0		
20	E2	TSJR	SET UP EQUIPMENT	04/14/80	04/25/80	5520		5520		240.0		240.0		
20	E2	TSSR	SET UP EQUIPMENT	04/14/80	04/25/80	5520		5520		160.0		160.0		
20	E3	ED M	CONDUCT TESTS	04/07/80	06/20/80	20240		20240		440.0		440.0		
20	E3	JOE	CONDUCT TESTS	04/07/80	06/20/80	3795		3795		110.0		110.0		
20	E3	MOLL	CONDUCT TESTS	04/07/80	06/20/80	20240		20240		440.0		440.0		
20	E3	TSJR	CONDUCT TESTS	04/07/80	06/20/80	5060		5060		220.0		220.0		
25	F0	MARV	DOCUMENT	04/07/80	05/02/80	3680		3680		80.0		80.0		
25	F0	TSJR	DOCUMENT	03/24/80	05/01/80	14720		14720		640.0		640.0		
25	F0	TSPR	DOCUMENT	04/07/80	05/02/80	3680		3680		80.0		80.0		
25	F0	TSSR	DOCUMENT	04/07/80	05/02/80	11040		11040		320.0		320.0		
*TOTAL 12			APPARATUS PHASE	12/31/79	06/20/80	167808		167808		4229		4229		
*TOTAL 01	EXP		EXPERIMENTAL WORK	12/31/79	06/20/80	370231		370231		8484		8484		
10	MATL-02	THEOR												
			THEORETICAL WORK	12/31/79	05/23/80	$80000				1500				

****
*THE THEORETICAL PART OF THE PROJECT WILL GO   *
* ON IN PARALLEL WITH THE EXPERIMENTAL PART.   *

Figure 9-12. Detailed task and subtask labor, schedule, and money report. (This computer-generated report is furnished courtesy of Atlantic Software, Inc. [ASI]. It is a sample output from Project Control/70 [PC/70], the proprietary project planning and control system that is the exclusive property of ASI. All rights are reserved.)

not to conflict with high priority projects (which usually results in low priority projects being late). "What if" capability is also often included, allowing managers to explore all the consequences of various scheduling options.

Highlights

- Resources, whether people or things, should be carefully allocated in a project.
- A network diagram can clarify resource allocation.

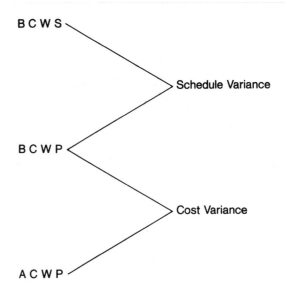

Figure 9-13. C/SCSC methodology.

BUDGET ITEM	TOTAL	JAN 1980	FEB 1980	MAR 1980	APR 1980	MAY 1980	JUN 1980	JUL 1980	AUG 1980	SEP 1980	OCT 1980	NOV 1980	DEC 1980
FORECAST BY FUNCTION													
BUI BUILD	72,650	15645	31515	25490									
DEB DEBUG	14,400			5760	8640								
DNL DIRECT NON LABOR COS	30,600	17600	11600	1000	400								
DOC DOCUMENT DESIGN	14,400				8080	6320							
EXP CONDUCT EXPERIMENT	45,151				16135	15818	13198						
FIN FINAL REPORT	6,500						3900	2600					
G&A GENERAL & ADMIN	61,446	11568	11288	12647	10932	8591	6420						
OBT OBTAIN MATERIALS	2,100	1105	920	75									
OVR OVERHEAD	190,069	33594	31712	38166	36734	28407	21456						
REP THEORETICAL REPORT	4,000					3100	900						
REV REVIEW LITERATURE	5,750	3900	1850										
SEL SELECT MATERIALS	1,650	1650											
STU THEORETICAL STUDY	23,550		2861	9976	10257	456							
TOTAL FORECAST	472,266	85062	91746	93114	91178	62692	45874	2600					

****

END OF REPORT

Figure 9-14. Project budget summary report. (Computer printout furnished courtesy of Nichols & Company, Culver City, California.)

Figure 9-15. Projected Six-month Work Load for Individual, Showing Conflict in Month 4.

Month & Hours Allowed	1	2	3	4	5	6
Task or Project	160	160	200	160	160	200
Materials Study	100	4	2	60	80	100
Ink Development	20	60	80	60	40	
Quill Development			40	40	40	
Chemical Society				40		
Total Hours	120	64	122	200		
Available or ⟨Conflict⟩	40	96	78	⟨40⟩	—	100

```
DECEMBER 28, 1979                        ATLANTIC SOFTWARE                              COPY 1  PAGE     1

                       P C / 7 0   R E S O U R C E   P L A N N I N G   R E P O R T

                                    SCHEDULED TO AVAILABILITY
RESOURCE-CHERYL WILLIAMS                                                      MANAGER-ED ROSS

C PR TASK ......DESCRIPTION........ ......START..... .....TARGET...... TASK AL P PASG PLAN DEC JAN FEB MAR APR MAY JUN JUL AUG SEP
O TY                                CURRENT  CALC/    CURRENT  CALC/   PREC GO L HDAY HRS   31  28  25  24  21  19  16  14  11  08
N                                            ACTUAL            COMPLETE     A DURA      79  80  80  80  80  80  80  80  80  80
D                                                                          N DAY


 40 ADMN-05SYMP
      SYMPOSIA ATTENDANCE
0 40   SY SYMPOSIA ATTENDANCE     05/05/0  05/05/0  05/09/0  05/09/0      LT A     40 |   |   |   |   | 40|   |   |   |   |

 20 INK -01
      INK DEVELOPMENT PROJECT
 20    A0 SELECT MATERIALS        01/14/0  01/14/0  05/13/0  05/13/0         A  3H 260 | 30| 60| 60| 60| 50|   |   |   |   |

 15 MATL-01EXPER
      EXPERIMENTAL WORK
 10    A0 SELECT MATERIALS        12/31/9  12/31/9  01/18/0  01/18/0         A 50P 60 | 60|   |   |   |   |   |   |   |   |
 10    B3    PROVIDE ASSISTANCE   01/28/0  01/28/0  02/18/0  02/18/0     B1  A  1H   4 |   | 4|   |   |   |   |   |   |   |
                                                                              MDAY
 10    B4    WRAP-UP              02/29/0  02/29/0  02/29/0  02/29/0     B3  A      2 |   |   | 2|   |   |   |   |   |   |
 20    E1    PLAN & SUPERVISE     04/07/0  04/07/0  06/20/0  06/20/0     B4  A 50P 220 |   |   |   | 40| 80| 80| 20|   |   |
                                                                        D0

 20 MATL-03REPORT                 (MATL-01EXPER         MATL-02THEOR        )
      FINAL REPORT
 10    K0 FINAL REPORT            06/23/0  06/23/0  06/27/0  06/27/0         A 50P 20 |   |   |   |   |   |   | 20|   |   |

 30 QUIL-01
      QUILL DEVELOPMENT PROJECT
 30    A0 SELECT MATERIALS        04/07/0  04/07/0  06/13/0  06/13/0         A     120 |   |   |   | 10| 30| 80|   |   |   |
                                                                   ------------------------------------------
RESOURCE NUMBER CHER   TOTAL              TOTAL HOURS SCHEDULED . . . . . . .  90  64  62 110 200 160  40

 AVAILABLE HOURS-   40.00               OPEN HOURS EACH PERIOD . . . . . . .  70  96  98  50  40-     120 160 160 160

                                        CUMULATIVE OPEN TIME   . . . . . . .  70 166 264 314 274 274 394 554 714 874


*****************************************************************************************************************
                COND-CONDITION CODE  L=CALCULATED START OR TARGET DATE IS LATER THAN YOUR PLAN
                                     E=CALCULATED TARGET DATE IS EARLIER THAN YOUR PLAN
                                     O=RESOURCE IS OVERSCHEDULED
                                     U=SIMULATION MODE, UPDATE THE PC/70 MASTER FILE
                                     D=SIMULATION MODE, DO NOT RETAIN DATA ON PC/70 MASTER FILE


*****************************************************************************************************************
```

Figure 9-16. Work load forecast for an individual, showing conflict. (This computer-generated report is furnished courtesy of Atlantic Software, Inc. [ASI]. It is a sample output from Project Control/70 [PC/70], the proprietary project planning and control system that is the exclusive property of ASI. All rights are reserved.)

- Each activity, critical path, and project has a time versus cost trade-off.

- All projects should contain contingency, which may be best inserted by adding tasks near the end.

- Computers can aid project planning in several ways, although care must be taken to avoid entering incorrect data and making programming errors.

Further Reading

R. H. Clough and G. A. Sears. *Construction Project Management*, 2nd ed. New York: Wiley-Interscience, 1979.

Chapter 7 is a thorough treatment of time reduction trade-off, using construction industry examples.

Cost/Schedule Control Systems Criteria—Joint Implementation Guide.
Published by Departments of the Air Force (AFSC/AFLC Pamphlet 173-5), Army (DARCOM-P 715-5), Navy (NAVMAT P5240), and Defense Supply Agency (DSAH 8315.2) (1 October 1976).

Cost/Schedule Management of Non-Major Contracts (C/SSR Joint Guide).
Published by Departments of the Army (Pamphlet DARCOM-P 715-13), Navy (NAVMAT P5244), Air Force (AFLCP 173-2 and AFSCP 173-3), and Defense Logistics Agency (DLAH 8315.3) (1 November 1978).

These two booklets provide an overview of C/SCSC.

J. A. Maciariello. *Program-Management Control Systems*. New York: Wiley-Interscience, 1978.

Chapter 8 is a good but brief treatment of resource allocation.

J. J. O'Brien, ed. *Scheduling Handbook*. New York: McGraw-Hill, 1969.

Chapter 6 is a thorough treatment of resource scheduling and contains many examples. Chapters 7 and 8 are a thorough treatment of cost and time planning, with many examples of computer printout.

Project Management Institute. *Survey of CPM Scheduling Software Packages and Related Project Control Programs*. Drexel Hill, Penn.: Project Management Institute (January 1980).

This publication contains the most complete listing of currently available scheduling and control software.

Part THREE

Implementation

CHAPTER **10**

Organizing the Project Team

The project team consists of those who work on the project and report administratively to the project manager. This is in distinction to the support team (people who work on the project but do not report administratively to the project manager) whom I discuss in Chapter 11. First, I review sources of project personnel and consider the frequent necessity to compromise by using whoever is available. Then I deal with how much control a project manager can exercise over project personnel and provide some practical tools to help him or her gain effective control. The last section discusses the use of task assignments both as a means to assign the work packages and to obtain commitments from personnel to carry out the work.

Sources of Personnel

The nature of personnel assignments varies.

Figure 10-1 shows eight categories of personnel assignment to projects. They result from all possible combinations of three factors: (1) whether personnel report directly to the project manager or are administratively assigned to someone else, (2) whether they work full-time or only part-time each day (or week or year) on the project, and (3) whether they work on the project from its inception to completion or for only some portion of the project.

The project team is composed of the people who report administratively to the project manager, (the four cells so designated on the left side of Figure 10-1). I consider this the project team because the project manager can assign work packages to these people rather than having to negotiate with other managers to obtain commitments for their work.

The amount of project labor obtained from each category depends on the project contractor's organizational form (that is, functional, project, or

Nature of Reporting Relationship / Duration of Project Assignment	Reports to Project Manager		Works on Projects but Reports to Another Manager	
	Works Only on Project	Also Has Other Assignment(s)	Works Only on Project	Also Has Other Assignment(s)
From Start to Finish	P	P	S	S
Only a Portion of Project's Duration	P	P	S	S

P = Project Team
S = Support Team

Figure 10-1.   The project team and the support team.

matrix) and project size. In a matrix organization, no one may be assigned to work for the project manager; the entire labor pool may be drawn from the support team. In a pure project organization, the vast majority of project labor, perhaps all of it, may be assigned to the project manager. This is especially likely for a large project of long duration. As a practical matter, small projects are not likely to have their own personnel, regardless of organizational form. The majority of those assigned to a project from start to finish is either managerial or administrative, as most other skills are required for only some portion of the project.

There are many sources of people, including the proposal team, other people already employed by the organization, and people from outside the organization (hired personnel, contract personnel, consultants, and subcontractors).

The Proposal Team

The proposal team is the best source of project personnel.

By far the best source of project personnel are those who worked on the proposal. They are familiar with the subject matter of the proposal and perhaps to some extent with the customer's specific problems. Being already "up to speed," they require minimal indoctrination. They will, for example, presumably understand the meaning of potentially ambiguous words (such as "gain").

Other Organization Employees

Other employees of the organization are the second best source of personnel. These people are at least familiar with company policies and procedures; they know where the library, the model shop, and such are located. Although they may not be familiar with the subject matter of the proposal, they are at least familiar with how the company does business and know its strengths and weaknesses. They know who to call for help and where to go to get something done. In fact, they have probably worked on similar projects in the past.

The project manager may know their strengths and weaknesses and thus be able to assign them to appropriate work packages. The project manager will not ask them to do more than their capabilities permit or give them a work package so trivial as to be demeaning or demotivating.

People from Outside the Company

There is a variety of outside sources for personnel. Consultants, contract ("body shop") personnel, and subcontractors can be obtained quickly whereas it often takes months to hire a new person. The newly hired person, who can work for and be fully under the administrative control of the project manager, may be thought of as part of the project team in the sense I am using that term. To hire a person, a project manager has to have a personnel requisition approved, typically must advertise the position, interview several people, make one or more offers to get an acceptance, and wait for the person to relocate (if required) before coming to work. Then there is an indoctrination period while the person becomes familiar with company practices. A project of short duration rarely can afford the time to hire personnel and thus depends on the support team.

Compromise _____

Staffing compromises are usually necessary.

It is indeed rare that a project manager can staff the project entirely with personnel who (1) already work for him or her, (2) worked on the proposal, and (3) represent exactly the right distribution of skills to carry out the project. Usually, the project manager must staff the project from whoever is currently available either full- or part-time. Many of these people will not completely meet the requirements. It is often a case of fitting square pegs in round holes.

Qualifications

The newly appointed project manager confronted with the urgent need to staff a project team is often victimized by other managers in the company who offer their "cats and dogs." These people may be marginally employed, so company management may pressure the project manager to accept them into his or her group.

This is a very tricky situation. There is pressure from above to accept the people and there is another manager offering them as freely available. But if these people are known to be marginal workers, it is probably better to terminate their employment than to shift them from one project to another, burdening these projects and retaining marginal workers for long periods of time. Nevertheless, it is common for a newly appointed project manager to be offered all kinds of personnel for transfer. On a short duration project, it may be better to accept these workers, unless they are clearly unqualified, than to recruit better qualified assistance.

Motivation

Some project personnel may be poorly motivated and some may be unrealistic.

Some projects that offer high pay (such as the trans-Alaska pipeline or projects requiring a great deal of overtime or shift premium work) frequently attract workers whose primary motivation is money. The project manager may be besieged by candidates who wish to go to work on his or her project. Their motivation, however, may not be best for the project. So confronted, the manager should seek to staff the project team with a few high quality people and confine the money seekers to support team roles, where they are someone else's problem.

Conversely, a project with high scientific content or one of national importance (the Apollo man-on-the-moon project) often attracts highly dedicated, altruistic people. A common correlate of this altruism is a lack of practicality, which the project manager must watch for and temper.

Some projects have an unsavory reputation (fairly or unfairly earned) that makes it very difficult to recruit personnel. They often require portions of the work be performed at an unattractive or remote location. To overcome this drawback, various inducements may be required.

Recruiting Qualified Help

Some compromise is clearly required in staffing the project team, but there may be some skill requirements that cannot be compromised. Imagine you are Mel Chase, SUPROMAC project manager for the materials study project I have been using as an example (Figure 10-2). Because Tom Richards is the only person in SUPROMAC capable of doing the theoretical

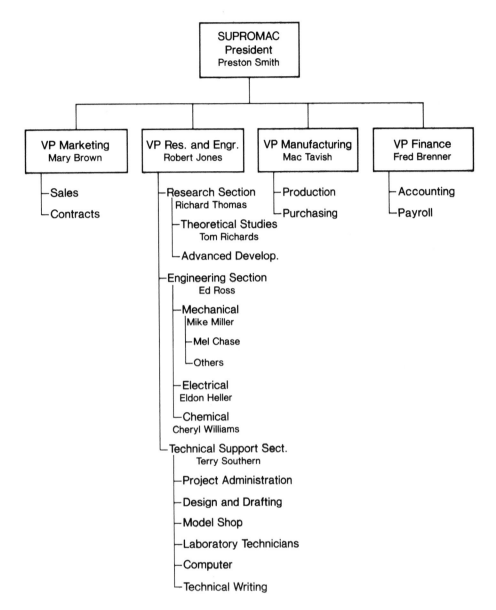

Figure 10-2. SUPROMAC organization chart.

study (tasks G, H, and J), you must have him conduct these tasks. You have two options: (1) Have the director of research transfer Tom Richards to your project team for the duration of the project. (2) Have Tom Richards perform the work without reassignment, as part of the support team.

Most project managers instinctively prefer option one because it improves project control. People on the project team cannot be given other distracting work assignments unless the project manager approves it, but people on the support team may be given other work that detracts from their ability to honor support commitments. Thus, you would first try to

Unless you have a matrix organization, you want personnel assigned to the project team.

persuade Richard Thomas to permit the transfer and then try to persuade Tom Richards to accept it. You could do this by stressing the importance of the project, the importance of Tom Richards's contribution to it, the reduced demand such a transfer would make on his supervisory time, and the temporary nature of the transfer. You might also stress how the experience Tom Richards would gain would benefit both him and the research section when the temporary transfer ended.

Nevertheless, such a transfer could well be undesirable for the project if you do not need Tom Richards 100 percent of each day. What would he do the rest of the time? It can also be undesirable if he is a difficult person to supervise. But if these are not obstacles, you should try to persuade Richard Thomas to approve the transfer. If your organization has a matrix form, of course, transfer is not possible; at most, you can obtain a firm commitment to assign a needed person as long as the project requires him or her.

Quiz 10-1

(A) Assuming the work required of Tom Richards will consume all his time, which of the eight categories in Figure 10-1 do these two options represent?

(B) Assuming the work required of Tom Richards will only consume 80 percent of his time each week, which of the eight categories in Figure 10-1 do these two options represent?

Control

Supervision

People must join and leave the project as needed.

In talking about the project team, I am talking about people who work for the project manager. They may not work full-time on the project, either for its entire duration or full-time within any given workday or workweek. Nevertheless, they are under the project manager's direct supervision, unless there are intermediate levels of supervision. Some of these people may have been transferred from other managers.

Projects go through different phases, which implies personnel must be changed. For instance, the creative design person, so valuable in the early phases of system design, is not needed when the project is moving toward completion and the team is trying to finish what has been designed rather than figure out additional clever ways to design it.

Thus, some people may have to be reassigned during the project. An administrator or junior project manager assigned to work under the project manager may be needed the entire time, but other personnel may need new assignments. They will either go to work on another project full-time after completing their work or work on two or three projects part-time. It is therefore important that the project manager exercise control over the timing of these assignments so as to have people with the right skills available when required and have other assignments for them when they are not required. This is one reason a resource allocation analysis is desirable.

Proximity

One of a project manager's most powerful tools for improving control of project personnel is to locate everyone in a common area. This aids communication, and where there is increased communication, there is increased understanding. This also assures the project manager everyone on the team understands the Triple Constraint.

Although the project manager has more control of hierarchically subordinate personnel and may therefore prefer to staff the project with them, this control is not total and it is unlikely the project can be fully staffed in this way.

Quiz 10-2

In what ways does the project manager lack control of the project team?

Task Assignments

All work assignments should be written.

I have previously emphasized use of the work breakdown structure and network diagrams to divide projects into small pieces of work. Each of these pieces, or tasks, has a corresponding cost estimate. In the ideal world, the person responsible for each task has prepared both the schedule and the budget estimate. They should also have played a significant role in defining the exact Triple Constraint of their small work package. In any case, the project manager must assign tasks to many different people. As these tasks are assigned, some give and take in the exact scope may be accepted, but whatever is finally agreed upon must be committed to paper. That is, there should be a minicontract between the project manager and the people responsible for tasks. This minicontract defines the Triple Constraint of the task.

The project team member who now has his or her task assignment should provide the project manager a detailed plan of how that task will be performed and periodically review progress against the plan. To the extent that the task performer has played a major role in creating and initiating the task assignment, he or she is likely to be highly motivated to carry it out. Conversely, if the task was assigned without negotiation, the person may have a low sense of involvement and be largely demotivated by the assignment.

Typical Problems

The usual problem, discussed earlier, is what to do with marginal personnel. This is one reason you should have inserted schedule and budget contingency—because sometimes you have personnel who must be used in an area outside their competency, which renders them temporarily marginal. In the case of truly marginal personnel, you can simply refuse to accept them on the project team.

Materials Study Project

Imagine SUPROMAC's proposal, and the resulting contract with NERESCO, designate Molly Cook (a noted mechanical expert) will work on the job, but she has just begun a long hospitalization. Your options include arranging for her to work while hospitalized, even though this may be inefficient and therefore more costly; trying to substitute a consultant or contract personnel; or trying to substitute less qualified SUPROMAC personnel.

Highlights

- The project team is people who work on the project and report administratively to the project manager.
- Sources of project personnel include the proposal team, others employed by the organization, and people from outside the organization.
- Compromise is required in forming project teams.
- People must join and leave the team as required during the project.
- Having team members in close proximity improves the project manager's control.

Further Reading ———————————————————

C. L. Buck. "Managing the Most Valuable Resource: People." *Project Management Quarterly,* vol. 8, no. 2 (June 1977), pp. 41–44.

This is a useful, brief discussion of building project teamwork.

C. Cammann and D. A. Nadler. "Fit Control Systems to Your Managerial Style." *Harvard Business Review*, vol. 54, no. 1 (January–February 1976), pp. 65–72.

This contains excellent suggestions for improving control of personnel.

C. C. Martin. *Project Management—How To Make It Work.* New York: AMACOM, 1976.

Chapter 7 has a good discussion of "people" issues in project management.

H. J. Thamhain and D. L. Wilemon. "Leadership, Conflict, and Program Management Effectiveness." *Sloan Management Review,* vol. 19, no. 1 (Fall 1977), pp. 69–89.

This has research data on effective management techniques for project managers.

CHAPTER 11

Organizing the Support Team

The support team is the people who work on the project either full-time or part-time for a part or all of the project but do not report administratively to the project manager. This chapter discusses how to obtain their involvement and commitment and how their efforts can and must be coordinated with the project team. Then I consider interaction between the project team and support groups and subcontractors.

Involvement and Commitment

As with the project team, the best way to develop a sense of involvement and obtain a commitment from the support team is to have had its members participate in the proposal. Participation also builds a team spirit that continues beyond the project. Failing this, their involvement in planning their own work and committing those plans to writing should also elicit involvement and commitment.

Early Support Group Involvement

Involve support groups as early as possible.

Project managers and the project team often ignore support requirements, which other groups must provide, until it is too late. Unless support personnel understand their services may be required, they cannot anticipate the extent to which they will be needed. Consequently, the support a project demands may not be available when needed. When support is sought tardily, support groups feel left out, and it may be difficult to obtain their commitment.

This kind of situation may arise because the project team has some degree of parochialism or is not aware what support is readily available. The project team may not understand the potential roles others can play or may assume it knows better than the support groups what kind of effort will be required. This latter situation frequently arises because the project team feels a support group will "gold plate" the amount of work they propose to do, exceeding project budgets.

As stated earlier, these problems can best be mitigated by involving support groups in the proposal phase. If this cannot be done, involve them as early as possible in the project work. Give them an opportunity to participate in planning their task and employing their best thinking and expertise.

The same applies to the time and cost estimates. The support group should make time and cost estimates for their task, and the project group should approve them. These estimates may require a negotiated revision to adjust other project tasks to accommodate support group plans if they differ from the project team's first estimate. This is a common occurrence. Support groups sometimes must perform their role at a pace dictated by other, higher priority commitments, thus scheduling your project support differently than you had planned. Sometimes the support group sees a completely different way to undertake its role, often to the project's advantage. Or the support group's experts may convince the project team their role must be broader than originally conceived. For all these reasons, involve support groups as early as possible.

Written Commitments

Put all agreements in writing.

Obtain meaningful commitments from support groups within your organization just as you do from outside subcontractors, namely, a written agreement. There must be a Triple Constraint and signatures by both parties. Such agreements lack legal standing and enforcement provisions, but if the support group manager must sign a written agreement, he or she will be motivated to make the group live up to its commitment.

Quiz 11-1

Why would a project manager prefer a large support team?

Coordination

Network diagrams aid coordination.

Once the support groups have been identified and their work has been planned properly and phased in with that of the project team, there is a continuing need to coordinate project team work. This is best done with network diagrams (Figures 11-1 and 11-2). In both figures, support group

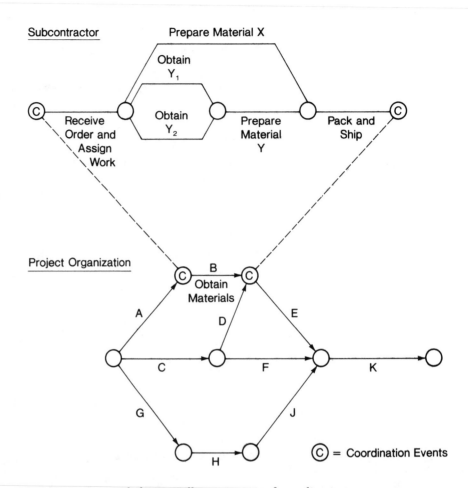

Figure 11-1. Network diagram illustrating use of coordination events.

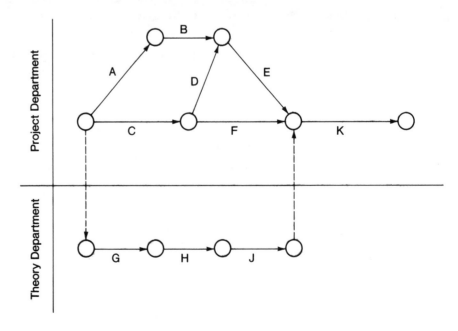

Figure 11-2. Network diagram illustrating use of spatial segregation of a support group's activities.

work has been segregated from the main part of the network. There are many other ways to do this, for instance, using distinctive line patterns for each support category. Where color copying machines are available, a color code may be used advantageously.

Change

Communication and coordination should be primarily in writing. Change should be accomplished by oral communication, over the telephone and/or at meetings involving as many people as required. But the change must then be embodied in the plan revisions.

Quiz 11-2

Once again imagine you are Mel Chase at SUPROMAC. A subcontractor is responsible for providing materials to you on task B, as illustrated in Figure 11-1. You now learn you will be late completing task D. Should you inform your task B subcontractor of this lateness?

Revision

Plan revisions must be written and distributed.

Once committed to paper, plans must be disseminated to and understood by all involved personnel. Plans must also be maintained in a current status. If any out-of-date project plans are allowed to remain in circulation, the credibility of all project plans will become suspect. Therefore, everyone who had the original plan must receive revisions. This can be facilitated by keeping an accurate distribution list.

Interaction with Support Groups

Project team and support group interaction can be difficult. All too often the support group is brought in too late, a situation that reminds me of a story. A commuter comes dashing onto the train platform just as the morning train into the city pulls out. A bystander, observing the commuter has just missed the train, comments, "Gee, that's too bad. If you'd simply run a little bit faster, you'd have caught the train." The commuter knows, of course, it is not a matter of having run a little bit faster but rather of having started a little bit sooner.

Project Actions

The tardy commuter's situation classically applies where the purchasing department is involved. Purchased materials arrive later than required, the project is delayed, and project people blame either the subcontractor for delivering late or the purchasing department for failing to place the order early enough. In fact, the blame lies with the people who did not requisition the purchase sufficiently early so the goods would be delivered on time. They need not run faster; they should have started earlier.

The experienced project manager copes with this problem in two ways. First, he or she makes certain the network diagram schedule allows enough time for the support groups to perform optimally. Second, the project manager makes certain all personnel know when task activities must be completed and holds the task managers accountable for meeting the schedule.

Support Team Viewpoint

These issues can be looked at in a different way, namely, from the point of view of the support groups. They are composed of professionals, in the previous example, purchasing professionals who wish to obtain the best quality of required goods at the lowest possible price within the other con-

Support groups labor under many constraints.

straints project personnel impose. They need time to perform their function in a professionally competent way. In the case of government contracts, there are even laws and regulations that require three competitive bids.

The same is true, of course, of any support group—technical writers, computer programmers, designers, draftspersons, or model shop personnel. Everyone wants to do a good job and wants sufficient time in which to do it. But departments have a work load imposed on them by others. They are trying to respond to many projects bringing work to them at random times and in variable amounts. Thus, support groups typically have some backlog they must work through before they can get to new requests. If they did not have this backlog, if they were sitting there idly waiting for work to arrive, they would not be utilizing a vital organization resource, their own time, in the most effective way.

Subcontractors

Subcontractors are basically no different than you. They have a contract from a customer, in this case, you or your project. They want to be responsive to you, but they have the same kind of problems you do: Personnel and resources frequently are not instantly available; they need time to plan their work; they have to interpret the Triple Constraint in the correct way, and so on.

Your support agreement is a written contract.

Just as a contract controls your relations with your customer, so subcontractors define their relationship to your project by the contract your company's purchasing department issues to them. Should a change be required, it is certainly all right to tell them about it. But the change becomes effective and meaningful only when it is converted into a contract change.

Another point to consider when working with subcontractors is that your request for a proposal can require periodic reviews be included in the contract. This is desirable, as it would be if your customer required periodic reviews of your work. You are trying to see how their work is progressing, to understand if changes will be called for as a result of what they are doing or problems they are encountering, in short, to stay abreast of their work.

But you must draw a fine line between giving new direction and simply keeping abreast of what they are doing. Remember the contract dictates the work and the progress reviews or monitoring activities are solely to find out if it is being done, not to provide daily, weekly, or monthly changes in direction.

Typical Problems

Working with the support team probably causes the greatest difficulty, especially for new, inexperienced project managers. The root of this problem is being dependent on nonsubordinates. Two other problems are closely related. First, to negotiate support agreements takes a lot of time, usually at the very busy project inception period. So it is done reluctantly or poorly or even omitted. In the latter situation, the project manager uses his or her own judgment of what the support group will do. Second, even when the support agreements have been intelligently negotiated, later events frequently require changes be made. Again, this is time-consuming and must be anticipated.

Materials Study Project

Consider the materials study project I have been using as an example. Let us make two further assumptions about it. First, again assume task B ("obtain materials") will require a subcontract to a material supply company. This procurement will be governed by a written contract or purchase order. Such a written instrument is valid only when it is accepted by the material supply company, usually acknowledged by the return of a signed copy. There can be no agreement unless both parties are satisfied by the contemplated Triple Constraint.

Second, assume Tom Richards remains assigned to Richard Thomas but will be responsible for the theoretical tasks (tasks G, H, and J). All too often this kind of agreement is only verbal. But why should a $77,740 theoretical effort (see Figure 8-12) be loosely defined when a much smaller material supply effort is governed by a legally binding agreement? Support group work is commonly authorized informally, and most of the time the results are a disappointment, if not a shock, to the project team.

Highlights

- Support teams do not work for the project manager in an administrative sense, but their participation and contributions are vital.

- Support groups should be involved in projects as early as possible and allowed to plan their task.

- Although they lack legal status, written agreements are an excellent way to obtain commitments from support teams.

- Coordination, a continuing need, is best provided by network diagrams.

- Every plan revision must be written and distributed to all concerned personnel.

Further Reading

R. D. Archibald. *Managing High-Technology Programs and Projects* New York: Wiley-Interscience, 1976.

Chapter 8 reviews many of the written devices the project manager can use to control the support team.

A. J. Melcher and T. A. Kayser. "Leadership Without Formal Authority—The Project Department." *California Management Review,* vol. 13, no. 2 (Winter 1970), pp. 57–64.

This is a case history, with some useful ideas on how to obtain cooperation from support groups.

CHAPTER 12

Role of the Project Manager

Although the project manager is clearly involved in all phases of the project and is ultimately responsible for satisfying the Triple Constraint, his or her interaction with the project and support teams is a key to the implementation phase. This chapter first examines the overriding importance of the project manager's ability to influence other team members. His or her leadership ability depends on motivational skills rather than on authority, regardless of how much hierarchical supervisory authority he or she has over project team members. I also briefly discuss how a manager can gain time to work more effectively with people. Because projects are one-time undertakings, team members must often develop creative solutions. I suggest ways to stimulate creativity.

Influence Rather Than Authority

Limits of Authority

The project manager lacks control.

As Chapters 10 and 11 noted, many people working on a project do not report directly to the project manager, and he or she does not have complete control even over those who do. In the first place, people are free to change jobs in our society. If given a command they do not like, some workers will simply quit. Or they may transfer to another division of the organization. Second, modern motivational theory indicates issuing commands is a poor means to encourage people to perform well on a job. McGregor's Theory X/Theory Y is but one manifestation of the thinking that underlies current managerial practice, which usually substitutes persuasion and participation for command.

Nevertheless, commands are still a way of life, to a greater or lesser extent, depending upon the specific organization and situation. If stated brutally or insensitively, they demotivate and create resentment. If stated politely and reasonably (which is difficult to accomplish), commands may be effective.

Need for Influence

Given these limits to hierarchical authority, project managers must operate by winning the respect of project and support team members. This accomplished, they will find their wishes are accepted voluntarily and frequently with enthusiasm.

A 1977 study by Thamhain and Wilemon identifies nine influence bases available to project managers:

There are nine ways to have influence.

> authority—the legitimate hierarchical right to issue orders
>
> assignment—the project manager's perceived ability to influence a worker's later work assignments
>
> budget—the project manager's perceived ability to authorize others' use of discretionary funds
>
> promotion—the project manager's perceived ability to improve a worker's position
>
> money—the project manager's perceived ability to increase a worker's monetary remuneration
>
> penalty—the project manager's perceived ability to dispense or cause punishment
>
> work challenge—an intrinsic motivational factor capitalizing on a worker's enjoyment of doing a particular task
>
> expertise—special knowledge the project manager possesses and others deem important
>
> friendship—friendly personal relationships between the project manager and others

The first clearly depends on higher management's decision to invest the project manager with power, regardless of power's intrinsic utility. The next five may or may not be truly inherent in the project manager's position; others' perception is most important in establishing their utility to the project manager. The seventh is an available tool anyone may use to influence others. The project manager must earn the last two.

There will be occasions when the project manager must negotiate with team members. A typical approach is to explain the rationale of the effort and to involve the people in planning the detailed work packages. Given this need to influence, an effective project manager must be a superb communicator. He or she must have verbal and written fluency and be persuasive to be effective.

Effective Managerial Behavior _____

A manager must plan and manage.

The project manager is a manager, not a doer. If the project manager is writing lines of computer code for a programming project, designing a circuit for a new product project, or nailing boards together for a construction project, who is planning the work of others? Who is deciding what approach to take to the support group manager so as to obtain the services of the most senior and best qualified person? And who is trying to devise a contingency plan in case the system test does not produce desirable results? The project manager must spend his or her time working with people and planning their work so nothing is overlooked and contingency plans are ready if needed.

On a very small project, the project manager's participation is also required as a worker, not merely as a manager. If not physically, then at least mentally, a project manager in this situation should have two hats, one labeled "project manager" and the other labeled "worker." The project manager must realize which function he or she is performing at any given moment and wear the appropriate hat.

Qualifications

The project manager should be chosen because of an interest and skill in human relations.

Generally speaking, one becomes a project manager because one has been an excellent programmer, circuit designer, or carpenter rather than because one has been trained or demonstrated competency as a project manager. In fact, one's demonstrated technical or professional skills are frequently problem-solving or performance skills that do not involve an ability to interact with others. But project managers need people skills rather than technical skills. Developing people skills can be extremely difficult for many technically trained people who become project managers. Physical systems tend to behave in repeatable and predictable ways; people do not. The same thing said to different people can produce different reactions. In fact, the same thing said to the same person at two different times can produce different reactions. This lack of predictability can be a major pitfall for many prospective project managers. Project managers must deal with both technical and emotional issues. If not already fluent with these human relations skills, they should take a course in behavioral psychology.

Managers manage and workers perform the tasks.

The project manager sets objectives and establishes plans, organizes, staffs, sets up controls, issues directives, spends time working with people, and generally sees the project is completed in a satisfactory way, on time, and within budget. The project manager does not do the work of others on the project. A project manager who is an excellent circuit designer may find it frustrating to watch a more junior person carry out the circuit design activities on the project. The junior person will take longer, make mistakes, and not do as good a job as could a project manager with that skill.

But if the project manager starts to do the circuit design, it demotivates the junior person and lessens the manager's time to function in the most vital role of all, namely, that of project manager.

Communication

Effective communication is one of the more difficult human endeavors. There are so many obstacles it is amazing any effective communication at all occurs. Words have different meanings, and people often have different perceptions. The project manager's reputation (be it as a jokester or as a very serious person) will alter the way any message is received. Everyone the project manager communicates with will tend to hear the message he or she wants or expects to hear, which is not necessarily the message the project manager is attempting to deliver.

Quiz 12-1

List several means to improve communication.

Communication must be worked at.

There is an aphorism about how to communicate: First you tell someone you intend to tell them, then you tell them, and then you tell them you told them. There is much truth in this. In addition to multiple message delivery, feedback, notices, and proximity can be used to improve project communication.

Feedback.   Communication is very much like a servomechanism in that it is not effective unless there is feedback. This means communication can be improved by asking the person to whom the message has been delivered to restate it in his or her own words. Another effective technique is to back up any verbal communication with a memo. This may also be done the other way around, first sending the memo and then having a meeting to discuss it. It is the duality of mode and the recipient's restatement that is most effective rather than simple redundancy.

Notices.   It is impractical constantly to meet with all participants on a very large project. Even on a smaller project, it may be disruptive to have numerous meetings. It is thus desirable to issue project notices and reminders of priority actions for any given period. Putting such notices on distinctively colored paper or preprinting the project name on the top will set them apart from the other mail.

Proximity.   Locating the people on the project near each other also aids communication. Because the people are close together, they can see each other more often, which makes communication easier and more frequent. And when people are in frequent contact, their point of view tends to become more uniform.

Follow-up

It is necessary to have some system of follow-up of the communications, be they face to face or written. Some people simply keep an action log, a chronological listing of all agreements reached with other people for which follow-up action is expected.

Follow up communications.

Somewhat more effective is a follow-up system keyed to the individual from whom action is expected. A filing card with each key person's name printed on the top may be used to record notations of actions expected of that person. A variant of this is keeping a folder for each key person in which you store records of all discussions or copies of memos for which follow-up action is required or requested. In either event, hold periodic meetings with each key person and use the filing card or folder to plan the topics to be discussed.

When it is known project managers (or any manager, for that matter) have such a consistent follow-up system, people who work for or with them will realize any statements made to them will be taken seriously. Therefore, commitments made to them will tend to receive serious and consistent attention.

Conflict Resolution

Projects are fraught with conflicts. They inevitably arise because projects are temporary entities within more permanent organizations. One root cause is thus competition for resources. Regardless of organizational form, project managers and functional managers tend to have momentary interests that are at odds, so project managers must be able to "stomach" conflict.

The project manager must cope with conflict.

The 1977 Thamhain and Wilemon study (as well as one published in 1975) reviews the causes of and ways to resolve conflict. Their findings indicate many things can be done to reduce conflicts, the simplest of which is having good plans, current and realistic schedules, and thorough communications.

Efficient Time Management

Given the wide range of project managers' duties (in a sense, they must be all things to all people), they can easily end up working nights and weekends unless they are very efficient in their use of time. Of course, they should not make the mistake of being efficient to the point of being ineffective. Effectiveness is achieving the desired results. Effectiveness is what counts, but project managers are more likely to be effective if they use their time efficiently.

The overriding issue in time management is "first things first." The project manager must know the most important things to do this year, this month, this week, today, and right now. Only when he or she has a clear perception of priorities can a project manager effectively manage his or her time.

Quiz 12-2

List several ways to manage your time efficiently.

Because project management involves intergrating the work of many people, numerous meetings will be held. Conducting them efficiently and effectively is essential. The following are keys to improving meetings:

Manage time efficiently.

- Know beforehand why the meeting is to be held and what outcome is expected.

- Determine the minimum number of people required.

- Choose a meeting location with room arrangement consonant with the meeting's purpose (for example, a round table arrangement for discussion among equals, a lecture hall arrangement, and so forth).

- Circulate an agenda with topic durations to all attendees, and perhaps discuss this individually with key participants ahead of time.

- Be prepared and open the meeting on time with a restatement of the purpose and agenda.

- If possible, ask each attendee (one at a time) for his or her views on each topic prior to topic completion.

- Verbally summarize what transpires at the meeting and later distribute published minutes to all attendees.

Theories of Motivation

Regardless of hierarchical authority, anyone can encourage or stimulate others to contribute to a project and improve their productivity. For project managers, many of whom lack direct authority over all the resources required for project success, an understanding of motivation is essential. A major element of the project manager role is to avoid demotivating others. There are many theories of motivation, four of which I shall briefly review.

Theory X/Theory Y

I have already mentioned Douglas McGregor's work in identifying two managerial styles, Theory X and Theory Y. Theory X is the authoritarian style, in which top management makes decisions and coerces workers to comply. Theory Y is the participative style, built upon the finding that people both enjoy and want to work. Theory X assumes external control of the worker; Theory Y assumes useful controls are within individuals and managers can draw upon workers' self-direction.

Participative decision making is best.

In working with the support team, over which he or she lacks control, the project manager should try to adopt the Theory Y style (and would probably be well advised to use it with the project team as well). Authoritarian behavior is not usually appropriate. Managerial behavior can be based on the assumption that others want to do a good job and eliciting their participation. To put it another way, consider how you would like to be managed and how you would respond.

Hierarchy of Needs

Abraham Maslow has developed a theory of the hierarchy of needs. This theory, too, holds that motivation is not external but rather arises within the worker if managerial actions are not inappropriate. The worker is motivated to achieve a specific goal because of an inherent internal need.

People have five levels of needs.

Each person has five levels of needs. The lowest of these is physiological or body needs (eat, sleep, have shelter, and so forth). A hungry person will have a goal to eat and will engage in the goal-directed activity of buying and preparing food to satisfy the hunger need. (In fact, if we try to prevent this person from satisfying the need, by denying him or her money to pay for the food, for instance, the person may engage in such antisocial behavior as robbery to satisfy the need.)

Once this first need is filled, continuing to offer more food, sleep, or shelter has no motivational value. Higher level needs now come into play. Second-level needs are safety and security; third-level needs are social; and fourth-level needs are esteem or ego. The fifth-level needs are for self-actualization or fulfillment. To take advantage of Maslow's findings, a project manager would have to understand the levels of need an individual has already satisfied. Then, he or she could offer satisfiers for unmet needs as an encouragement. Americans generally have unfilled needs on levels three, four, or five; therefore, the project manager would have to offer satisfiers aimed at these levels.

Motivational Factors

Achievement and recognition are the most powerful motivators.

Frederick Herzberg has done an excellent study on work and motivation, examining specific factors that motivate workers. He found many things done (company policies, supervision, work conditions, and salary, for instance) are not motivational at all. He called these "hygiene factors." The absence of hygiene factors is demotivating, but their presence is not motivating.

Instead, there have to be motivational factors present to foster high individual productivity. The key motivational factors are achievement, recognition, the work itself, responsibility, advancement, and growth. Achievement and recognition are short term, and the others are long term in their impact. Thus, it is important to give workers recognition frequently (but not routinely) for significant accomplishments.

Behavior Modification

People's behavior can be modified.

B. F. Skinner devised a theory of behavior modification that advocates positive reinforcement, namely, rewards for "good" behavior. Using Skinner's theory, one would induce people to behave differently (that is, consonant with project goals) by rewarding them when they act appropriately. "Rewards" typically are consistent with Herzberg's findings, namely, a sense of achievement and recognition.

Thus, if a designer does a fine job on your project, it is appropriate to send her a memo and send a copy to her boss (or vice versa) and perhaps to her personnel folder as well. Conversely, if you have been practicing behavior modification and positive reinforcement consistently, you do not have to do anything if on another occasion she does a poor job. The absence of positive reinforcement will be message enough. Further, that absence may very well motivate the designer to ask you how her performance fell short.

Very early in my industrial career, the president of my company sent the following letter (on engraved, personal stationery) to me at my home just after the project team of which I was a member shipped the first unit of an advanced system:

> Dear Milt:
>   I would like to extend to you my hearty congratulations for your contributions to the outstanding technical success of the Satrack Program. I know that you must feel proud of being a member of the team who accomplished a marked advance in the state of the art of aspheric manufacture.
>   Our Company is now considered to be in the forefront of this development activity, and it has been through your contributions that we have achieved this position.
>   I know that your efforts were great and there were many long evenings and weekends which you personally sacrificed. It is indeed

gratifying that we have the people with the spirit to undertake such a challenging problem and carry forth to a successful conclusion.

Sincerely yours,

The recipient of such a letter will become motivated to put in similar extraordinary efforts in the future and probably will continue to have family support for that effort.

Other examples of positive reinforcement include awards (wall plaques, luncheons or dinners, trips, and so forth) or a story or picture in the company newspaper.

Stimulating Creativity

The project manager must also stimulate creativity. This is not merely applicable to high-technology projects; it is often required on all projects. Even two similar projects, for instance, building two bridges over the same river, can encounter different soil conditions requiring an innovative approach in one case. In general, the less precedent for the project, the more creativity will be required.

Motivation

Positive reinforcement and brainstorming will stimulate creativity.

Creativity may be stimulated simply by managing in a way consistent with Herzberg's and Skinner's findings. Encouragement by providing recognition and appreciation is the most straightforward technique to stimulate creativity. In addition, one must provide a favorable atmosphere. In a sense, we are looking at positive reinforcement again. People are permitted to fail when asked to produce creative results and are not castigated for doing so. Rather, they are praised when they succeed.

Brainstorming

Brainstorming techniques are often used to deal with some intractable problem. The conventional method for brainstorming is to advise perhaps a half-dozen people of the problem and after one or two days convene a brainstorming meeting. At this meeting, restate the problem and reiterate the ground rules:

1. Absolutely no criticism (including smirking) is permitted.
2. The more ideas produced, the better is the session.
3. Novel, unusual (even impractical) ideas are desired.
4. Improvement or combination of prior ideas is also desirable.

Use a tape recorder to permit more leisurely subsequent consideration of the ideas thus generated.

An alternative method that may work better in some situations is to have a facilitator talk to a few people individually and ask for their ideas on solving the problem. After three or four people have been interviewed, you have a list of ideas to use to start the brainstorming session (like pump priming), which is then carried out in the normal way.

Typical Problems

Project managers are not normally selected from a pool of trained, qualified people. Rather, projects arise within (or descend upon) the organization, and a person who has demonstrated technical proficiency is asked to become project leader.

Such people are often good "doers" and have technical skills and may think they want to be a project manager, but they usually take the job not knowing what is involved. They may get along with others (as opposed to being hermitlike) but be unable to cope with the inevitable conflicts that bedevil the project manager. What then happens is the organization has a poor project manager and has lost the services of a good technical resource.

One cure for this problem is to be sure candidates for project management read books such as this prior to being offered jobs as project managers. After that, assuming a continuing interest in the job, the selected candidates should be sent to any one of the plethora of seminars on project management. These seminars, typically of two to five days duration, are given throughout the world.

Materials Study Project

At SUPROMAC, Ed Ross has been concerned for some time about the development of more project managers and has periodically conducted in-house seminars on project management. Thus, Mel Chase, who has demonstrated competency as a mechanical engineer as well as exhibiting drive and personal ambition, attended such a seminar before he was asked to manage the NERESCO materials study project.

Unfortunately, such prior training and care in project manager selection is exceptional. Most organizations select a good, professionally competent worker and let him or her struggle with the unfamiliar role.

Highlights

- There are many limits to authority, so project managers should learn how to wield influence.
- Managers must confine themselves to planning and let others perform the tasks.
- Human relations skills are vital to a project manager.
- Effective communication can be aided by feedback, issuing notices, and locating workers near each other.
- Familiarity with theories of motivation will help managers do their job.
- Creativity can be stimulated by positive reinforcement and brainstorming.

Further Reading

R. D. Archibald. *Managing High-Technology Programs and Projects.* New York: Wiley-Interscience, 1976.

Chapter 3 is an excellent overview of the many role issues confronting project managers.

V. G. Hajek. *Management of Engineering Projects.* New York: McGraw-Hill, 1977.

Chapter 1 is only five pages long, but it has an overview of the project manager's role, stressing contractual involvement.

P. Hersey and K. H. Blanchard. *Management of Organization Behavior: Utilizing Human Resources,* 3rd ed. Englewood Cliffs, N.J.: Prentice-Hall, 1977.

This is a very good and reasonably nontechnical review of motivation and organizational behavior.

F. Herzberg. "One More Time: How Do You Motivate Employees?" *Harvard Business Review,* vol. 46, no. 1 (January–February 1968), pp. 53–62.

This is a classic, brief article that summarizes job factors that are "satisfiers" and "dissatisfiers."

C. C. Martin. *Project Management—How to Make It Work.* New York: AMACOM, 1976.

Chapter 7 is a good practical summary of project manager problems.

H. J. Thamhain and D. L. Wilemon. "Conflict Management in Project Life Cycles." *Sloan Management Review*, vol. 16, no. 3 (Spring 1975), pp. 31–50.

H. J. Thamhain and D. L. Wilemon. "Leadership, Conflict, and Program Management Effectiveness." *Sloan Management Review*, vol. 19, no. 1 (Fall 1977), pp. 69–89.

The first article reviews the kinds of conflict project managers encounter and some ways to cope with it. The second article measures which influencing techniques are most effective in given situations.

Part FOUR

Control

CHAPTER 13

Control Tools

The next phase of project management is control. First this chapter discusses various control techniques. Then there is a detailed consideration of the use of reports. Last, the special case of controlling several projects simultaneously is discussed.

Control Techniques

Controls tell you if the project plan is being followed.

The first, and in many ways most important, control is a well-publicized plan for all three dimensions of the Triple Constraint. A work breakdown structure, a network diagram that indicates every element of it, and a cost estimate for each activity indicates how the project should be carried out. Any deviation—and there usually is at least one—from this three-dimensional plan indicates the need for corrective action. Without such a plan, control is impossible.

There are several restrictive control tools available, such as withholding resources or discretionary authority. When the project manager uses these controls, he or she is assured people working on the project request the use of these resources or authorities, thus providing visibility. As an example, the project manager could require any expenditure in excess of $1,000 receives his or her specific approval. Or the project manager could require any drawing release to need his or her signature. These kinds of controls go beyond the project plan in that they make project workers seek out the project manager for approval during the performance of each project activity or task. Anyone's failure to request approval of a planned major purchase tells the project manager the project has deviated from plan.

This kind of restrictive control may well be appropriate with an inexperienced team or on a difficult project. But it is normally appropriate only for very small projects. If essentially all decisions on a large project must flow through the manager, the project will get bogged down by his or her lack of time to review a myriad of documents for approval. An effective variation on this restrictive approval control approach is to insist on independent inspection and quality control approvals or on test data as means to verify progress.

Another project control method is to place trust entirely in the person carrying out a particular task. This method is fine if that person is able to recognize deviations from plan and realizes they must be reported promptly to the project manager. The person must also be capable of reporting the problem clearly. Because these three preconditions are rarely satisfied, this control tool should not normally be used.

Control is best exercised by examining the status of tasks.

A far better approach is for the project manager to examine the work being done under the direct control of the project team and support teams. This kind of control is based on the Theory Y assumption that people working on project tasks will be trying to do a good job (which can often become a self-fulfilling prophecy) rather than on the Theory X assumption that people will not do a good job. These examinations of activity work are accomplished by reading reports and conducting project reviews.

Reports

Reports may concern performance, schedule, or cost.

Reports fall into three broad categories: those concerned with the accomplishments along the performance axis, those concerned with schedule progress, and those concerned with cost. Reports may be written as summaries to provide an overview or be detailed about a particular task activity or some other element of project work. Reports may be strictly for the use of the organization performing the project or be intended for people outside, such as the customer or cocontractors. If the project organization is an industrial company such as SUPROMAC, there is a wide spectrum of people to whom reports might be addressed, as shown in Figure 13-1.

Problems

The project manager cannot depend entirely on reports. In the first place, they may be inaccurate, a common failing of cost reports, which are prone to arithmetical errors and keypunching errors if a computer-based system is being employed. On the other two axes, the people who write reports are prone to unwarranted optimism. Project workers generally assume a well-advanced task is nearly complete; in fact, no task is complete until it is truly finished. Thus, most task reports will indicate a task is 80 or

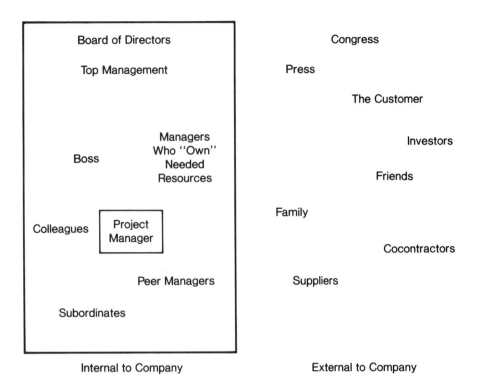

Figure 13-1. Report recipients.

90 percent complete, implying it will require additionally only a small fraction of the time already spent. Unless the task is as simple as drilling a hundred holes in a plate, it is normally impossible to measure what percentage of the task is truly complete. In general, completing any given task requires more time than the person working on it forecasts. For instance, a report that X lines of code have been written for computer program originally planned to be Y lines long tells you nothing about the percentage of completion. You know you are truly complete only when Z lines of code (which may be either more or less than the Y lines planned) actually run properly and adequately.

Even though the task manager's report expresses a high degree of confidence the task will be completed when scheduled, such a promise is not deliverable. Reports are one-way communication and lack the give and take possible in a meeting, so it is hard to judge the status of a task in progress solely from written data.

Quiz 13-1

Why would the project illustrated in Figure 13-2 be difficult to control?

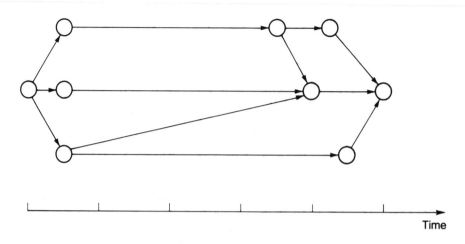

Figure 13-2. Time-based network diagram.

Dividing a project into many small tasks aids determinations of its status.

If the work breakdown structure divides the project into many small tasks, the manager can look at each of them individually and decide whether they are complete. Only those tasks for which all work has been done are considered complete. No other task, regardless of the amount of effort put in so far, is complete. A task that is 80, 90, 99 percent complete is not finished. This two-state (bivalued) approach to examining tasks simplifies the project manager's job tremendously. He or she can accept as complete only those tasks for which reports (oral or written) guarantee the activity is complete. With many small tasks rather than only a few larger ones, there is much less uncertainty about overall project status.

Detail Level

Reports should always be as brief as possible. Because many people concerned with the project will wish to receive reports, there is a tendency to try to circulate one report to many recipients. This is a mistake. Many who wish to be kept abreast of progress are not interested in small details. This is especially true of busy management, both project organization and customer, for whom the project manager should prepare brief summary level reports. Such reports might also be circulated to people concerned with some specific aspects of the project but who do not require all the detail in any particular report.

Pictures, demonstrations, and models should also be encouraged, especially for high-technology or geographically remote projects. It is often hard for people not intimately concerned with the project to visualize the expected outcome or even the concept. For them, tangible descriptions, pictures, and such are by far the most appropriate means for providing reports. If your organization has closed-circuit television, this may be an excellent use of it.

It is always important to avoid the pitfall of excessive reporting. Clearly, this is a gray area requiring judgment. The "convenience" of copying machines can easily lead to too many copies of overly detailed reports being circulated to too many people.

Cost Reports

Cost planning and reporting is important because it provides a guide for management action. It permits comparison of actual accomplishments in terms of costs incurred and planned accomplishments. Thus, it aids in determining whether there will be a cost overrun or underrun at completion. In some instances, it may aid in determining whether a specific task is on schedule.

Unfortunately, in many organizations, there is a tendency to look at actual cost versus planned cost as virtually the only measure of project progress. This is useless because there may be offsetting overruns and underruns.

Multiple Projects

The value of summary status indicators is questionable.

As a project manager, you may eventually be responsible for more than one project. You may have many project managers reporting to you or there may be so many task managers reporting to you on a single project that you cannot personally attend all the task reviews and critically examine all the necessary detail. In this case, you must receive some kind of summary information that indicates the status of the several projects (or the many tasks) for which you have responsibility. When you cannot personally get into details, you are completely at the mercy of those who summarize information for you. Robert A. Howell indicates one way you might receive summary briefing information. In essence, his proposal is that for every project (or task) for which you have responsibility, there should be a red, yellow, or green status indicator for each of the technical, schedule, and cost dimensions of the job. He also suggests these for funding status and would display in this summary form whether project review meetings have been held and at what point the program plan obtained approval. Such a system is certainly graphic, but it is no better than the judgment of the person who prepares the information.

Personal reviews are best.

Probably a better approach is to visit the various project reviews personally. Imagine you have three projects reporting to you, each of which is being managed by another project manager who reviews it monthly. You might sit in on each of these in a rotating fashion, so you attend the review of each project once every three months.

Typical Problems

Problems arise because of too much or too little control. The former may demotivate personnel, consume too much time, or cost too much.

Inadequate control, based perhaps on the naive optimism that the project will be performed in accordance with plan, can lead to disaster. The following (edited) quotation comes from a memo (written thirteen months after the start of the project) in my files:

> Several major factors have contributed to the increase in the development cost:
>
> A. The accessories were far more complex than anticipated at the time the original plan was prepared. There was not, at that time, any defined level of performance for these accessories; the feasibility of the accessories had not been studied. The estimates for the optical systems and mechanical components of the accessories were inadequate until several months of feasibility study had been performed and the products fully defined. Even after they were defined, all of the accessories have had to go through repeated design iterations. In October, all of the accessory designs were rejected. The Head Adapter and the Lamp Housing required mechanical design rework to reduce their size. In addition, the Lamp Housing required optical redesign to accommodate additional optical features necessary for a smaller, more compact package. The Head Adapter was finally approved in mid-December; however, the base was not approved until mid-January. The Lamp Housing received verbal approval only last week. The Accessory, as designed in this project, was found to be completely unacceptable, requiring total redesign, forcing its removal from this project (all future efforts on the Accessory will be covered by a separate project and are excluded from this summary).
>
> The original plan of last February (13 months ago) contained approximately 600 hours of optical and mechanical design for the Accessories. In our revised plan, including labor to date, the optical and mechanical design is approximately 2400 hours; the difference is 1800 hours plus drafting time.
>
> B. The original plan called for 670 hours for Industrial Design. Because the designs have been subjected to repeated revisions, the revised plan, including labor hours spent to date, puts Industrial Design at approximately 1700 hours; an increase of 1030 hours.
>
> C. The layout and design of the Indicator Dial required considerably more time than that provided in the original plan. The Dial design was rejected several times, which added approximately 800 hours.
>
> D. The custom microcircuit for the digital meter version added coordination time with the vendors and with purchasing of approximately 300 hours.
>
> E. It was assumed in the original plan that the proprietary microcircuit would be available as an input to this project. Delays in receiving properly functioning devices made the timing critical. Therefore, coordination with the vendor and evaluation of sample devices of about 400 hours was performed on this project.

F. Due to the complexity of the mechanical design, we added preparation of a tooling plan, preliminary tool design, and coordination to the project. This had added approximately 450 hours. (We will also do the tool design, but that work is covered under a separate project.)

G. The revised plan contains 90 hours for planning and supervision; that time is now charged to the project rather than handled as indirect overhead.

H. The original plan was based on burdened labor rates that were in effect when the plan was prepared. The change in burdened labor rates since then has added approximately 20 percent to the project cost.

I. Personnel being shifted temporarily to other projects has caused approximately 200–300 hours to be added.

J. Approximately 340 hours were added to Support Engineering time to better match experience on other projects.

K. The original plan allowed for about 800 hours for project administration. The actual and planned hours now represent an increase of approximately 800 hours due to slightly higher monthly hours plus the longer duration of the project.

L. Compared to the original plan, a higher level of Technical Documentation hours have been expended. Additional drafting time associated with the accessory mechanical designs and redesigns (due to size rejections) is approximately 600 hours. Other factors were the low estimates for standard parts drawings and reworking circuit layouts due to mechanical and size limitations. These other factors represent approximately 1200 hours.

This project has gotten into severe cost (approximately quadrupled) and schedule difficulties, and it basically got that way by slipping one day at a time. Controls, exercised on a continuing basis, could have detected deviations from plan in time to redirect—or terminate—the project.

Materials Study Project

Mel Chase has to decide how to control the theoretical portion (tasks G, H, and J) of the materials study project. Because much of the work will be abstract, which makes Mel uncomfortable, he opts to trust the task performer, Tom Richards. A discussion with Tom has made Mel confident the three critical conditions are satisfied: Tom can recognize if there is a problem; Tom knows a deviation must be reported promptly; and Tom both writes and speaks clearly. As further assurance and control, Mel asks Tom also to provide a brief written note on work status each month.

Highlights _____

- Comparison with the project plan provides the basis for control.

- Project managers may exercise control by requiring their approval or trusting task managers, but the best approach is to examine the status of tasks.

- Reports, which may concern any axis of the Triple Constraint and be detailed or general, provide a means to examine the status of tasks.

- Managers in charge of several projects can best exercise control by periodic personal reviews.

Further Reading _____

R. D. Archibald. *Managing High-Technology Programs and Projects.* New York: Wiley-Interscience, 1976.

Chapters 8 and 9 provide several illustrations of control techniques.

R. H. Clough and G. A. Sears. *Construction Project Management*, 2nd ed. New York: Wiley-Interscience, 1979.

Chapters 9 and 10 stress time and cost control, also illustrating several reporting techniques.

J. Gido. *An Introduction to Project Planning.* Schenectady, N.Y.: General Electric, 1974.

Chapter 5 briefly treats control, with concentration on the schedule aspect.

Robert A. Howell. "Multiproject Control." *Managing Projects and Programs Series.* Cambridge, Mass.: Reprint from *Harvard Business Review* (no. 21300) 1971.

This article clearly illustrates a method for controlling several projects simultaneously. As noted in this chapter, there are some problems with Howell's approach, but it is still the best concept if there are several projects.

R. Pilcher. *Appraisal and Control of Project Costs.* London: McGraw-Hill, 1973.

Chapters 11 and 12 provide a detailed discussion of cost controls.

J. D. Wiest and F. K. Levy. *A Management Guide to PERT/CPM*, 2nd ed. Englewood Cliffs, N.J.: Prentice-Hall, 1977.

Chapter 6 is a brief discussion of PERT/Cost as a control tool.

CHAPTER 14

Reviews

There are two kinds of project reviews: periodic (typically monthly) and topical. Reviews are the most important control tool available to the project manager; they assure he or she and the project team will actually be meeting to discuss progress. This chapter deals with both types of reviews and the general necessity to conduct reviews.

The Necessity for Reviews

Reviews are your off-course alarm.

Having reviews is very much like having a navigator on an airplane. Reviews and a navigator are unnecessary if everything is proceeding according to plan. The purpose of both is to uncover deviations and correct them. Experienced project managers know the project will not proceed as planned, but they do not know how it will deviate. Only the naive project manager believes the plan is sufficient and no further navigation is necessary to arrive at the project's Triple Constraint point destination.

The project manager's boss and other senior management will frequently want to know about project status. Although this may not be true for relatively insignificant projects within an organization, it is a very common situation for commercial development projects where company money is at stake and for larger projects being performed on contract for others. The customer, too, may wish to have periodic or topical reviews. These requirements and their nature and thoroughness should have been included in the negotiated contract for the work. The people working on the project will also wish to have reviews of the overall project from time to time. This is their means of learning whether their effort has to be adjusted from plan to conform with some new reality or everything is still proceeding according to the original plan (which never occurs). Reviews with the project personnel in attendance are a means for communication and can provide motivation.

The Conduct of Reviews _____

Whether reviews are periodic or topical, they should be planned. Certain questions are almost always appropriate to raise.

Planning

Reviews may be thought of as a very small project. The goal is acquisition of all relevant information. There is a schedule and cost. The schedule may be a simple statement that the review will consume two hours on a particular afternoon. The cost depends on the number of people who participate and preparation time.

Think of a review as a small project.

There should be a plan for reviews. Everyone involved should understand the Triple Constraint for the review and be prepared to carry out their assignment. This means the project manager must make specific assignments to various individuals, who must know how much time and what level of detail is appropriate for their participation. Reviews may also be thought of as a particular kind of meeting. As such, all the care of preparation and follow-up discussed in Chapter 12 is relevant.

Questions

The smart project manager learns to ask questions at project reviews. This need is illustrated by another Vermont story:

> A farmer and his hired hand were by the road when a motorist inquired if he was on the right road for Jericho Center, and the farmer gave affirmative reply. After he had driven on, the hired man remarked, "You didn't tell him the bridge was out." "Nope," said the farmer. "He didn't ask."
>
> (Quoted from *What the Old Timer Said* by Allen R. Foley, published by The Stephen Greene Press, 1971. Copyright © 1971 by Allen R. Foley. Reproduced by permission.)

In common with the motorist in this tale, you may find yourself headed in the wrong direction of your project unless you learn to ask questions.

Ask "why" questions.

You are not asking questions to embarrass or pillory anyone but rather to find out how the project is deviating from plan so you can take corrective action. Thus, ask questions nonthreateningly. Such nondirective questions often start out with "why." A very good question is, "Why are you doing that?" You can follow this with successive "why" questions. Some other helpful questions to ask are the following:

- What persistent problems do you have, and what is being done to correct them?

- Which problems do you anticipate arising in the future?

- Do you need any information you do not have now?

- Are there any resources (people or things) you do not yet have and you believe you will need?

- Are there any personnel problems now or that you anticipate?

- Do you know of any things that will give you schedule difficulties in completing your task? If so, what are they?

- Is there any possibility your task will be completed early?

- Will your task be completed within the allowed budget, or do you anticipate some overrun?

- Is there any possibility your task will be completed with an underrun?

- Is there any possibility completion of your task will lead to any technological breakthroughs for which patents might be appropriate?

- Has any work done on your task led to any competitive edge we might use to gain other business elsewhere?

Plan to conduct project review meetings and expect problems to surface.

The thing to remember about project reviews and these questions is that you are almost assuredly going to hear some bad news. Most of us do not cope with bad news in a very positive way, so the project review can easily become a recrimination and blaming session. This will not be productive. It will destroy the review and much additional effort on the project. Be businesslike and factual in conducting the reviews, and keep asking questions to gather information. If it is appropriate to assess blame, do that in a different meeting, preferably privately with the person who must be blamed.

Periodic Reviews

In general, every project should be reviewed once a month. It may be appropriate to review some projects once a year or once every three months; others may require weekly or even daily reviews. Unless there are compelling reasons to do otherwise, schedule periodic reviews for a few days after the monthly project cost reports are available.

Periodic reviews catch deviations from plan before they become major disasters. In the case of the overrun project discussed in Chapter 13, periodic project reviews could have caught the deviations at the end of one or two months, when something might have been done about them, rather than at the end of thirteen months, when the accumulated deviation from plan was so severe.

Task Review

A task is in one of two conditions: complete or not complete. For tasks whose performance axis dimension has been completed, examine the actual versus planned cost and schedule, as illustrated in Figure 14-1. Unless there is something unique about the cost deviations on any completed activity, the accumulated actual cost versus plan can be used to project the cost at the end of the project. In Figure 14-1, actual cost for the five complete tasks ($42,000) is less than planned cost ($44,100), and the ratio of these indicates final actual costs will be 97.5 percent of plan.

Watch the critical path.

Actual versus plan ratio may not be meaningful in the case of schedule variations because many of the completed tasks will not be on the critical path. An activity not on the critical path will often be completed later than plan simply because it was not necessary to complete it within the planned time. Thus, the project manager can make predictions about the schedule only by looking at those completed tasks on the critical path.

It is appropriate to ask which incomplete tasks are in progress and which have not yet been started. For those under way, find out whether there have already been any difficulties that would preclude their being completed on time or within the cost plan.

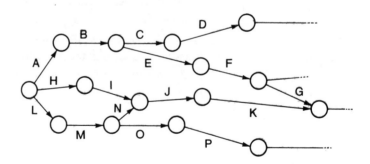

1 - Identify technically complete activities.
2 - Examine actual versus planned cost and schedule:

Completed Activity	Cost			Schedule		
	Act	Plan	Var	Act	Plan	Var
A	3,000	3,200	200	7	6	⟨1⟩
B	4,100	2,900	⟨1,200⟩	9	5	⟨4⟩
C	6,000	8,400	2,400	6	11	5
D	9,700	12,600	2,900	12	17	5
E	19,200	17,000	⟨2,200⟩	24	23	⟨1⟩

Figure 14-1. Measuring progress.

Quiz 14-1

If you were managing the project illustrated in Figure 14-1, what concerns might you have?

In the case of cost review, it is necessary to examine the details of each task individually as shown in Figure 14-2. The project manager who looks only at the overall project may be deceived. Project cost can appear to be in harmony with the plan, but that may conceal compensating task overruns and underruns or other difficulties that must be explored.

Commitments

Project cost reports are always plagued by certain problems. First, they are not issued instantly at the end of the month. It takes time to gather the data, process it, print it out, and distribute it, whether the system is manual or electronic. Second, these reports are never the highest priority in any corporation's accounting department, coming after payroll and usually after customer billing. Thus, project cost reports typically follow completion of the monthly period by two or three weeks (at least a week and a half, and in some cases, five or six weeks).

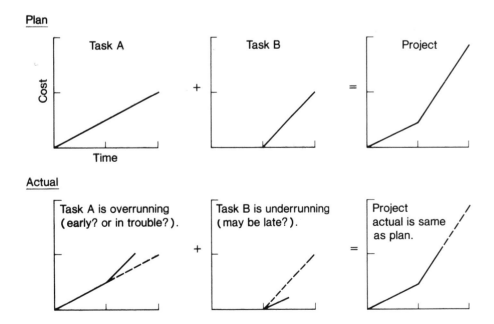

Figure 14-2. Details matter.

Commitments are future costs.

In addition, cost reports are nothing but a record of the apparent charges to a project, which may be in error. Even if the cost charges to the project are correct, they do not necessarily reflect the corresponding amount of performance accomplishment. Even if the actual costs for each task agree completely with the plan for each task, there is no assurance the work accomplishment has a corresponding degree of completion. Within an individual task, where there is no detailed further subtask breakdown, the project manager has only judgment to guide whether progress and cost are consistent. But if a project is divided into many tasks, that ambiguity is removed because the project manager can look at completed tasks and compare their actual cost with plan. In looking at these costs for tasks, the manager must also look at commitments. Commitments are obligations for which the project will be billed but which are not yet reflected on the actual cost reports. Figure 14-3 illustrates two common problems.

A task apparently completed with an underrun may in fact have outstanding bills charged against it. To preclude surprises, look at the commitments charged against that task. You may do so with either a manual or computer-based commitment report. If these reports do not exist, the project manager must maintain these manually to avoid unpleasant surprises.

To summarize, review the Triple Constraint:

- technical dimension
    Task is either complete or not.

- schedule dimension
    Compare actual and planned time for completed tasks.
    Slippage is significant only if the schedule is delayed.

Month	Event	Commitment Report	Cost Report
1	$10K purchase order issued	$10,000	-0-
2	$1K trip authorized	11,000	-0-
3	Traveler paid $900	10,000	$900
4	Vendor delivers	10,000	900
5	Vendor sends bill	10,000	900
6		10,000	900
7	Vendor's bill paid	-0-	10,900

Figure 14-3.   Commitments are future costs.

- cost dimension

  Compare actual and planned cost for completed tasks.

  Include commitments.

Cost to Complete

Periodically, the project manager should request estimates of the cost (and time) to complete all incomplete tasks. You might do so quarterly or semi-annually and also whenever the plan is revised substantially.

Do not make these estimates by simple subtraction of cost to date from the planned cost, as in method one in Figure 14-4. Have each task manager totally reestimate the task in light of everything now known, as shown by method two in the figure. Unfortunately, this often indicates the project will overrun its budget, but it is important to learn of that possibility early enough to do something about it.

Quiz 14-2

Why should the project manager ask for estimates of time and cost to complete the project?

Follow-Up Actions

Follow up reviews.

During any review, a variety of actions will be identified to cope with the various problems uncovered. The project manager should always record these actions, the person responsible, and the expected completion date. This might be done on a register (Figure 14-5). All concerned people should receive copies, and the status of these action assignments should be reviewed no later than the next project review.

Figure 14-4. Estimated Cost to Completion.

Method 1		Method 2	
Plan (or Allowed) Cost	= $10,000	Task Q	= $1,632
Cost to Date	= 6,000	Task R	= 2,149
Cost to Complete	= $4,000	Task S	= 1,910
		Cost to Complete	= $5,691

Assigned Actions for Completion		
Project: _____		
Action	Responsibility	Due

Figure 14-5.   Typical action follow-up form.

Topical Reviews

There are many kinds of topical reviews. The one used depends on the undertaking and customer requirements. Many hardware projects have the following types of reviews:

1. conceptual design

2. preliminary design

3. critical design

4. manufacturing

5. preshipment

6. management

7. customer

A software project would typically have different types of reviews, as would a construction project.

All these reviews are often mandated in the contract and may be a precondition to carrying out further work on the project. In such a case, the reviews themselves would clearly be designated as task activities on the network diagram and be considered major project milestones.

Major review presentations can be an opportunity.

Such reviews are often onerous, but they may stimulate participation and involvement on the part of all people working on the project. For this to happen, the project manager must solicit ideas from all project personnel as to what should be discussed during the review. Rough ideas for the review should be delineated in a smaller group of key staff. At this point, the manager should delegate portions of the review to other people. (Be sure there are not so many people making presentations at the formal review that it becomes a circus.) Next conduct a trial run with a fairly large group of project participants invited to criticize. Following this, materials can be prepared for the formal presentation, before which it is desirable to conduct a second dry run with a peer management group that represents the same range of skill backgrounds as the audience that will attend the formal review. The people attending this dry run review will provide additional insights as to how materials can be better presented or changed. If possible, videotape the presentation for later review.

Now you are ready to conduct the formal review, after which it is desirable to conduct the entire review again for the benefit of everyone working on the project. They are just as interested as you in the kinds of questions the important people asked and will find it just as interesting and motivating to spend some time hearing what happened and getting an overview of the particular issues covered in the review.

Typical Problems

Reviews are plagued by two common problems. First, there is always a concern as to whether the information being presented or discussed is accurate. Cost reports, as previously noted, are especially prone to error. Beyond this, there is often speculation about the exact status of some task, test, component, or report. Clearly, good planning for reviews can reduce if not eliminate this problem.

The second problem is the poorly conducted review. Aimless discussion or recriminations are common. Running a review like any other well-planned meeting greatly reduces the possibility of getting off the track.

Materials Study Project

Imagine SUPROMAC management requires a preshipment review before the final report (task K) can be sent to NERESCO. Because this is not shown explicitly as a separate task, it must be integral in the task (that is, comparable to typing, editing, binding and so forth). Thus, when the project enters the last month, Mel Chase might prudently begin to schedule the appropriate manager's time to participate in the review.

Highlights

- Reviews uncover the inevitable deviations from plan and allow a consensus as to the needed corrective action.
- Reviews, like projects, must be planned.
- Ask nondirective questions and expect problems to surface at project review meetings.
- Periodic reviews should be conducted as appropriate for the project, but one a month is a good rule of thumb.
- The kind of topical review used depends on the project and the customer's requirements.
- Questionable accuracy and poor procedures are common problems with reviews.

Further Reading

There does not appear to be any extensive, systematic discussion of reviews per se as a control tool, although the following books include brief mention and limited further treatment:

B. N. Abramson and R. D. Kennedy. *Managing Small Projects.* Redondo Beach, Calif.: TRW Systems Group, 1975.

R. D. Archibald. *Managing High-Technology Programs and Projects* (Chapter 9). New York: Wiley-Interscience, 1976.

V. G. Hajek. *Management of Engineering Projects* (Chapter 14). New York: McGraw-Hill, 1977.

D. B. Uman. *New Product Programs: Their Planning and Control* (Chapter 6). New York: American Management Association, 1969.

M. Zeldman. *Keeping Technical Projects on Target.* New York: AMACOM, 1978.

CHAPTER 15

Cost Reports

Actual project costs must be measured to control the cost dimension and may reveal schedule or performance dimension problems. I discuss these topics and include typical examples of cost reports, which are normally generated as computer printout, in this chapter.

Computer Cost Reports

Variance from plan is a danger signal.

Large organizations commonly have computer-generated reports that summarize project cost. They may also cover schedule deviations. There is a variety of report systems available for purchase or lease. Figure 15-1 shows how such reports can be useful for project control. Actual cost (and schedule) data are collected from labor time cards, purchase orders, and other direct charges to the project. These are compared with plans, noted variances are analyzed, and required corrective actions may then lead to replanning. Comparing reality to the plan may suggest certain trends will lead to future variances, which again is a cause for replanning. To be useful, this comparison must be done for each cost center (for example, department) and work breakdown task.

The project manager must steer a careful line between having too many forms and too much information and having too little information to control the project, although it is probably better to have more information than less. Neither the project manager nor top management should be trapped into believing actual cost data (which can be reported with great precision) are the only measure of project health (which requires difficult three-dimensional measurements).

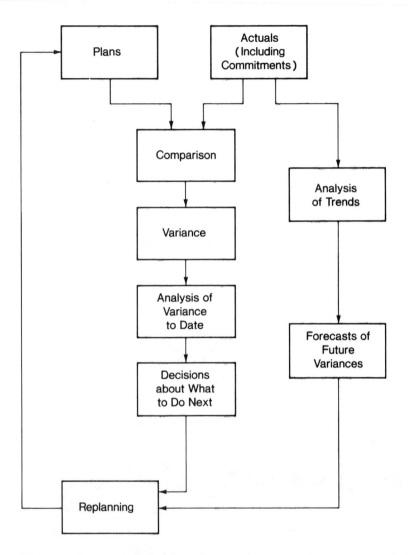

Figure 15-1. Replanning is called for whenever future trends or past actuals indicate significant deviation from plan.

Control

This section reviews a few of the cost reports for the materials study project, illustrating some issues in project control. These reports are typically prepared with a computer, working with the planning data base previously discussed. But it is not absolutely necessary to use a computer, although the amount of data to be handled can otherwise be a substantial burden, even to a well-qualified project cost accountant.

Variances Due to Timing

Figure 15-2 is the project cost report for task B within the chemical group, at the end of the first month. Typically, this report would be available

PROJECT COST REPORT

PROJECT_____MATERIALS STUDY_____ TASK__B-OBTAIN MATERIALS__ DEPARTMENT__CHEMICAL___

CATEGORY		MONTH 1 - JAN			TOTALS TO DATE		
		PLAN	ACTUAL	VARIANCE	PLAN	ACTUAL	VARIANCE
HOURS	SR. PROF.	40	40	0	40	40	0
	JR. PROF.						
	SR. TECH.						
	JR. TECH.						
DOLLARS	LABOR	1,000	1,000	0	1,000	1,000	0
	OVERHEAD	1,000	1,000	0	1,000	1,000	0
	NONLABOR	4,400	0	4,400	4,400	0	4,400
	PRIME COSTS	6,400	2,000	4,400	6,400	2,000	4,400
	G & A	960	300	660	960	300	660
	TOTAL COSTS	7,360	2,300	5,060	7,360	2,300	5,060

Figure 15-2. Cost report for first month for task B work by the chemical group.

A variance between actual cost and plan may be due to payments being made later than plan rather than work variances.

about the middle of the second month (February, in this case). The planning numbers are consistent with Figure 8-8. In this case, labor and the overhead thereon are in accordance with plan. But there is a favorable variance in the nonlabor expense. That is, there was a plan to spend $4,400, but nothing has been spent.

Figure 15-3 shows the corresponding task and period commitment report for the chemical group. Commitments in the amount of $4,400 have been incurred. Thus, the cost variance merely indicates bills have not yet been paid rather than being a variance due to activities not yet undertaken. To put it another way, it is anticipated the $4,400 expense will occur later.

It is impossible to make intelligent use of project cost reports without also examining commitment reports. Actual computer reports can flag this kind of information as well (see Figure 15-4).

Figures 15-5 and 15-6 are the same reports for the end of the second month. Once again, the labor hours and costs as well as the overhead are in accordance with the plan. In this case, there is an unfavorable variance during the second month with regard to nonlabor costs because the travel voucher is paid now but the plan had the expense in the first month. For the totals to date, that is, through the end of the second month, the nonlabor variance is favorable. This favorable variance is composed of the unpaid $4,000 purchase order, which is variance only because of payment timing, and a $50 favorable variance because the travel voucher payment was $50 less than plan.

Figure 15-3. Commitment Report for First Month for Task B Work by the Chemical Group.

PROJECT COMMITMENT REPORT

MONTH ___1___

PROJECT _Materials Study_   TASK _B—Obtain Materials_   DEPARTMENT _Chemical_

Commitment Date	Item	Amount	Estimated Payment Date
21 Jan 80	P.O.—Material Supply Co.	$4,000.	30 Apr 80
21 Jan 80	Travel Auth.—C. Williams	400.	15 Feb 80
		$4,400.	

FEBRUARY 22, 1980   ATLANTIC SOFTWARE   COPY 1 PAGE 1

P C / 7 0   R E S O U R C E   S T A T U S   R E P O R T

RESOURCE-CHERYL WILLIAMS   MANAGER-ED ROSS

PR TY	TASK NUMBER	........DESCRIPTION......	...........DATE.......... STARTED	TARGET	COMPLETE	........DOLLARS......... CURRENT BUDGET	TO/DATE	CURRENT FORECAST	..........HOURS............. THIS WEEK	BUD-GET	TOTAL T/D	TO FINISH	PCT COMP LETE	HOURS VARI-ANCE
40	ADMN-05SYMP													
		SYMPOSIA ATTENDANCE	05/05/80	05/09/80										
40	SY	SYMPOSIA ATTENDANCE	05/05/80	05/09/80		2300		2300		40.0		40.0		
	*TOTAL	SYMPOSIA ATTENDANCE				$2300		$2300		40.0		40.0		
20	INK -01													
		INK DEVELOPMENT PROJECT	01/14/80	05/13/80										
20	A0	SELECT MATERIALS	01/14/80	05/13/80		14950	5060	14950	88.0	260.0	88.0	172.0	34	
	*TOTAL	INK DEVELOPMENT PROJECT				$14950	$5060	$14950	88.0	260.0	88.0	172.0		
15	MATL-01EXPER													
		EXPERIMENTAL WORK	12/31/79	06/20/80										
10	A0	SELECT MATERIALS	12/31/79	01/18/80	01/16/80	3450	3450	3450	60.0	60.0	60.0		CPT	
10	BT	NON-LABOR TRAVEL			02/22/80	400	350	350					CPT	NOBGT

```
*****************************************************
* 1-21-80    TRAVEL EXPENSES EXPECTED TO REMAIN *
*            WITHIN $400 BUDGET. PAYMENT DUE    *
*            ABOUT 2-15-80.                     *
* 2-1-80     TRANEL EXPENSES ACTUALLY ONLY $350 *
* 2-1-80     TRAVEL EXPENSES ACTUALLY ONLY $350. *
*****************************************************
```

PR TY	TASK NUMBER	DESCRIPTION	STARTED	TARGET	COMPLETE	CURRENT BUDGET	TO/DATE	CURRENT FORECAST	THIS WEEK	BUD-GET	TOTAL T/D	TO FINISH	PCT COMP LETE	HOURS VARI-ANCE
15	B1	SUPPLIER MEETINGS			01/25/80		2300	2300	40.0		40.0		CPT	NOBGT
10	B3	PROVIDE ASSISTANCE	01/28/80	02/18/80	02/21/80	230	230	230	4.0	4.0	4.0		CPT	
10	B4	WRAP-UP	02/29/80	02/29/80		115		115		2.0		2.0		
20	E1	PLAN & SUPERVISE	04/07/80	06/20/80		12650		12650		220.0		220.0		
	*TOTAL	EXPERIMENTAL WORK				$16845	$6330	$19095	104.0	286.0	104.0	222.0		40-
20	MATL-03REPORT													
		FINAL REPORT	06/23/80	06/27/80										
10	K0	FINAL REPORT	06/23/80	06/27/80		1150		1150		20.0		20.0		
	*TOTAL	FINAL REPORT				$1150		$1150		20.0		20.0		
30	QUIL-01													
		QUILL DEVELOPMENT PROJECT	04/07/80	06/13/80										
30	A0	SELECT MATERIALS	04/07/80	06/13/80		6900		6900		120.0		120.0		
	*TOTAL	QUILL DEVELOPMENT PROJECT				$6900		$6900		120.0		120.0		
T O T A L		CHERYL WILLIAMS				$42145	$11390	$44395	192.0	726.0	192.0	574.0		40-

Figure 15-4. Commitment notation in computer cost and schedule report. (This computer-generated report is furnished courtesy of Atlantic Software, Inc. [ASI]. It is a sample output from Project Control/70 [PC/70], the proprietary project planning and control system that is the exclusive property of ASI. All rights are reserved.)

PROJECT COST REPORT

PROJECT___MATERIALS STUDY___   TASK__B-OBTAIN MATERIALS__ DEPARTMENT__CHEMICAL___

CATEGORY		MONTH 2 - FEB			TOTALS TO DATE		
		PLAN	ACTUAL	VARIANCE	PLAN	ACTUAL	VARIANCE
HOURS	SR. PROF.	4	4	0	44	44	0
	JR. PROF.						
	SR. TECH.						
	JR. TECH.						
DOLLARS	LABOR	100	100	0	1,100	1,100	0
	OVERHEAD	100	100	0	1,100	1,100	0
	NONLABOR	0	350	⟨350⟩	4,400	350	4,050
	PRIME COSTS	200	550	⟨350⟩	6,600	2,550	4,050
	G & A	30	83	⟨53⟩	990	383	607
	TOTAL COSTS	230	633	⟨403⟩	7,590	2,933	4,657

Figure 15-5. Cost report for second month for task B work by the chemical group.

Figure 15-6. Commitment Report for Second Month for Task B Work by the Chemical Group.

PROJECT COMMITMENT REPORT

MONTH_____2_____

PROJECT Materials Study   TASK B—Obtain Materials   DEPARTMENT Chemical

Commitment Date	Item	Amount	Estimated Payment Date
21 Jan 80	P.O.—Material Supply Co.	$4,000.	30 Apr 80
21 Jan 80	Travel Auth.—C. Williams	All	Paid
		$4,000.	

Variances Due to Actual Work Not as Per Plan

Figures 15-7 and 15-8 are the project cost reports at the end of the third and fourth months for the same task. In this case, labor hours exceed plan in the third month with attendant unfavorable cost variances, which happen to offset exactly the previous favorable variance on nonlabor due to

PROJECT COST REPORT

PROJECT_____MATERIALS STUDY_____ TASK__B-OBTAIN MATERIALS_ DEPARTMENT___CHEMICAL___

CATEGORY		MONTH 3 - MAR			TOTALS TO DATE		
		PLAN	ACTUAL	VARIANCE	PLAN	ACTUAL	VARIANCE
HOURS	SR. PROF.	2	3	⟨1⟩	46	47	⟨1⟩
	JR. PROF.						
	SR. TECH.						
	JR. TECH.						
DOLLARS	LABOR	100	125	⟨25⟩	1,150	1,175	⟨25⟩
	OVERHEAD	100	125	⟨25⟩	1,150	1,175	⟨25⟩
	NONLABOR	0	0	0	4,400	350	4,050
	PRIME COSTS	200	250	⟨50⟩	6,700	2,700	4,000
	G & A	30	38	⟨8⟩	1,005	405	600
	TOTAL COSTS	230	288	⟨58⟩	7,705	3,105	4,600

Figure 15-7. Cost report for third month for task B work by the chemical group.

PROJECT COST REPORT

PROJECT_____MATERIAL STUDY_____ TASK__B-OBTAIN MATERIALS_ DEPARTMENT___CHEMICAL___

CATEGORY		MONTH 4 - APR			TOTALS TO DATE		
		PLAN	ACTUAL	VARIANCE	PLAN	ACTUAL	VARIANCE
HOURS	SR. PROF.	0	0	0	46	47	⟨1⟩
	JR. PROF.						
	SR. TECH.						
	JR. TECH.						
DOLLARS	LABOR	0	0	0	1,150	1,175	⟨25⟩
	OVERHEAD	0	0	0	1,150	1,175	⟨25⟩
	NONLABOR	0	4,000	⟨4,000⟩	4,400	4,350	50
	PRIME COSTS	0	4,000	⟨4,000⟩	6,700	6,700	0
	G & A	0	600	⟨600⟩	1,005	1,005	0
	TOTAL COSTS	0	4,600	⟨4,600⟩	7,705	7,705	0

Figure 15-8. Cost report for fourth month for task B work by the chemical group.

the travel variance. In the fourth month, the purchase order is paid, and the net variance for the task becomes zero.

Figures 15-2 through 15-8 illustrate that variances occur because of the payment timing and that actual performance differs from plan. They also indicate the necessity of examining the details in project cost reports and commitment reports to understand the reported variances and their significance.

Actual work may differ from plan.

Figure 15-9 is a detailed schedule status report and Figure 15-10, a combined schedule and cost analysis report. These two reports are typical computer outputs. Each computer-based system differs in detail, so the project manager should understand exactly how the reports are prepared (that is, to what errors the reports are prone) as well as the specific meaning of each column of data.

```
FEBRUARY 22, 1980                          ATLANTIC SOFTWARE                      PC700375   03/05/80   PAGE   7

                      P C / 7 0   C P M   D E T A I L   S T A T U S   R E P O R T

CRIT  RA  TASK RESC ........DESCRIPTION........  ............D A T E S...........  DAYS   UNITS   DAYS      CRITICAL
PATH  NK   ID  ID                                 E A R L Y          L A T E       FLOAT   TO     DUR-    CONSTRAINT
                                                 START   TARGET   START   TARGET          PLAN   ATION   ...................

 *    05   E1 MEL    PLAN & SUPERVISE             04/08/80 06/24/80 04/03/80 06/19/80   5-    430    78    TASK DEPENDENCY    D0
 *    05   F2 TSJR   SET UP EQUIPMENT             04/14/80 04/25/80 04/14/80 04/25/80   0     240    12    TASK START DATE  04/14/80
                                                                                                         PHD CODE H024
 *    05   E2 TSSR   SET UP EQUIPMENT             04/14/80 04/25/80 04/14/80 04/25/80   0     160    12    TASK START DATE  04/14/80
                                                                                                         PHD CODE H016
 *    05   E3 ED M   CONDUCT TESTS                04/09/80 06/24/80 04/04/80 06/19/80   5-    440    77    TASK DEPENDENCY    D0
 *    05   E3 JOE    CONDUCT TESTS                04/09/80 06/24/80 04/04/80 06/19/80   5-    110    77    TASK DEPENDENCY    D0
                                                                                                         PHD CODE H002
 *    05   E3 MOLL   CONDUCT TESTS                04/09/80 06/24/80 04/04/80 06/19/80   5-    440    77    TASK DEPENDENCY    D0
 *    05   E3 TSJR   CONDUCT TESTS                04/09/80 06/24/80 04/04/80 06/19/80   5-    220    77    TASK DEPENDENCY    D0
                                                                                                         PHD CODE H004
                                                                                              ------
                                                                                               5983

 *    01  MATL-02THEOR
                      THEORETICAL WORK            02/26/80 05/26/80 02/22/80 05/23/80   4-           91
 *    02   H0 ADPR THEORETICAL STUDY              02/26/80 04/21/80 02/23/80 04/18/80   3-    632    56    TASK DEPENDENCY    G0
 *    02   H0 MEL  THEORETICAL STUDY              02/29/80 04/18/80 02/22/80 04/11/80   7-     24    50    TASK DEPENDENCY    G0
                                                                                                         PHD H003 AND DAY F
 *    02   H0 TOM  THEORETICAL STUDY              02/26/80 04/21/80 02/23/80 04/18/80   3-    320    56    TASK DEPENDENCY    G0
 *    03   J0 TOM  REPORT THEORY                  04/22/80 05/26/80 04/18/80 05/23/80   4-    200    35    TASK DEPENDENCY    H0
                                                                                              ------
                                                                                               1176

 *    02  MATL-03REPORT
                      FINAL REPORT                06/25/80 07/01/80 06/20/80 06/27/80   5-            7    MATL-01EXPER
 *    00   K0 CHER FINAL REPORT                   06/25/80 07/01/80 06/20/80 06/27/80   5-     20     7    PROJECT DEPENDENCY
                                                                                                         PHD CODE P050
 *    00   K0 ED M FINAL REPORT                   06/25/80 07/01/80 06/20/80 06/27/80   5-     40     7    PROJECT DEPENDENCY
 *    00   K0 ELDN FINAL REPORT                   06/25/80 07/01/80 06/20/80 06/27/80   5-     40     7    PROJECT DEPENDENCY
 *    00   K0 MEL  FINAL REPORT                   06/25/80 07/01/80 06/20/80 06/27/80   5-     40     7    PROJECT DEPENDENCY
 *    00   K0 TSJR FINAL REPORT                   06/25/80 07/01/80 06/20/80 06/27/80   5-    120     7    PROJECT DEPENDENCY
                                                                                                         PHD CODE H024
 *    00   K0 TSPR FINAL REPORT                   06/25/80 07/01/80 06/20/80 06/27/80   5-     40     7    PROJECT DEPENDENCY
 *    00   K0 TSSR FINAL REPORT                   06/25/80 07/01/80 06/20/80 06/27/80   5-     80     7    PROJECT DEPENDENCY
                                                                                                         PHD CODE H016
                                                                                              ------
                                                                                                380

     TOTAL NETWORK                               02/25/80 07/01/80 01/21/80 06/27/80         7539


 NETWORK NUMBER - 01     NETWORK PRIORITY - 10     NETWORK DEMAND START - 12/31/79     NETWORK DEMAND TARGET - 06/27/80
```

Figure 15-9. Typical schedule status report. (This computer-generated report is furnished courtesy of Atlantic Software, Inc. [ASI]. It is a sample output from Project Control/70 [PC/70], the proprietary project planning and control system that is the exclusive property of ASI. All rights reserved.)

```
                        ---- RESOURCES ----   ---- COST ---   ------- SCHEDULE --------   -------- DEPENDENCY --------- OPTIONS ERR
TASK  FUNC  DETAIL      DAILY   TOTAL   %      TOTAL    %      START   FINISH  DAYS   %     DATE     PROJECTS/TASKS

            *** ACTIVITY   0300   TOTAL VALUE ***

            ORIG PLAN                         14,375          2JAN80  21FEB80  51
            FORECAST                          14,375   100    2JAN80  21FEB80  51   100
            SCH NEXT WK     21.0               1,710    12                     0
            VARIANCE                                                           0

************************************************************************************************************************************

ACTIVITY
0400  OBT  OBTAIN MATERIALS      MEL CHASE      (MC)

0410  OBT  OBTAIN MATERIALS      MEL CHASE      (MC)
            DELAY DAYS                                        22JAN80  28JAN80   6
            ORIG PLAN    1.0    6.0             150           28JAN80   3MAR80  36                                              W 11
            FORECAST     1.0    6.0  100        150   100     28JAN80   3MAR80  36   100    (0100)
            SLACK DAYS                                         4MAR80   2JUL80 120           PROJ 100   CMPL

************************************************************************************************************************************

0420  OBT  OBTAIN MATERIALS      MOLLY COOK     (MK)
            DELAY DAYS                                        22JAN80  30JAN80   8
            ORIG PLAN    2.0   40.0             800           30JAN80  26FEB80  28                                              L 05
            FORECAST     2.0   40.0  100        800   100     30JAN80  26FEB80  28   100    (0100)
            SLACK DAYS                                        27FEB80   2JUL80 126           PROJ 100   CMPL

************************************************************************************************************************************

0430  DNL  DIRECT NON LABOR COS, ROBERT JONES   (RJ)
            OBTAIN MATERI AL (MECH)
            DELAY DAYS                                        22JAN80  23JAN80   1
            ORIG PLAN    5     200             200           23JAN80  27JAN80   5                                              F
            FORECAST     5     200   100       200   100     23JAN80  27JAN80   5   100    (0100)
            SLACK DAYS                                        28JAN80   2JUL80 156           PROJ 100   CMPL

************************************************************************************************************************************

0440  OBT  OBTAIN MATERIALS, AT  CHERYL WILLIAMS (CW)
            SUPPLIER
            DELAY DAYS                                        22JAN80  23JAN80   1
            ORIG PLAN    8.0   40.0           1,000          23JAN80  29JAN80   7
            FORECAST     8.0   40.0  100      1,000   100    23JAN80  29JAN80   7   100    (0100)
            SLACK DAYS                                          -        -      0            PROJ 100   TASK 0450

************************************************************************************************************************************

0450  OBT  OBTAIN MATERIALS, AT  CHERYL WILLIAMS (CW)
            SUPPLIER
            DELAY DAYS                                        29JAN80   4FEB80   6
            ORIG PLAN    1.0    6.0             150            4FEB80  10MAR80  36                                              W 11
            FORECAST     1.0    6.0  100        150   100      4FEB80  10MAR80  36   100
            SLACK DAYS                                        11MAR80   2JUL80 113           PROJ 100   CMPL


30DEC79   FOR MECH    MEL CHASE      RPT 06  ----PROJECT ANALYSIS---- PAGE 7 PROJ 100  PRTY 5  NEED 30JUN80 DETAIL 8
TIME STAMP 01/22/80 101251
```

Figure 15-10. Typical schedule and cost analysis report. (Computer printout furnished courtesy of Nichols & Company, Culver City, California.)

Variances Due to Overhead Rate Changes

Figure 15-11 is the project report for task E in the technical support section as reported at the end of the fourth month. In this report, there are favorable variances in labor but an unfavorable variance in overhead. How can this be? If labor is favorable, why should overhead be unfavorable?

Figure 15-12 shows the cause of this. A planned overhead (namely, 100 percent) was based on a planned work load for the technical support section (or perhaps the entire research and engineering division). But the actual overhead at the end of the fourth month is higher (namely, 130 percent) because the work load base for the entire section has been reduced from plan. The overhead expenses have been somewhat reduced but not in the same proportion as the direct labor because overhead is

PROJECT COST REPORT

PROJECT_____MATERIALS STUDY_____   TASK__E-EXPERIMENT_____   DEPARTMENT_TECHNICAL SUPPORT

CATEGORY		MONTH 4 - APR			TOTALS TO DATE		
		PLAN	ACTUAL	VARIANCE	PLAN	ACTUAL	VARIANCE
HOURS	SR. PROF.						
	JR. PROF.						
	SR. TECH.	200	120	80	200	120	80
	JR. TECH.	400	400	0	400	400	0
DOLLARS	LABOR	7,000	5,800	1,200	7,000	5,800	1,200
	OVERHEAD	7,000	7,540	⟨540⟩	7,000	7,540	⟨540⟩
	NONLABOR	0	0	0	0	0	0
	PRIME COSTS	14,000	13,340	660	14,000	13,340	660
	G & A	2,100	2,001	99	2,100	2,001	99
	TOTAL COSTS	16,100	15,341	759	16,100	15,341	759

Figure 15-11. Cost report for fourth month for task E work by the technical support section.

Figure 15-12. Cause of Unfavorable Overhead Variance.

Planned

Project Example $100,000 Labor Cost	Project Otherone $300,000 Labor Cost
Overhead ($200,000 Fixed + $200,000 Variable) / $400,000 = 100%	

Revised

Project Example $100,000 Labor Cost	Project Otherone $150,000 Labor Cost
Overhead ($200,000 Fixed + $125,000 Variable) / $325,000 = 130%	

Factors outside the manager's control may cause costs to vary from plan.

partially composed of fixed expenses that cannot be reduced. Thus, the actual overhead rate turns out in this case to be 130 percent rather than the planned 100 percent. (Such a change in overhead is extreme; I use it simply to dramatize the possible effect of overhead rate changes.) The variance could be summarized as follows:

- Joe Senior was planned full-time but was not released from his previous project at the start of month **4**. If labor is not added, the project will be late.

- Overhead is now 130 percent, not 100 percent as planned. This will cause a cost overrun unless compensating savings can be found.

Quiz 15-1

What are some reasons for overhead rate changes?

Figure 15-13 is the project cost report for this task in the technical support department at the end of the fifth month. The senior technician category continues to have a favorable variance, which is partially offset by an unfavorable variance in the junior technician category and a continuing unfavorable variance in the overhead. The overhead variance is again attributable solely to the overhead rate now being 130 percent rather

PROJECT COST REPORT

PROJECT_____MATERIALS STUDY_____ TASK_E-EXPERIMENT_____ DEPARTMENT_TECHNICAL SUPPORT

CATEGORY		MONTH 5 - MAY			TOTALS TO DATE		
		PLAN	ACTUAL	VARIANCE	PLAN	ACTUAL	VARIANCE
HOURS	SR. PROF.						
	JR. PROF.						
	SR. TECH.	40	20	20	240	140	100
	JR. TECH.	80	120	⟨40⟩	480	520	⟨40⟩
DOLLARS	LABOR	1,400	1,500	⟨100⟩	8,400	7,300	1,100
	OVERHEAD	1,400	1,950	⟨550⟩	8,400	9,490	⟨1,090⟩
	NONLABOR	0	0	0	0	0	0
	PRIME COSTS	2,800	3,450	⟨650⟩	16,800	16,790	10
	G & A	420	518	⟨98⟩	2,520	2,519	1
	TOTAL COSTS	3,220	3,968	⟨748⟩	19,320	19,309	11

Figure 15-13. Cost report for fifth month for task E work by the technical support section.

than 100 percent per plan. Examination of these variances might lead to the following kind of information:

- Joe Senior is sick.

- A speedy juniorwoman, previously unplanned, has been added to complete the work on schedule.

- Overhead is still 130 percent, but final dollars are okay.

The junior technician was able to accomplish in fewer hours the work previously planned for a senior technician. This net effective saving in labor hours was sufficient to compensate for the increased overhead dollars. The end result in this case is a small, favorable variance.

Management Information

One of the attractive aspects of computer-based control systems is the variety of summary reports they make conveniently available. Figure 15-14 shows how schedule and cost status for several projects can be distilled for management review.

Typical Problems

Cost reports are late and sometimes incorrect.

In addition to management's tendency to presume cost status is the only measure of a project's progress, a problem previously mentioned, there are two other common problems. First, cost reports are never available immediately after the end of the reporting period (typically the fiscal or calendar month). They are usually issued about two or three weeks after the close of the report period. Thus, there is always a time lag with which the project manager must contend. This problem cannot be solved but must be accepted because of other accounting priorities. An alert project manager can recognize the situation and make full use of other available data to stay more current, including weekly labor distribution reports (indicating who did or did not charge time to the project), purchase orders, travel vouchers, and drawing releases.

The second problem is that cost reports often have errors, such as charges that should have been allocated to other projects or overhead accounts. The project manager or an administrative assistant must study the reports carefully and not merely accept them as gospel.

```
FEBRUARY 22, 1980                          ATLANTIC SOFTWARE                                    COPY 1  PAGE    1

                                  P C / 7 0   E X E C U T I V E   S U M M A R Y

PR  PROJECT NUMBER AND DESCRIPTION    ...........DATE............  .........DOLLARS........  ................HOURS..............  PCT  HOURS
TY                                    STARTED   TARGET   COMPLETE  CURRENT TO/DATE CURRENT  THIS   CURRENT  TOTAL  TO      CPT  VARI-
                                                                   BUDGET          FORECAST WEEK   BUDGET   T/D    FINISH       ANCE

    ADMN-01HOLVAC
            HOLIDAY-VACATION-PAIDTIME 12/31/79 12/26/80             100000          100000          2000           2000

    ADMN-02SICK
            SICK LEAVE & PERSONAL     12/31/79 12/26/80             39500    368    39868    8      900      8      900      1   8-

40  ADMN-05SYMP
            SYMPOSIA ATTENDANCE       05/05/80 05/09/80             2300            2300            40             40
*TOTAL ADMN  PROJECT                  12/31/79 12/26/80            $141800  $368  $142168    8      2940     8      2940         8-

20  INK -01
            INK DEVELOPMENT PROJECT   01/14/80 05/13/80             14950   5060   14950    88      260      88     172      34
*TOTAL INK   PROJECT                  01/14/80 05/13/80            $14950  $5060  $14950    88      260      88     172      34

10  MATL      MATERIALS STUDY                  06/29/80            $500000                           10500

    *************************************************
    *THE PROJECT CONSISTS OF 3 PARTS :             *
    * EXPERIMENTAL; THEORETICAL; AND REPORT.       *
    *************************************************

15  MATL-01EXPER
            EXPERIMENTAL WORK         12/31/79 06/20/80             370231  123652 370925   2504    8484    2504    5983     30   3-

    *************************************************
    *THIS PROJECT PART CONSISTS OF 2 PHASES :      *
    * SELECTING MATERIALS; BUILDING THE APPARATUS  *
    *************************************************

10  MATL-02THEOR
            THEORETICAL WORK          12/31/79 05/23/80             79890   19726  80078    329     1500    329     1176     22   5-

    *************************************************
    *THE THEORETICAL PART OF THE PROJECT WILL GO   *
    * ON IN PARALLEL WITH THE EXPERIMENTAL PART.   *
    *************************************************

20  MATL-03REPORT
            FINAL REPORT              06/23/80 06/27/80             14950           14950           380            380
*TOTAL MATL  MATERIALS STUDY          12/31/79 06/27/80            $465071 $143378 $465953  2833    10364   2833    7539     27   8-

30  QUIL-01
            QUILL DEVELOPMENT PROJECT 04/07/80 06/13/80             6900            6900            120            120
*TOTAL QUIL  PROJECT                  04/07/80 06/13/80            $6900           $6900           120            120
```

Figure 15-14. Typical management summary of schedule and cost status on several projects, including some task detail. (This computer-generated report is furnished courtesy of Atlantic Software, Inc. [ASI]. It is a sample output from Project Control/70 [PC/70], the proprietary project planning and control system that is the exclusive property of ASI. All rights are reserved.)

Materials Study Project

All the examples in this chapter have been based on the materials study project. I have not yet discussed the manager's desire to understand subordinates' contributions to projects underway. Again, the ability of computers to sort stored data in a wide variety of ways makes it easy to provide such status reports to managers.

Figures 15-15 and 15-16 show two reports Ed Ross could review. They cover Mel Chase's work status on the schedule and cost dimensions. It is also easy to provide support team managers with similar reports on their subordinates' work, as shown in Figure 15-17.

```
FEBRUARY 22, 1980                    ATLANTIC SOFTWARE                         COPY 1  PAGE    1

                    P C / 7 0·  R E S O U R C E   P L A N N I N G   R E P O R T
                              SCHEDULED TO AVAILABILITY
RESOURCE-MEL CHASE                                                   MANAGER-ED ROSS

C PR TASK .......DESCRIPTION.......  .......START......  ......TARGET......  TASK AL P PASG PLAN FEB MAR APR MAY JUN JUL AUG SEP OCT NOV
O TY                                 CURRENT   CALC/     CURRENT   CALC/     PREC GO L HDAY HRS   25  24  21  19  16  14  11  08  06  03
N                                              ACTUAL              COMPLETE            A DURA      80  80  80  80  80  80  80  80  80  80
D                                                                                     N DAY


  15 MATL-01EXPER
        EXPERIMENTAL WORK
L 20  C1   PLAN & SUPERVISE          12/31/9   12/31/9A 03/21/0L 03/25/0              160 |146| 14|   |   |   |   |   |   |   |   |
  10  B4   WRAP-UP                   02/29/0   02/29/0  02/29/0  02/29/0   B3          2 | 2|   |   |   |   |   |   |   |   |   |
L 20  D0 DEBUG                       03/24/0L  03/25/0  04/04/0L 04/08/0   C6         74 |   | 74|   |   |   |   |   |   |   |   |
L 20  E1   PLAN & SUPERVISE          04/07/0L  04/08/0  06/20/0L 06/24/0   B4        430 |   | 60|160|160| 50|   |   |   |   |   |
                                                                          D0            |   |   |   |   |   |   |   |   |   |

  10 MATL-02THEOR
        THEORETICAL WORK
L 15  H0 THEORETICAL STUDY           02/08/0L  02/13/0A 04/11/0L 04/18/0   G0      3H 24 | 12| 12|   |   |   |   |   |   |   |
                                                                                 FDAY    |   |   |   |   |   |   |   |   |   |

  20 MATL-03REPORT                   (MATL-01EXPER          MATL-02THEOR        )
        FINAL REPORT
L 10  K0 FINAL REPORT                06/23/0L  06/25/0  06/27/0L 07/01/0              40 |   |   |   |   | 40|   |   |   |   |
                                                                                    --------------------------------------------

RESOURCE NUMBER MEL    TOTAL                  TOTAL HOURS SCHEDULED . . . . . . .  160 160 160 160  90

AVAILABLE HOURS-   40.00                      OPEN HOURS EACH PERIOD . . . . . . .              70 160 160 160 160 160

                                             CUMULATIVE OPEN TIME  . . . . . . .              70 230 390 550 710 870
```

```
**************************************************************************************************
          COND-CONDITION CODE  L=CALCULATED START OR TARGET DATE IS LATER THAN YOUR PLAN
                               E=CALCULATED TARGET DATE IS EARLIER THAN YOUR PLAN
                               O=RESOURCE IS OVERSCHEDULED
                               U=SIMULATION MODE, UPDATE THE PC/70 MASTER FILE
                               D=SIMULATION MODE, DO NOT RETAIN DATA ON PC/70 MASTER FILE


**************************************************************************************************
```

Figure 15-15. A subordinate's project schedule status, as provided to the manager. (This computer-generated report is furnished courtesy of Atlantic Software, Inc. [ASI]. It is a sample output from Project Control/70 [PC/70], the proprietary project planning and control system that is the exclusive property of ASI. All rights are reserved.)

Highlights

- Computer-generated cost reports show variances from plan, which usually require corrective action.

- Reports can show variances due to timing, actual work deviating from plan, or overhead rate changes.

- Three problems with cost reports are that management tends to assume they are the only measure of progress, they never appear immediately after the reporting period, and they may contain errors.

```
FEBRUARY 22, 1980                        ATLANTIC SOFTWARE                      COPY 1  PAGE   1
                          P C / 7 0   R E S O U R C E   S T A T U S   R E P O R T

RESOURCE-MEL CHASE                                            MANAGER-ED ROSS

PR  TASK  ........DESCRIPTION.....  ...........DATE..........  ........DOLLARS........  ..........HOURS...........  PCT  HOURS
TY  NUMBER                          STARTED TARGET  COMPLETE   CURRENT  TO/DATE CURRENT THIS   BUD-  TOTAL   TO    COMP VARI-
                                                               BUDGET           FORECAST WEEK  GET   T/D  FINISH  LETE ANCE

15 MATL-01EXPER
        EXPERIMENTAL WORK           12/31/79 06/20/80
10    A0  SELECT MATERIALS          01/04/80 01/18/80 01/16/80    345     345      345    6.0    6.0    6.0            CPT
10    B1   SUPPLIER MEETINGS        01/23/80 01/24/80 01/24/80    460     460      460    8.0    8.0    8.0            CPT
10    B3   PROVIDE ASSISTANCE       01/28/80 02/18/80 02/22/80    230     173      173    3.0    4.0    3.0            CPT   1.0
10    B4  WRAP-UP                   02/29/80 02/29/80             115              115           2.0           2.0
20    C1   PLAN & SUPERVISE         12/31/79 03/21/80          23518   15008    24208  261.0  409.0  261.0  160.0    62   12.0-
20    D0  DEBUG                     03/24/80 04/04/80           4255             4255          74.0          74.0
20    E1   PLAN & SUPERVISE         04/07/80 06/20/80          24725            24725         430.0         430.0
   *TOTAL  EXPERIMENTAL WORK                                 $53648  $15986  $54281  278.0  933.0  278.0  666.0          11-

10 MATL-02THEOR
        THEORETICAL WORK            12/31/79 05/23/80
15    G0  STUDY LITERATURE          12/31/79 02/01/80 01/29/80   1725    1783     1783   31.0   30.0   31.0            CPT   1.0-
15    H0  THEORETICAL STUDY         02/08/80 04/11/80            1725     575     1955   10.0   30.0   10.0   24.0     29   4.0-
   *TOTAL  THEORETICAL WORK                                  $3450   $2358   $3738   41.0   60.0   41.0   24.0           5-

20 MATL-03REPORT
        FINAL REPORT                06/23/80 06/27/80
10    K0  FINAL REPORT              06/23/80 06/27/80           2300             2300          40.0          40.0
   *TOTAL  FINAL REPORT                                      $2300           $2300          40.0          40.0

T O T A L    MEL CHASE                                     $59398  $18344  $60319  319.0 1033.0  319.0  730.0          16-
```

Figure 15-16. A subordinate's project cost status, as provided to the manager. (This computer-generated report is furnished courtesy of Atlantic Software, Inc. [ASI]. It is a sample output from Project Control/70 [PC/70], the proprietary project planning and control system that is the exclusive property of ASI. All rights are reserved.)

```
FEBRUARY 22, 1980                        ATLANTIC SOFTWARE                      COPY 1  PAGE   1
                          P C / 7 0   R E S O U R C E   S T A T U S   R E P O R T

RESOURCE-TOM RICHARDS                                         MANAGER-RICHARD THOMAS

PR  TASK  ........DESCRIPTION.....  ...........DATE..........  ........DOLLARS........  ..........HOURS...........  PCT  HOURS
TY  NUMBER                          STARTED TARGET  COMPLETE   CURRENT  TO/DATE CURRENT THIS   BUD-  TOTAL   TO    COMP VARI-
                                                               BUDGET           FORECAST WEEK  GET   T/D  FINISH  LETE ANCE

10 MATL-02THEOR
        THEORETICAL WORK            12/31/79 05/23/80
15    G0  STUDY LITERATURE          12/31/79 02/01/80 02/08/80  11500   11500    11500  200.0  200.0  200.0            CPT
15    H0  THEORETICAL STUDY         02/11/80 04/18/80          23000    4600    23000   80.0  400.0   80.0  320.0     20
15    J0  REPORT THEORY             04/21/80 05/23/80          11500            11500         200.0         200.0
   *TOTAL  THEORETICAL WORK                                 $46000  $16100  $46000  280.0  800.0  280.0  520.0

T O T A L    TOM RICHARDS                                  $46000  $16100  $46000  280.0  800.0  280.0  520.0
```

Figure 15-17. Report to a support team manager, showing the status of a subordinate's work on a project for another manager. (This computer-generated report is furnished courtesy of Atlantic Software, Inc. [ASI]. It is a sample output from Project Control/70 [PC/70], the proprietary project planning and control system that is the exclusive property of ASI. All rights are reserved.)

Further Reading

R. H. Clough and G. A. Sears. *Construction Project Management*, 2nd ed. New York: Wiley-Interscience, 1979.

Chapter 10 has an extensive discussion of the project cost system in the construction industry, with much that is generally applicable in any industry.

J. A. Maciariello. *Program-Management Control Systems*. New York: Wiley-Interscience, 1978.

Chapter 11 contains a good overview of PERT/COST and C/SCSC cost control approaches.

R. Pilcher. *Appraisal and Control of Project Costs*. London: McGraw-Hill, 1973.

Chapter 11 provides a clear and thorough discussion of cost control, with an emphasis on the need to tie this into the work breakdown structure and network diagram.

CHAPTER **16**

Handling Changes

Change is a reality of project management. This chapter first reviews why project plans are altered and then discusses techniques for implementing changes.

Reasons for Changes _____

Deviations from project plan occur because Murphy was an optimist. Or there is Rosenau's law of revolting developments: There will be at least one. A large body of data supports this assertion. Table 16-1 summarizes overrun data from a variety of sources. These data convincingly demonstrate that presumably conscientious program managers have been confronted with changes in many situations. This has led to missing both the schedule and cost dimensions of the Triple Constraint, with the overruns typically being a factor of approximately two above plan.

Change is a constant on projects.

Although not illustrated in Table 16-1, Mansfield's data also show the situation is somewhat worse than average for large projects and better than average for small projects. This seems to make sense; intuition tells us the more ambitious undertaking is less likely to be estimated accurately. This is another reason to break a large project down into many small tasks. It will be easier to estimate a small task accurately.

Real Changes in the Planned Project

One of the causes of both time and cost overruns is that deviations from the plan occur in the job. They may be externally imposed, by the customer, for instance. They might include a request for extra flexibility in a computer program, a request to add traffic islands on a bridge, or perhaps a request for an additional flight experiment on a space payload.

Table 16-1. Time and Cost Overrun Data, Expressed as Multiple (X) of Plan.

Project Type	Time	Cost	Source
50 new products (new chemical entities, compounded products, or alternate dosage forms) in ethical drug firm	1.78X	1.61X	E. Mansfield et al., *Research and Innovation in the Modern Corporation*, W. W. Norton, New York, 1971, p. 89
69 new products in proprietary drug laboratory	2.95X	2.11X	E. Mansfield et al., op. cit., pp. 102 & 104
20 management information systems projects	2.10X	1.95X	R. F. Powers & G. W. Dickson, "MisProject Management? Myth, Opinions, and Reality," *California Management Review*, XV, no. 3, 147–156 (Spring 1973)
34 Department of Defense systems from "planning estimate" from "development estimate"	– –	 2.11X 1.41X	G. R. McNichols, D.O.D. Report (November 1974), as quoted in R. A. Brown, "Probabilistic Models of Project Management with Design Implications," *IEEE Trans. Engr. Mgmt.*, vol. EM-25, no. 2, 43–49 (May 1978)
10 major construction projects completed 1956–1977	–	3.93X	W. J. Mead et al. (1977), as quoted in E.W. Merrow et al., "A Review of Cost Estimation in New Technologies," Rand Corporation Report R-2481-DOE (July 1979), p. 38
10 energy process plants	–	2.53X	E. W. Merrow et al., op. cit., p. 87

Quiz 16-1

List some possible changes of scope for the materials study project that might lead to a schedule or cost change.

In addition, schedule changes can be imposed, and these frequently have attendant cost implications. If the customer's plant is shut down by a strike or for some other reason the customer does not wish to receive the project output on a stipulated date, there is typically a cost consequence. Conversely, the customer may impose a change in project funding. Although a delay in project funding to the project organization may not appear to change the total available funding, it almost always is accompanied by a schedule rearrangement, which normally leads to undesirable cost consequences.

Changes can be imposed indirectly.

Environmental, health, and safety regulations that change during the course of the project may cause other changes in scope. Inflation may exceed plan, causing a cost problem, particularly on major construction projects originally planned to take several years. There may be changes in resource availability, either people or facilities. These do not constitute changes in project scope, but they do constitute changes from plan that will have an impact, usually unfavorable, on schedule and cost.

Estimation Inaccuracy

Several factors affect estimation accuracy. Of these, an imperfect definition of project scope is the most common. Either a customer or the contractor may be the cause of the error, but it usually is attributable to both.

Uncertainty and "buy-ins" can cause poor estimates.

There may also be poor estimates of either time or cost. The rush to prepare a proposal and submit it in accordance with the bidding requirements may preclude there being sufficient time to do a good job of estimating. There is so much inherent uncertainty in some tasks of some projects that a poor estimate is almost a foregone conclusion.

Many jobs are proposed with deliberate underestimates of the amount of time or money it will take to perform them. This is the so-called "buy-in" situation in which a bidder attempts to win a job by making a low bid. This does not require an illegal misrepresentation, although that may be the case. It may result from a deliberate attempt to make optimistic assumptions about all the uncertainties in the proposed project as well as to omit all contingency from the estimates. In a sense, the bidder is making an estimate of time and cost that could occur perhaps 1 or 0.1 percent of the time rather than attempting to make an estimate near the mid range of possibilities. Buy-in bids are much more prevalent where the contemplated contract will be a cost reimbursable form and the bidding contractor will not bear the financial burden of having made a low bid. They can also occur in a fixed price contract situation where the bidding contractor is confident the customer will request changes in scope. Such changes will provide a "get well" opportunity: Increases in both time and cost for the main project can be added onto or concealed in renegotiations necessitated by changes of scope.

Adopting Changes

At this point, it should be clear projects normally require changes of plan, although the specific reason or reasons cannot be forecast. The original plan should have included contingency for each dimension of the Triple Constraint, as discussed in Chapter 9. The next chapter reviews several

Unless you want people to continue to work on the basis of the previous plan, inform everyone of revisions.

methods to solve the problems caused by the occurrence of revolting developments, stressing the importance of developing and considering alternatives. Once the best alternative has been identified, the change must be adopted.

Figure 16-1 is a typical task authorization form. Each organization has its own detailed version, but the essential elements are a description of the Triple Constraint, which defines the task being authorized, and a place for the person authorizing the work and the person accepting responsibility for the work to sign. This form thus constitutes a "contract," defining in writing the agreement reached to authorize a task to be performed within the same organization in support of a project. In the case of a subcontractor, the subcontract document authorizes the task.

TASK AUTHORIZATION			PAGE OF
TITLE			
PROJECT NO.	TASK NO.	REVISION NO.	DATE ISSUED
STATEMENT OF WORK:			
APPLICABLE DOCUMENTS:			
SCHEDULE START DATE: COMPLETION DATE:			
COST:			
ORIGINATED BY: DATE:		ACCEPTED BY: DATE:	
APPROVED BY: DATE:		APPROVED BY: DATE:	
APPROVED BY: DATE:		APPROVED BY: DATE:	

Figure 16-1. Typical task authorization form.

Changes, just like originally intended work, must be defined, planned, implemented, and controlled before they can be completed. Thus, some, if not all, of the originally issued task authorizations must be changed when a change has occurred and a decision has been made as to how to alter the plan to carry out the remainder of the project. This may seem to be a lot of work, but it is far less onerous to take the time to make sure each agreement with people working on the project has been changed than to discover later some people have been working according to their prior understanding of the project plan.

Figure 16-1 shows a one-page form, but an actual task authorization, in common with a subcontract, might be many pages long. The form might be part of a carbon set, providing copies for the initiator, the task manager, and the project cost accounting section.

Hence, the task authorization documents initially used to authorize work are also a major change control document. A large project may generate many of these, and the amount of time it takes to issue them may be so great as to advise there first be telephonic or other speedy notice of forthcoming changes.

Quiz 16-2

You are managing a computer programming project, and after a few months' effort, you realize the amount of core memory required for the program will exceed the specified amount. When do you inform your customer of this?

Typical Problems

Quiz 16-2 illustrates one of three key problems changes can cause. There is always a reluctance to tell the customer and your boss a revolting development has occurred and many reasons to justify delay. But you should deliver the bad news carefully, thoughtfully, and promptly, before someone else does it.

A second problem is task authorizations are often verbal rather than written. Because they promote misinterpretation, verbal authorizations should be avoided. But they are employed in the real world of project management. When you must use them, be sure you are clear, ask for feedback, and then try for written confirmation.

The third problem with changes is their impact on resource allocation. There is nothing to do but face up to the reality that resources must be rescheduled, as inconvenient as this may be.

Materials Study Project

The experimental effort (task E) on the materials study project has run into difficulty because one of the materials was found to be impure. SU-PROMAC is anxious to obtain follow-on work from NERESCO, so there is a reluctance to inform the customer. Viable alternatives that avoid that necessity are desired. In this instance, properly purified materials can be obtained quickly, and means to recover lost time must then be devised. Two possibilities are using overtime and adding a second shift.

Highlights

- Changes will occur on every project, but smaller projects face fewer difficulties from them than do larger projects.
- Changes may result from customer requests; extenuating circumstances, such as a strike; altered environmental, health, or safety regulations; inflation; or resource unavailability.
- Uncertainty and buy-ins can result in inaccurate estimations.
- Authorization documents can be used to communicate planning and change control.
- Three problems changes can cause are managers may be reluctant to inform the customer and higher management of them, verbal authorizations often cause misunderstanding, and resources must be reallocated.

Further Reading

R. D. Archibald. *Managing High-Technology Programs and Projects.* New York: Wiley-Interscience, 1976.

Chapter 8, section 2 very briefly discusses change control.

P. W. Metzger. *Managing a Programming Project.* Englewood Cliffs, N.J.: Prentice-Hall, 1973.

Pages 87–89 and 159–161 discuss change control and implementation.

CHAPTER 17

Problem Solving

This chapter is concerned with how to solve problems as your project encounters changes during execution. First I discuss some general approaches to coping with problems. Then I describe decision trees, a powerful analytic technique for problem analysis. Following that, I review use of a matrix array and then discuss the kind of meetings in which problem-solving approaches are most likely to be effective.

The General Approach

Good solutions require a seven-step approach.

In general, the options available are either deductive or inductive logic. In the former, the solution is derived by reasoning from known scientific principles, using analytical techniques, and the conclusions reached are necessary and certain if the premises are correct. In practice, the project manager is rarely confronted with problems for which this approach is appropriate and must rely on inductive techniques, for which the scientific method is the typical prototype. Inductive methods reach conclusions that are probable. This straightforward approach entails seven steps, described in the following sections.

State the Real Problem

The key to problem solving is understanding the real problem rather than the apparent symptoms. Smoke may be emerging from the hardware you built or the computer may refuse to obey a subroutine command, but the actual problem may be an overheated component or an improper line of code in the computer program. You will have to decide how and perhaps why these particular problems occurred.

Gather the Relevant Facts

A fact-gathering phase is usually necessary to clarify the problem. People trained in engineering and science tend to want to engage in this step ad infinitum. Although it may take a good deal of time to locate information sources, there is also a law of diminishing returns. Because you will never have a 100 percent certainty of obtaining all the information, you must learn to exercise judgment as to when to truncate a search for additional information. At that point, you begin to converge on a solution using the information already gathered.

Propose a Solution

Once a plausible or possible solution has been identified, the winners and losers rapidly separate in their approach to problem solving. The losers inevitably adopt the first solution that comes to mind, possibly leaping out of the frying plan and into the fire. Admittedly, the pressures to come up with a solution quickly are great. No one likes to walk into his or her boss's or customer's office and say, "We have a problem." Such a crisis generates psychological pressure in the project manager to come up with a solution quickly so he or she can say, "We have a problem, but don't worry about it because we have a pretty good solution in mind." But it is best to take a different approach.

Develop Several Alternative Solutions

Developing alternatives is the key to problem solving.

The winning approach to problem solving is to develop several alternative solutions. Thus, when the problem has arisen and must be reported, the successful project manager will say, "We have a problem. We may have a possible solution, but I am going to take three or four days and consider other alternatives. Then I will report to you on the options and our recommended course of corrective action." Although such an approach to reporting the bad news may be initially uncomfortable, it is invariably associated with reaching better solutions.

Adopt the Best Alternative

After deciding what is the best alternative, you must adopt a course of action.

Tell Everyone

As an effective project manager, you have earlier made certain everybody involved in your project knew the original project plan. Now, because you have changed one or more dimensions of the Triple Constraint, you must tell everyone what the new plan is. As discussed in the previous chapter, if you fail to do this, there will be some people working in accordance with obsolete direction, producing something useless and out of date.

Audit the Outcome

As you implement the best alternative solution, watch how it is working out. Auditing will improve your ability to solve problems by showing you how your solutions actually work out. And as you learn more about the problem you are solving and the approach you have adopted, a better alternative may become clear, which may necessitate a further change in the plan.

Quiz 17-1

Consider the series of numbers 1, 2, 3, 4, __, __. What numbers go next in the series?

Decision Trees

Choosing the best alternative often requires estimating the possible outcomes and their probabilities. An organized way to cope with the situation is to use a decision tree. This technique is both simple and powerful. If you use it often enough, it will improve your average performance in adopting alternatives. Consider the decision whether to go to a movie or walk on the beach. This decision and its possible outcomes are shown in Figure 17-1.

Decision trees require you to quantify the outcome.

Each possibility has chance future events, which have to do with the quality of the movie or the weather. There are also different outcomes, which are illustrated. Outcomes such as those shown, which have more than one dimension to them (happiness and money, in the figure) must be reduced to a single numeric value. This can be done by utility or preference techniques, which I shall not discuss.

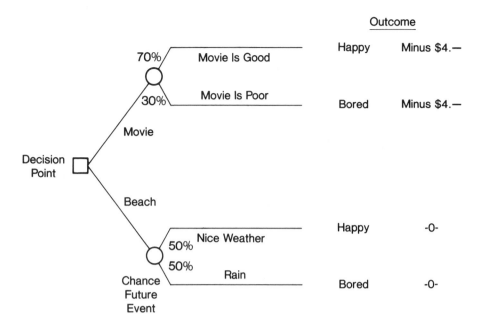

Figure 17-1. A decision tree.

Figure 17-2 is a general representation of the kind of decision tree with which you must work. A decision tree always starts with a decision for which there are two or more possible choices. Each choice may be followed by chance future events or subordinate choices (decisions) in any order and with two or more branches following each node. There is a single numeric value outcome, which is typically the present value of the cash flows along the various branches to that outcome.

Decision trees are used routinely in many situations, such as the decision whether to drill an oil well at a given location or whether to locate a new warehouse in a new geographic region. In both of these typical situations, the correctness of the decision depends on the probabilities of things happening in the future (oil being found or business growth), and decision trees are designed to maximize the likelihood of choosing the correct course of action.

Consider the following situation, which often confronts a project manager. You have just received an unsolicited request for a proposal that will yield a $300,000 before-tax profit if you can win the job. Checking with the marketing manager, you learn your company and two others were both solicited suddenly and you all have an equal opportunity of winning the job. Thus, you appear to have one chance in three of winning $300,000 if you write the proposal.

After discussing this, you and the marketing manager realize you have the opportunity to construct a working model for $45,000 and doing so increases the odds of your winning to fifty-fifty. The decision with which you are confronted is whether to build a working model (at a cost of

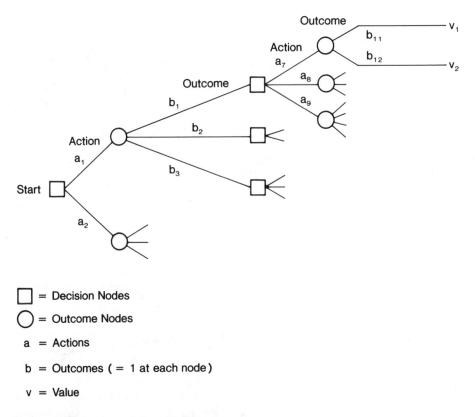

= Decision Nodes

= Outcome Nodes

a = Actions

b = Outcomes (= 1 at each node)

v = Value

Figure 17-2. A generalized decision tree.

There are two ways to draw decision trees.

$45,000) to increase the odds of winning a $300,000 before-tax profit from one in three to one in two. Figure 17-3 shows the decision tree and the problem analysis for this situation. Figure 17-4 is an alternative representation. In both cases, the branch in which the model is built has a higher value than the branch in which the model is not built. Therefore, your decision would be to build the model because it has a higher expected value. Note this does not guarantee you will win the job. Rather, it gives you a higher expected dollar value. If you use decision trees in enough cases, you will do better over the long run. But you might very well build the model and still lose the job, thus ending up losing $45,000. (Note that for simplicity I have ignored the cost of writing the proposal in both situations.)

Quiz 17-2

Imagine you start with the preceding proposal decision tree, but you and the marketing manager continue to discuss the situation prior to deciding whether to build the model. You realize whether or not you build the model, if you lose the proposal, you will have an opportunity to write a further proposal to the winning contractor. Such a further

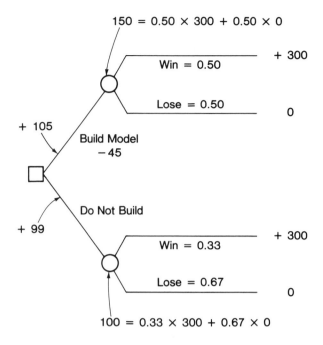

Figure 17-3. Decision tree for illustrative example (thousands of dollars omitted).

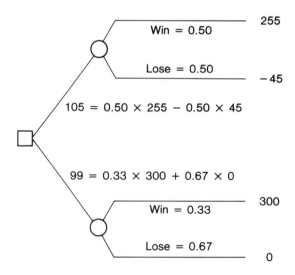

Figure 17-4. Alternative representation of Figure 17-3 decision tree.

proposal will cost you an additional $10,000, but if you write it after losing, you will have an 80 percent chance to win a subcontract (worth $100,000 in before-tax profit) from the winning contractor. Is it still attractive to build the model? Why or why not?

Matrix Array

A matrix must list all significant criteria.

Quantitative

In situations where decision trees are not practical or are unwieldy for the analysis and comparison of alternatives, the matrix array may be a satisfactory aid. Figure 17-5 illustrates a quantitative weighting (or scoring) array. The key considerations in the particular problem are listed on the left margin. In a computer programming project, the performance criteria might include processing speed, size of memory required, or similar considerations. For an airborne piece of equipment, performance issues might be weight, size and reliability. In addition to performance target criteria, the listing should include the schedule and cost implications of adopting that particular solution.

Next, weighting factors (the sum of which is equal to one) are attached to each criterion (or target). Then a percentage, indicating the degree to which the solution satisfies the particular criterion target, is entered for each solution. Finally, each percentage for each solution in the body of the matrix is multiplied by the corresponding weighting factors, and the result is entered at the bottom of the solution column (for example, for solution approach 2, $0.20 \times 90\% + 0.15 \times 70\% + 0.15 \times 50\% + 0.20 \times 70\% + 0.30 \times 80\% = 74\%$). There are four problems with this approach:

Criteria	Weighting Factor	Solution Approach 1	Solution Approach 2	Solution Approach 3
Performance Target A	0.20	60%	90%	80%
Performance Target B	0.15	90%	70%	70%
Performance Target C	0.15	90%	50%	90%
Schedule Target	0.20	70%	70%	90%
Cost Target	0.30	90%	80%	70%
Weighted Percentage Value		80%	74%	79%

Figure 17-5. Quantitative decision matrix.

1. Deciding on weighting factors may be difficult.

2. Choosing percentages may be difficult, especially for the schedule and cost targets where the solution approach may exceed plan.

3. The highest ranking or weighted percentage value may still be inadequate.

4. It does not consider people, in particular, the possibility that one solution approach is championed by an ambitious person who will work nights and weekends to accomplish it.

Quiz 17-3

Replace the five weighting factors in Figure 17-5 with 0.2, 0.1, 0.2, 0.3, and 0.2, respectively, and calculate the weighted percentage value for each solution.

Qualitative

Because of the manipulation to which the quantitative approach is subject, it is often better to use a slightly more qualitative matrix. Such a matrix can explicitly consider people issues, especially where there are advocates for or opponents to a particular solution approach. Figures 17-6, 17-7, and 17-8 illustrate this technique. Note three aspects of this approach:

1. Numbers are used whenever possible.

2. People are given explicit consideration.

3. The summary identifies both favorable and unfavorable issues.

Also, this kind of matrix can always be used, even early in the decision analysis, before all relevant numerical data are available.

Figure 17-6 shows a qualitative matrix array for the problem of selecting a three-axis "frictionless" support for an airborne instrument with ±5 degrees of freedom in three directions. The original perceptions of the factors to be considered are typed in the left margin. The first two solution approaches are listed. Both have many drawbacks. In Figure 17-7, a third alternative solution is identified, pointing out the need to consider one more factor (outgassing). Figure 17-8 shows a reasonably adequate solution for which the schedule must be studied further or perhaps accelerated.

Be honest about solution shortfalls.

To use this kind of matrix, list each solution across the top. You must do this conscientiously. When you write down the first solution and it clearly falls short with regard to one or more of the key criteria, seek additional solutions designed to overcome the shortfall of the ones pres-

Approach / Consideration	Conventional Outer-Ring Gimbal	Internal Gimbal				
Weight (Lbs)	50?	20?				
Size	Huge	Should Be OK				
Reliability	Bearings	Bearings				
Coercion (In-Lbs)	1?	1?				
Schedule	Quick	Less Quick				
Cost	Low	Higher				
People						
Pro						
Con	Weight, Size, Coercion	Weight, Coercion				

Figure 17-6. Qualitative matrix array.

ently conceived. Usually, after you have written down two, three, or four solutions, each of which has one or more aspects of shortfall, you will identify some hybrid or new variant that comes close to satisfying all the key considerations identified. Even if the matrix array does not lead to a hybrid that clearly satisfies all significant considerations, using the array will clarify available trade-offs and options.

Problem-Solving Meeting Styles

Problem-solving approaches have appropriate meeting styles.

C. J. Margerison, in *Managerial Problem Solving*, points out five approaches to problem solving, and for each there is a meeting style most likely to result in an effective solution. Table 17-1 summarizes Margerison's ideas. If the information to solve the problem is readily available, a solution-centered approach to problem solving may be adapted. Three of these are indicated. If the managerial authority is accepted and the manager has the information and the ability to solve the problem, a directive approach

Approach / Consideration	Conventional Outer-Ring Gimbal	Internal Gimbal	Gas Bearing			
Weight (Lbs)	50 ?	20 ?	10-20			
Size	Huge	Should Be OK	OK, But Also Has Pump			
Reliability	Bearings	Bearings	Pump			
Coercion (In-Lbs)	1 ?	1 ?	Nil			
Outgassing	Oil	Oil	Support Gas			
Schedule	Quick	Less Quick	8-12 Months			
Cost	Low	Higher	Still Higher			
People			Jack			
Pro			Coercion			
Con	Weight, Size, Coercion	Weight, Coercion	Weight, Gas, Reliability, Time			

Figure 17-7.   Qualitative matrix array with a third alternative solution identified.

is appropriate and a command meeting, one in which the manager issues orders, is the most appropriate meeting style. This does not mean a different meeting style cannot be used, but a command meeting will most likely produce an effective solution.

Typical Problems

In most project management problem-solving situations, it is not possible to find *the* answer, only a most acceptable (or least objectionable) answer. This may be caused by inherent uncertainty or lack of quantitative data. It is thus a matter of judgment about when to choose among the identified solutions and when to keep looking for more, better solutions. Honest people will differ (as they will in their perception of the problem and their evaluation of solution alternatives), and this must be both expected and tolerated. Use of a qualitative matrix or a purely qualitative decision tree can reduce, if not eliminate, this problem.

Approach / Consideration	Conventional Outer-Ring Gimbal	Internal Gimbal	Gas Bearing	2 Horizontal Flexures + Vertical Mercury	3 Equal (35.2°) Flexures	1 Horizontal + 2 45° Flexures
Weight (Lbs)	50 ?	20 ?	10-20	~ 10	5-10	5-10
Size	Huge	Should Be OK	OK, But Also Has Pump	Reasonable	Small	Small
Reliability	Bearings	Bearings	Pump	Mercury Spillage	∞	∞
Coercion (In-Lbs)	1 ?	1 ?	Nil	~ 0.01	~ 0.01	~ 0.01
Outgassing	Oil	Oil	Support Gas	Mercury Vapor	Nil	Nil
Schedule	Quick	Less Quick	8-12 Months	3-4 Months	5-6 Months	4-5 Months
Cost	Low	Higher	Still Higher	~ $15K	~ $25K	~ $20K
People			Jack	Hy	Mike	Mike
Pro			Coercion	Time & Cost, Coercion	Weight, Size, Reliability, Coercion	Weight, Size, Reliability, Coercion
Con	Weight, Size, Coercion	Weight, Coercion	Weight, Gas, Reliability, Time	Mercury	Harder to Make Parts	Time = ?

Figure 17-8. Qualitative matrix array with one reasonably adequate solution.

Materials Study Project

Considering the materials study project problem from the prior chapter, a qualitative matrix (Figure 17-9) suggests overtime is the least objectionable solution.

Highlights

- The seven steps in problem solving are identify the problem, collect the data, devise a solution, search for alternative solutions, adopt the best solution, implement the solution, and audit the outcome.
- Decision trees help you choose the best alternative.
- Matrices, another aid to alternative selection, may be qualitative or quantitative.

Table 17-1. Effective Meeting Styles. (Adapted From C. J. Margerison, *Managerial Problem Solving*, McGraw-Hill Book Co. (UK) LTD., © 1974. Reproduced By Permission.)

	Approach to Problem Solving	Characteristics	Appropriate Meeting Style
Solution Centered —Information Available	Directive	Managerial authority accepted and manager has both information & ability to solve problem	Command—issue orders
	Negotiative	Bargaining with different objectives but common interests	Negotiative—different groups horse trading to reach aggreement
	Prescriptive	Solution solicited— presented answer may be tentative trial	(Negotiative—or) Collegiate—peers reaching decision by consensus
Problem Centered —Information Needed	Consultative	Trust exists and information sharing useful to diagnose problem	Advisory—exchange information and make subsequent decision
	Reflective	Useful if unclear problem and nonjudgmental restatements are acceptable	Advisory is best

- There are appropriate meeting styles for different problem-solving approaches.

Further Reading

V. G. Hajek. *Management of Engineering Projects.* New York: McGraw-Hill, 1977.

Section 14.11 is a good one-page summary of decision making to solve problems.

C. J. Margerison. *Managerial Problem Solving.* Maidenhead, Berkshire, England: McGraw-Hill, 1974.

This is an outstanding book on all aspects of problem solving.

P. G. Moore and H. Thomas. *The Anatomy of Decisions.* New York: Penguin, 1976.

This is a well-written, clear, complete treatment of decision trees. It is brief but thorough.

Solution / Consideration	Overtime	Second Shift
Performance	OK	OK
Schedule	OK	OK, but must train crew
People	Same as original plan	Need leader and two technicians
Cost	Overtime premium	Shift premium
Pro	People available	Less costly
Con	Overtime premium exceeds shift premium	Extra people training time

Figure 17-9. Qualitative matrix for the materials study project problem cited in Chapter 16.

Part FIVE

Completion

CHAPTER **18**

Finishing the Project

The fifth and last step in project management is project completion. To introduce this topic, this chapter first discusses project life cycles. This discussion reviews activities required to complete the project. Then the consequences of project completion are discussed, and it is shown all personnel do not necessarily have the same stake in ending the project.

Project Life Cycle

Phases

That projects have different phases emphasizes that personnel needs will change throughout the project life cycle.

Figure 18-1 shows a project life cycle. The three phases are arbitrary, but they are sufficient to illustrate the point that project activities change during the duration of any project. This has implications for the illustrated personnel head count and means the kind of personnel used in different phases will have to change. For instance, creative designers, very useful in the early phases, can easily become an obstacle to completion if they are retained during the later phases.

Termination

There is a variety of ways to stop projects. Resources can be withdrawn, for instance, by reassigning personnel or required facilities. Higher priority projects may gain at the expense of a low priority project, which may be allowed to wither on the vine. These approaches are not as desirable as an orderly and carefully planned termination. Project success, that is, satisfying the Triple Constraint, can be obtained only by this latter approach. During the last few months of a project, weekly reviews may be required; and during the last few weeks, daily reviews may be required.

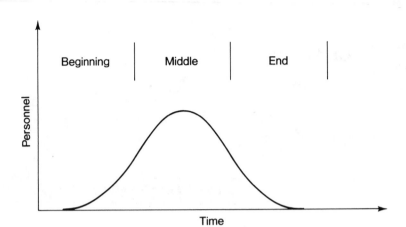

	Beginning	Middle	End
Construction	Site	Erection	Landscaping
Product Development	R&D, Market Research	Engineering and Manufacturing	Product Introduction
Aerospace System	Engineering	Assembly	Customer Test and Sign-off

Figure 18-1. Project life cycle.

Acceptance

The goal of project management is to obtain customer acceptance of the project result. This means the customer agrees the performance dimension specification of the Triple Constraint has been met. Unless the criteria for acceptance have been clearly defined in documentation agreed to by the customer and the contractor, there will be discord at the end of the project. When agreement is lacking, the customer will typically want more (unless it costs unacceptable amounts of time or money) and the contractor will argue for less.

Therefore, the acceptance phase must start with the initial contractual definition of the work to be undertaken. This is not to say there cannot be changes of scope during the contract to alter or clarify the acceptance criteria. In the materials study project, the customer could have asked that more materials be tested. If SUPROMAC had agreed to this, a contract amendment (more materials, more time, more money) could have been negotiated.

In some projects, it may be impossible at the beginning to agree upon final acceptance criteria. This is typical of high-technology projects. When this is the case, the contract should call for an initial effort phase of an adequate duration to clarify the entire system design and acceptance criteria. At the end of this first phase, a customer review is conducted and a contract is negotiated for the final phase of work, including acceptance criteria for the end of the project. This approach requires the customer to bear a large risk during the initial phase because the contractor may decide during the initial phase that the final phase is too extensive and costly. Nevertheless, there is no reasonable alternative to this two-phase approach.

Because there are many possible completion points and delivery conditions for a project, it is necessary to think these through. Completion of the Apollo lunar project would differ depending on whether it was defined as the launch to the moon, the manned landing, the astronaut recovery, or the completion of rock analysis.

Objectively measurable criteria for completion (such as move these two hundred books to the next room before 9:30) are best. Subjective criteria (such as paint an attractive portrait of me) are risky. The former allow little or no room for ambiguity; in the latter, the customer and contractor could easily have different standards.

Completion requires objective and measurable criteria be attained, which ideally solves the customer's problem.

It is also important to be clear about what the project output is supposed to accomplish. For instance, three very different results occur when the product performs the specified functions, the product was built according to the specified designs, or the product really solved the customer's problem.

Project completion clearly depends upon precise wording of the acceptance criteria. There should be no room for doubt or ambiguity, although in practice this is extremely difficult to accomplish at project inception. Both parties may enter into a contract with goodwill, but the contractor may have assumed and perhaps even included in the contract the jointly agreed priority to use customer facilities to validate product output. Such a priority can easily become an ambiguous issue toward the end of the project. Other difficulties in wording arise when the word "appropriate" is used. Appropriate tests or demonstrations that seem clear and simple at the beginning of a project have a way of becoming the opposite toward the end.

Delivery

Delivery may or may not be completion. Project completion often requires the product function after delivery to a location the customer designates. Even if not explicitly the case, there may be an implied warranty that requires it. Thus, responsibility for delivered goods after they leave the contractor's facility is always an issue to be considered at project inception. Once the contractor has turned over possession of the goods, the contractor's control is greatly diminished. Therefore, it is important to have clearly stipulated conditions for acceptance, including payment terms.

Quiz 18-1

The customer has witnessed final system tests at your company and accepts the system. After delivery to the customer's plant, the system does not perform adequately. What do you do?

Documentation Reports

It is not at all uncommon for a project to require the delivery of documentation as well as some other tangible output. Such documentation, in addition to a final report, might include a spare parts list, instruction manuals, and as-built drawings. Even the format may be specified.

Because furnishing these items may delay completion of the principal project output, they should be identified as a separate line item in the original contract. Thus, billing for the principal portion of the contract may accompany its delivery and billing for the documentation reports may follow later.

Completion Consequences

Project completion may be viewed as a boon or doom. The customer, the contracting organization, the project manager, and the project personnel may not all see it the same way.

Four Affected Parties

Everyone does not have the same stake in completion, and the project manager must understand the differences.

For the project manager, completion may be an opportunity for promotion, but many project personnel may find themselves laid off if there is no other work. If the project was badly managed, its manager may receive a less favorable assignment in the future and personnel who did an outstanding job may have a choice future assignment. The contracting organization's view of project completion depends on customer approval and project profitability. The customer may be unhappy because he or she specified the wrong acceptance criteria but admit the contractor has met the specifications.

Thus, there is no reason to assume all four parties will have the same view of project completion. Project managers must realize they may have a very different stake in ending the project than the other three parties.

Completion consequences are also influenced by the reasons for termination. It is certainly best to end the project because all the objectives have been satisfactorily achieved. It is a bad situation if one or more dimensions of the Triple Constraint have been missed substantially.

Personnel Reassignment

Project completion requires reassignment of people. We have now come full circle. The (temporary) project is no longer imposed on the rest of the (permanent) contracting organization. This frequently will necessitate a reorganization of the parent entity because the mix of remaining project work is such that the previously satisfactory orgainzation is no longer appropriate.

A person's perception of what will happen when the project ends will affect his or her work as termination approaches.

The other crucial aspect of personnel reassignment is timing. If a person's next assignment is a choice one, he or she will normally be anxious to start and will lose interest in completing the present project. Conversely, if someone's next project assignment is undesirable, he or she may stall. When no assignment is obvious and layoff or termination is probable, personnel may even attempt sabotage to stretch out the present project assignment.

The project manager can cope with these tendencies to some extent by selecting the time he or she informs project personnel of their next assignment. But if the contracting organization has a reputation for terminating personnel at the end of projects, there is little a project manager can do. The best situation is one in which all project personnel can count on their good work being recognized and appreciated and there being a selection of future assignments.

Even if no specific new project assignment is available when personnel need reassignment, there are still options. For example, personnel can write an unsolicited proposal, prepare an article for publication, work on an in-house development effort, or attend a short course or seminar. Temporary assignments such as these can be used constructively to fill in valleys in the project work load. They also can be used as a motivational tool if they are authorized so as to make participation a mark of recognition for a job well done.

Increasing the Odds of Success _____

There are both external and internal factors that influence how well a project satisfies its Triple Constraint.

External Factors

A knowledgeable customer, high priority, and clear objectives aid successful completion.

Customers for projects seem to be divided into two broad categories. Knowledgeable and shortsighted. The shortsighted customers tend to emphasize the buyer versus seller relationship and to some extent create an adversary relationship between the two organizations. Conversely, knowledgeable customers realize their stake in project success is ultimately just as great as that of the performing contract organization. Thus, a knowledgeable customer will become involved in the project in an effective, as opposed to a destructive, manner. Such a customer will specify expected reviews and include them in the original job definition. Beyond this, he or she will attempt to ask the tough questions and to carry out probing reviews of the contractor's work, not to embarrass but to help assure all significant issues have been dealt with appropriately. Any required changes will be negotiated intelligently.

High priority projects inevitably seem to have better outcomes than lower priority projects because they tend to win all competitions for physical and human resources. This is not to say low priority projects lack top management support; top management clearly wants all projects to succeed, but the lower priority projects are at a relative disadvantage.

Clear and stable project objectives are a sine qua non of project success. Project objectives can and do change during the course of many projects, but not on a daily or hourly basis. Thus, committing these objectives to writing helps assure they are fixed in everyone's mind, and revising them when they must occasionally change is also a clear requirement of success.

Internal Factors

A good leader, a balanced team, the right-sized work packages, careful replanning, and orderly termination contribute to project success.

A qualified, experienced, competent leader is vital, as is a balanced team. Having a team with a balance of skills and getting teamwork from it can be somewhat contradictory. People with very similar backgrounds tend to get along better, so it is easier to promote teamwork in a group composed entirely of, for instance, electrical engineers. Nevertheless, a successful project usually requires a team be composed of more than electrical engineers. Thus, the project manager is confronted with merging people with diverse backgrounds into an effective and harmonious team.

Having the properly sized work packages helps you avoid two potential problems. Complex, difficult work packages should not be assigned to junior people and simple work packages should not be assigned to senior people, who will not be challenged by them.

Because projects will almost never be carried out exactly in accordance with the original plan, replanning is a constant requirement in project management. Project termination, especially the reassignment of personnel, requires active planning well before scheduled completion.

Typical Problems

Sometimes not only subordinate personnel but also the project manager must change during the project's life. The manager for the initial phases may be great at the inception but become stale with time or bored by routine wrap-up activities. The solution in this case is to change project managers, and both upper management and the project manager must be alert to this possibility.

Materials Study Project

SUPROMAC can complete the materials study project by submitting its written report to NERESCO. However, even if that is the only contractual obligation, it may be better to present it as part of an oral briefing in order to (1) improve communication by allowing some give-and-take discussion and (2) provide an opportunity to increase the customer's happiness with the results.

Highlights

- Although the project life cycle starts with the definition phase and ends with the completion phase, project completion and customer acceptance depend on agreements reached during the definition phase.
- Personnel needs may change throughout the project life cycle.
- It is best to end a project because all dimensions of the Triple Constraint have been satisfied.
- The project manager must realize project completion may not be good for all involved parties and plan for an orderly end well in advance of its scheduled time.
- Both internal and external factors contribute to project success.

Further Reading

V. G. Hajek. *Management of Engineering Projects*. New York: McGraw-Hill, 1977.

Chapters 19 and 20 provide a reasonable treatment of the completion phase.

P. W. Metzger. *Managing a Programming Project.* Englewood Cliffs, N.J.: Prentice-Hall, 1973.

Chapters 5, 6, and 7 give a detailed overview of the completion phase for programming projects and have broader generality as well.

CHAPTER 19

After Completion

Projects end with their completion, but there frequently are postcompletion activities that are necessary to the project and may be viewed as part of it. They are not, however, necessarily part of the basic contract. These are discussed in this chapter.

Continuing Service and Support

Some projects require postcompletion service and support.

Continuing service and support may be an obligation. If they are, it must be understood who is to pay for them and when. This is often left to be negotiated when the project is completed. Negotiating at this time may be desirable because of an initial inability to see what may be involved, but it leaves a potential Pandora's box at the end of the project.

The contractor should view continuing service and support as an opportunity and not merely as an obligation. His or her employees will be working with the customer's personnel, providing continuing service and support, if it is included in the project. In so doing, they will have informal opportunities to explore ideas with the customer's personnel and hear about real problems the customer is facing. Thus, these contacts provide the basis for future business opportunities.

Ownership Rights

Patents and special facilities required for contract performance have ownership value. In general, if it is a cost reimbursable contract in which the customer pays all costs incurred, ownership rights revert to the customer at the end of the job. If it is a fixed price contract, ownership rights generally revert to the contractor unless otherwise stipulated in the initial

Patent rights and hiring policies must be outlined in the contract.

contract. These can be points of contention unless they are discussed and clearly resolved in the initial contract. In any event, patent applications must be filed if any seem justified. The party of ultimate ownership must expect to pay for this activity.

There is also the issue of people. Obviously, neither the customer nor the contractor owns any people. But "no compete" clauses in recruiting customer personnel into the contractor organization or vice versa are often in the initial contract. If they were not, the customer might hire the contractor's personnel to perform the continuing service and support the contracting organization presumed it was going to perform and be reimbursed for.

Audits

A project is not complete until the customer pays the bill.

There often are postcompletion audits, especially in contracts performed for governmental entities. It is therefore absolutely essential to retain records for the required duration and even more important to file and document them in an organized and thorough way. Many of the people who could explain some audited item may no longer be available when the audit is performed, so the contractor might lose an important claim if this is not done. Some portion of the final payment on a contract may be withheld until the audit is completed. Therefore, a final financial summary may not be possible until the audit is performed, and this can be months or even years after the other work is finished.

Quiz 19-1

What can you do if your customer does not pay?

People Issues

After being assured all project personnel have been reassigned (or laid off or terminated if necessary), the project manager has two other things to do. First, send personal letters of thanks, appreciation, or praise to project personnel. Second, send a brief wrap-up report to your management, and it is smart to cite your own successful performance in this.

Typical Problems

Basically, the problem here is simply doing it all. The press or excitement of new things to do often leads to the omission of some postcompletion activities. The solution is to recognize your responsibility in getting these things done.

Materials Study Project

In the case of the materials study project, SUPROMAC could use the final report to submit either an oral or a preliminary written proposal for further work. Assuming it is well received, they could continue to discuss this with NERESCO until a new project is defined and initiated.

Highlights

- Continuing service and support activities may lead to future business opportunities.
- Contracts often include assignment of patent rights and "no compete" personnel recruitment clauses.
- Records must be carefully kept in case there is a postcompletion audit.
- Managers should send letters of appreciation to project personnel and a wrap-up report to the boss.

Further Reading

R. D. Archibald. *Managing High-Technology Programs and Projects.* New York: Wiley-Interscience, 1976.

Chapter 10 is a very short recap of some terminal activities.

V. G. Hajek. *Management of Engineering Projects.* New York: McGraw-Hill, 1977.

Chapter 21 is a very brief recap of a few terminal activities.

M. Silverman. *Project Management—A Short Course for Professionals.* New York: Wiley Professional Development Programs, 1976.

Chapter 10 briefly discusses phase out, mostly covering the people issues.

Part SIX

Other Issues

20

Small Projects

Relative to large projects, small projects have both advantages and disadvantages. Being smaller, they are easier to understand and less likely to get into difficulty. But there is less time and money to recover from anything that goes wrong and they inevitably lack high priority.

Simplified Management

Small projects have a Triple Constraint to plan and control.

Figure 20-1 is a form that can be used to plan and control small projects. It shows the plan for the three research tasks of the materials study project (assuming for the purpose of illustration this is a small task within the research group). The form allows the work breakdown items and the schedule to be entered in either a network diagram or a bar chart form. The overall plan for labor and nonlabor cost may also be entered. As actual costs are incurred, they can be entered and variances noted. In this particular form, the labor categories do not exactly match those previously used, but the form is merely illustrative and could be changed to include any categories. Note also that the form uses months for the time horizon across the top. This could be changed to weeks, quarters, or any other convenient time frame. For small tasks, it is certainly permissible to lump future periods in yearly intervals because by definition the amount of effort on a small project is not very great and this is perhaps sufficient time resolution for such future periods.

Problems

There are four causes for the problems unique to small projects: tight schedules, tight budgets, small teams, and low priority.

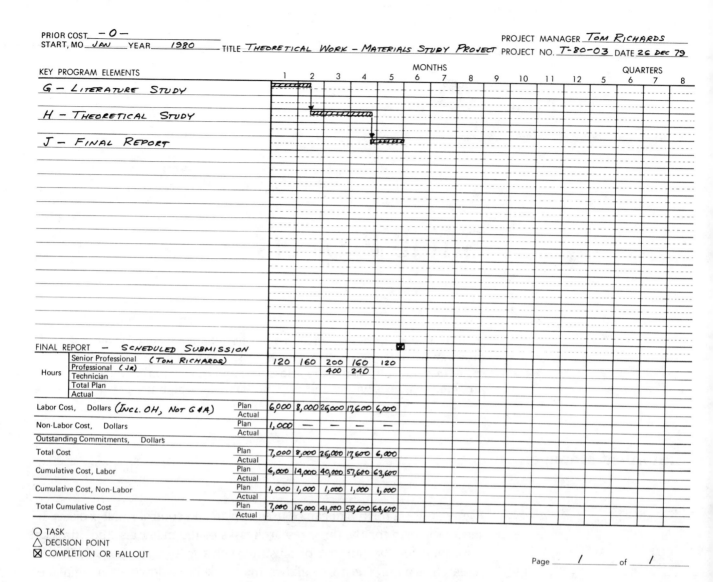

PRIOR COST ___-O-___
START, MO __JAN__ YEAR ___1980___ TITLE _THEORETICAL WORK – MATERIALS STUDY PROJECT_

PROJECT MANAGER _TOM RICHARDS_
PROJECT NO. _T-80-03_ DATE _26 DEC 79_

KEY PROGRAM ELEMENTS					MONTHS											QUARTERS			
	1	2	3	4	5	6	7	8	9	10	11	12	5	6	7	8			
G – LITERATURE STUDY																			
H – THEORETICAL STUDY																			
J – FINAL REPORT																			

FINAL REPORT — SCHEDULED SUBMISSION

Hours		1	2	3	4	5												
	Senior Professional (TOM RICHARDS)	120	160	200	160	120												
	Professional (JR)			400	240													
	Technician																	
	Total Plan																	
	Actual																	

Labor Cost, Dollars (INCL. OH, NOT G&A)	Plan	6,000	8,000	26,000	17,600	6,000												
	Actual																	
Non-Labor Cost, Dollars	Plan	1,000	—	—	—	—												
	Actual																	
Outstanding Commitments, Dollars																		
Total Cost	Plan	7,000	8,000	26,000	17,600	6,000												
	Actual																	
Cumulative Cost, Labor	Plan	6,000	14,000	40,000	57,600	63,600												
	Actual																	
Cumulative Cost, Non-Labor	Plan	1,000	1,000	1,000	1,000	1,000												
	Actual																	
Total Cumulative Cost	Plan	7,000	15,000	41,000	58,600	64,600												
	Actual																	

○ TASK
△ DECISION POINT
⊠ COMPLETION OR FALLOUT

Page ___1___ of ___1___

Figure 20-1. Simplified form for small project planning and control.

Tight Schedules

A small project typically is planned to have a shorter schedule than a large project. Thus, the inevitable "getting up to speed" consumes a larger fraction of the available time. A one-week or a one-month delay on a long program is less significant than the same delay on a two-, three-, or four-month program, a typical period for a small project. The implication is small projects must be initiated at the very first opportunity and the project manager must devote a relatively large amount of effort to assuring schedule compliance.

Tight Budgets

A small project budget will be less than a large project budget. Hence, the absolute amount of money available for contingency must necessarily be

*Small projects lack time,
money, personnel, and priority.*

less. When the inevitable revolting development occurs, there is less maneuvering room in which to cope with the consequences. The typical two-week lag in cost reports represents a significantly larger fraction of the overall project time and again leads to less reaction capability when some revolting development is discovered. Thus, extremely close attention to cost is required, on a weekly, if not on a daily basis.

Small Teams

A large project can typically have the full-time attention of a functional expert (for instance, a thermodynamicist), whereas a small project must make do with the part-time assignment of such specialists. Thus, the small project must compete against other projects for specialists' time. In some cases, especially where computer programming is called for, this can be a major problem. Each time a person begins a particular programming task, he or she will spend a certain amount of time "getting up to speed." Thus, time is lost in reindoctrination. The problem may be worse with computer programming, but it is not confined to that specialty. Confronted with this reality, the effective project manager should attempt to bargain for full days whenever part-time resources are required.

Priority

Studies have shown that high priority projects are more likely than low priority projects to be completed successfully because they will normally win each competition for any key resource. If you have a low priority project and another person has a high priority project and you both request the model shop make parts for your projects, the person with the high priority project will have his or her needs satisfied first. And it is unlikely a small project will ever have the same significance for an organization as a large project, which means low priority is more common on small projects than on large projects.

Quiz 20-1

You are spending half your time managing a small four-month project and spending the other half working on a much larger project. After two months, you discover the small project is running late and will require three-quarters of your time to complete it on schedule. What do you do?

Typical Problems _____

Beware that small projects do not escalate.

There is another, insidious problem, namely, that of projects starting small and escalating. Again, "staying on top" helps as does switching to more extensive, formal project management techniques as the project grows.

Materials Study Project _____

As shown in Figure 20-1, Tom Richards is to perform the theoretical work on the materials study project (tasks G, H, and J). If he gets ill, quits, or is reassigned to a higher priority project, there is very little time in which to recover (that is, only the slack time until the project's final report, task K).

Highlights _____

- Four causes of the problems unique to small projects are tight schedules, tight budgets, small teams, and low priority.
- Another problem associated with small projects is a tendency for the project to grow.

Further Reading _____

B. N. Abramson and R. D. Kennedy. *Managing Small Projects.* Redondo Beach, Calif.: TRW Systems Group, 1975.

Although somewhat specific to TRW, this short booklet has some useful pointers.

M. Zeldman. *Keeping Technical Projects on Target.* New York: AMACOM, 1978.

This is a graphic, manual system that may be helpful for controlling small projects, although the system illustrated in Figure 20-1 seems preferable.

CHAPTER 21

Northeast Research Laboratory Case

This entire chapter is a case study. Skim it to gain a sense of what it is about. Then read it to define the problems and recommend solutions to them. (An analysis of the case is printed with the other quiz answers.)

Quiz 21-1 The Northeast Research Laboratory (B) Case

On a Friday morning in late December, 1973, Sam Lacy, Head of the Physical Sciences Division of Northeast Research Laboratory (NRL) thought about two letters which lay on his desk. One, which he had received a few weeks before, was a progress report from Robert Kirk, recently assigned project leader of the Exco Project, who reported that earlier frictions between the NRL team and the client had lessened considerably, that quality research was under way, and that the prospects for retaining the Exco project on a long-term basis appeared fairly good. The other letter, which had just arrived in the morning's mail, came from Gray Kenney, a Vice President of Exco, and stated that the company wished to terminate the Exco contract effective immediately.

Lacy was puzzled. He remembered how pleased Gray Kenney had been only a few months before when the Exco project produced its second patentable process. On the other hand, he also recalled some of the difficulties the project had encountered within NRL which had ultimately led to the replacement of project leader Alan North in order to avoid losing the contract. Lacy decided to call in the participants in an effort to piece together an understanding of what had happened. Some of what he learned is described below. But the problem remained for him to decide what he should report to top management. What should he recommend to avoid the recurrence of such a situation in the future?

Company Background

Northeast Research Laboratory was a multidisciplinary research and development organization employing approximately 1,000 professionals. It was organized into two main sectors, one for economics and business administration and the other for the physical and natural sciences. Within the physical and natural sciences sector, the organization was essentially by branches of science. The main units were called divisions and the subunits were called laboratories. A partial organization chart is shown in Exhibit 1.

Most of the company's work was done on the basis of contracts with clients. Each contract was a project. Responsibility for the project was vested in a project leader, and through him up the organizational structure in which his laboratory was located. Typically, some members of the project team were drawn from laboratories other than that in which the project leader worked; it was the ability to put together a team with a variety of technical talents that was one of the principal strengths of a multidisciplinary laboratory. Team members worked un-

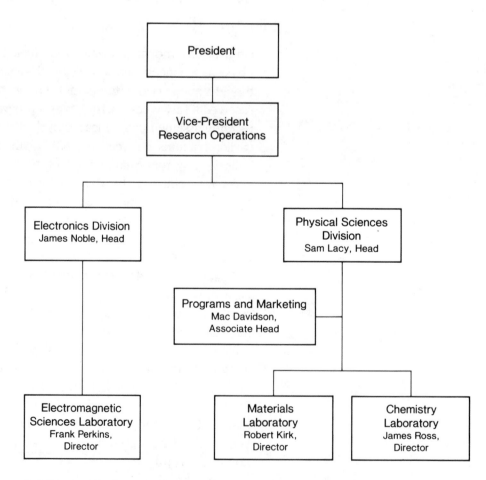

Exhibit 1. Northeast Research Laboratory (B) organization chart (simplified).

der the direction of the project leader during the period in which they were assigned to the project. An individual might be working on more than one project concurrently. The project leader could also draw on the resources of central service organizations, such as model shops, computer services, editorial, and drafting. The project was billed for the services of these units at rates which were intended to cover their full costs.

Inception of the Exco Project

In October, 1972, Gray Kenney, Vice President of Exco, had telephoned Mac Davidson of NRL to outline a research project which would examine the effect of microwaves on various ores and minerals. Davidson was Associate Head of the Physical Sciences Division and had known Kenney for several years. During the conversation Kenney asserted that NRL ought to be particularly intrigued by the research aspects of the project, and Davidson readily agreed. Davidson was also pleased because the Physical Sciences Division was under pressure to generate more revenue, and this potentially long-term project from Exco would make good use of available manpower. In addition, top management of NRL had recently circulated several memos indicating that more emphasis should be put on commercial rather than government work. Davidson was, however, a little concerned that the project did not fall neatly into one laboratory or even one division, but in fact required assistance from the Electronics Division to complement work that would be done in two different Physical Sciences Laboratories (the Chemistry Laboratory and the Materials Laboratory).

A few days later Davidson organized a joint client-NRL conference to determine what Exco wanted and to plan the proposal. Kenney sent his assistant, Tod Denby, who was to serve as the Exco liaison officer for the project. Representing NRL were Davidson; Sam Lacy; Dr. Robert Kirk, director of the Materials Laboratory (one of the two Physical Sciences laboratories involved in the project); Dr. Alan North, manager of Chemical Development & Engineering (and associate director of the Chemistry Laboratory); Dr. James Noble, Executive Director of the Electronics Division; and a few researchers chosen by Kirk and North. Davidson also would like to have invited Dr. James Ross, director of the Chemistry Laboratory, but Ross was out of town and couldn't attend the pre-proposal meeting.

Denby described the project as a study of the use of microwaves for the conversion of basic ores and minerals to more valuable commercial products. The study was to consist of two parts:

Task A—An experimental program to examine the effect of microwaves on some 50 ores and minerals, and to select those processes appearing to have the most promise.

Task B—A basic study to obtain an understanding of how and why microwaves interact with certain minerals.

It was agreed that the project would be a joint effort of three laboratories: (1) Materials, (2) Chemistry, and (3) Electromagnetic. The first two laboratories were in the Physical Sciences Division, and the last was in the Electronics Division.

Denby proposed that the contract be open-ended, with a level of effort of around $10,000–$12,000 per month. Agreement was quickly reached on the content of the proposal. Denby emphasized to the group that an early start was essential if Exco were to remain ahead of its competition.

After the meeting Lacy, who was to have overall responsibility for the project, discussed the choice of project leader with Davidson. Davidson proposed Alan North, a 37-year-old chemist who had had experience as a project leader on several projects. North had impressed Davidson at the pre-proposal meeting and seemed well suited to head the interdisciplinary team. Lacy agreed. Lacy regretted that Dr. Ross (head of the Laboratory in which North worked) was unable to participate in the decision of who should head the joint project. In fact, because he was out of town, Ross was neither aware of the Exco project nor of his laboratory's involvement in it.

The following day, Alan North was told of his appointment as project leader. During the next few days, he conferred with Robert Kirk, head of the other Physical Sciences laboratory involved in the project. Toward the end of October Denby began to exert pressure on North to finalize the proposal, stating that the substance had been agreed upon at the pre-proposal conference. North thereupon drafted a five-page letter as a substitute for a formal proposal, describing the nature of the project and outlining the procedures and equipment necessary. At Denby's request, North included a paragraph which authorized members of the client's staff to visit NRL frequently and observe portions of the research program. The proposal's cover sheet contained approval signatures from the laboratories and divisions involved. North signed for his own area and for laboratory director Ross. He telephoned Dr. Noble of the Electronics Division, relayed the client's sense of urgency, and Noble authorized North to sign for him. Davidson signed for the Physical Sciences Division as a whole.

At this stage, North relied principally on the advice of colleagues within his own division. As he did not know personally the individuals in the Electronics Division, they were not called upon at this point. Since North understood informally that the director of the Electromagnetic Sciences Laboratory, Dr. Perkins, was quite busy and often out of town, North did not attempt to discuss the project with Perkins.

After the proposal had been signed and mailed, Dr. Perkins was sent a copy. It listed the engineering equipment which the client wanted purchased for the project and prescribed how it was to be used. Perkins worried that performance characteristics of the power supply (necessary for quantitative measurement) specified in the proposal were inadequate for the task. He asked North about it and North said that the client had made up his mind as to the microwave equipment he wanted and how it was to be used. Denby had said he was paying for that equipment and intended to move it to Exco's laboratories after the completion of the NRL contract.

All these events had transpired rather quickly. By the time Dr. Ross, director of the Chemistry Laboratory, returned to the Institute, the proposal for the Exco project had been signed and accepted. Ross went to see Lacy and said that he had dealt with Denby on a previous project and had serious misgivings about working with him. Lacy assuaged some of Ross's fears by observing that if anyone could succeed in working with Denby it would be North—a flexible man, professionally competent, who could move with the tide and get along with clients of all types.

Conduct of the Project

Thus the project began. Periodically, when decisions arose, North would seek opinions from division management. However, he was somewhat unclear about whom he should talk to. Davidson had been the person who had actually appointed him project leader. Normally, however, North worked for Ross. Although Kirk's laboratory was heavily involved in the project, Kirk was very busy with other Materials Laboratory work. Adding to his uncertainty, North periodically received telephone calls from Perkins of the Electronics Division, whom he didn't know well. Perkins expected to be heavily involved in the project.

Difficulties and delays began to plague the project. The microwave equipment specified by the client was not delivered by the manufacturer on schedule, and there were problems in filtering the power supply of the radio-frequency source. Over the objection of NRL Electromagnetic Sciences engineers, but at the insistence of the client, one of the chemical engineers tried to improve the power supply filter. Eventually the equipment had to be sent back to the manufacturer for modification. This required several months.

In the spring of 1973, Denby, who had made his presence felt from the outset, began to apply strong pressure. "Listen," he said to North, "top management of Exco is starting to get on my back and we need results. Besides, I'm up for review in four months and I can't afford to let this project affect my promotion." Denby was constantly at NRL during the next few months. He was often in the labs conferring individually with members of the NRL teams. Denby also visited North's office frequently.

A number of related problems began to surface. North had agreed to do both experimental and theoretical work for this project, but Denby's constant pushing for experimental results began to tilt the emphasis. Theoretical studies began to lapse, and experimental work became the focus of the Exco project. From time to time North argued that the theoretical work should precede or at least accompany the experimental program, but Denby's insistence on concrete results led North to temporarily deemphasize the theoretical work. Symptoms of this shifting emphasis were evident. One day a senior researcher from Kirk's laboratory came to North to complain that people were being "stolen" from his team. "How can we do a balanced project if the theoretical studies are not given enough manpower?" he asked. North explained the client's position and asked the researcher to bear with this temporary realignment of the project's resources.

As the six-month milestone approached, Denby expressed increasing dissatisfaction with the project's progress. In order to have concrete results to report to Exco management, he directed North a number of times to change the direction of the research. On several occasions various members of the project team had vigorous discussions with Denby about the risks of chasing results without laying a careful foundation. North himself spent a good deal of time talking with Denby on this subject, but Denby seemed to discount its importance. Denby began to avoid North and to spend most of his time with the other team members. Eventually the experimental program, initially dedicated to a careful screening of some 50 materials, deteriorated to a somewhat frantic and erratic pursuit of what appeared to be "promising leads." Lacy and Noble played little or no role in this shift of emphasis.

On June 21, 1973, Denby visited North in his office and severely criticized him for proposing a process (hydrochloric acid pickling) that was economically infeasible. In defense, North asked an NRL economist to check his figures. The economist reported back that North's numbers were sound and that, in fact, a source at U.S. Steel indicated that hydrochloric acid pickling was "generally more economic than the traditional process and was increasingly being adopted." Through this and subsequent encounters, the relationship between Denby and North became increasingly strained.

Denby continued to express concern about the Exco project's payoff. In an effort to save time, he discouraged the NRL team from repeating experiments, a practice that was designed to insure accuracy. Data received from initial experiments were frequently taken as sufficiently accurate, and after hasty analysis were adopted for the purposes of the moment. Not surprisingly Denby periodically discovered errors in these data. He informed NRL of them.

Denby's visits to NRL became more frequent as the summer progressed. Some days he would visit all three laboratories, talking to the researchers involved and asking them about encouraging leads. North occasionally cautioned Denby against too much optimism. Nonetheless, North continued to oblige the client by restructuring the Exco project to allow for more "production line" scheduling of experiments and for less systematic research.

In August, North discovered that vertile could be obtained from iron ore. This discovery was a significant one, and the client applied for a patent. If the reaction could be proved commercially, its potential would be measured in millions of dollars. Soon thereafter, the NRL team discovered that the operation could, in fact, be handled commercially in a rotary kiln. The client was notified and soon began planning a pilot plant that would use the rotary kiln process.

Exco's engineering department, after reviewing the plans for the pilot plant, rejected them. It was argued that the rotary process was infeasible and that a fluid bed process would have to be used instead. Denby returned to NRL and insisted on an experiment to test the fluid bed process. North warned Denby that agglomeration (a sticking together of the material) would probably take place. It did. Denby was highly upset, reported to Gray Kenney that he had not received "timely" warning of the probability of aggolmeration taking place, and indicated that he had been misled as to the feasibility of the rotary kiln process.[1]

Work continued, and two other "disclosures of invention" were turned over to the client by the end of September.

Personnel Changes

On September 30, Denby came to North's office to request that Charles Fenton be removed from the Exco project. Denby reported he had been watching Fenton in the Electromagnetic Laboratory, which he visited often, and had observed that Fenton spent relatively little time on the Exco project. North, who did not know Fenton well, agreed to look into it. But Denby insisted that Fenton be removed immediately and threatened to terminate the contract if he were allowed to remain.

North was unable to talk to Fenton before taking action because Fenton was on vacation. He did talk to Fenton as soon as he returned, and the researcher admitted that due to the pressure of other work he had not devoted as much time or effort to the Exco work as perhaps he should have.

Three weeks later, Denby called a meeting with Mac Davidson and Sam Lacy. It was their first meeting since the pre-proposal conference for the Exco project. Denby was brief and to the point:

[1]Ten months later the client was experimenting with the rotary kiln process for producing vertile from iron ore in his own laboratory.

Denby: I'm here because we have to replace North. He's become increasingly difficult to work with and is obstructing the progress of the project.

Lacy: But North is an awfully good man . . .

Davidson: Look, he's come up with some good solid work thus far. What about the process of extracting vertile from iron ore he came up with. And . . .

Denby: I'm sorry, but we have to have a new project leader. I don't mean to be abrupt, but it's either replace North or forget the contract.

Davidson reluctantly appointed Robert Kirk project leader and informed North of the decision. North went to see Davidson a few days later. Davidson told him that although management did not agree with the client, North had been replaced in order to save the contract. Later Dr. Lacy told North the same thing. Neither Lacy nor Davidson made an effort to contact Exco senior management on the matter.

Following the change of project leadership, the record became more difficult to reconstruct. It appeared that Kirk made many efforts to get the team together, but morale remained low. Denby continued to make periodic visits to the Institute but found that the NRL researchers were not talking as freely with him as they had in the past. Denby became skeptical about the project's value. Weeks slipped by. No further breakthroughs emerged.

Lacy's Problem

Doctor Lacy had received weekly status reports on the project, the latest of which is shown in Exhibit 2. He had had a few informal conversations about the project, principally with North and Kirk. He had not read the reports submitted to Exco. If the project had been placed on NRL's "problem list," which comprised about 10 percent of the projects which seemed to be experiencing the most difficulty, Lacy would have received a written report on its status weekly, but the Exco project was not on that list.

With the background given above, Lacy reread Kenney's letter terminating the Exco contract. It seemed likely that Kenney, too, had not had full knowledge of what went on during the project's existence. In his letter, Kenney mentioned the "glowing reports" which reached his ears in the early stages of the work. These reports, which came to him only from Denby, were later significantly modified, and Denby apparently implied that NRL had been "leading him on." Kenney pointed to the complete lack of economic evaluation of alternative processes in the experimentation. He seemed unaware of the fact that at Denby's insistence all economic analysis was supposed to be done by the client.

NORTHEAST RESEARCH LABORATORY (B)
Weekly Project Status Report

PROJECT/ACCOUNT STATUS REPORT	ORG	PROJ/ACCT SUB	W/O	WEEK ENDING DATE	TYPE	REV TYPE	PLACE	CLIENT	BILL SITE	MO/YR
	325	3273 000000		12-22-73	PROJ	INDUS	SCA	YD	3	ON DOMESTIC

DEPARTMENT	SUPERVISOR	LEADER	START DATE	STOP WORK DATE	BURDEN %	OVERHEAD %	FEE %
PHYSICAL SCI	CHEMISTRY LAB	ROBERT KIRK / ROBERT KIRK	11-06-72 -	11-06-74	28.00	105.00	15.00

EXCO

PROJECT TITLE: MICROWAVES IN CONVERSION OF BASIC ORES AND MINERALS

Cost Categories

COST CATEGORIES	OBJECT CODE	DOLLARS PTD	13 WK	TO DATE	LABOR HOURS ESTIMATE	TO DATE	BALANCE
SUPERVISOR	(11, 12)			560			36
SENIOR	(13)	192		17986			1348
PROFESSIONAL	(14)	150		16787			1678
TECHNICAL	(15)	629		5299			1037
CLER/SUPP	(16, 17, 18)			301			84
OTHER	(10, 19)	72		72			12
LABOR (S.T.)		943		41005			1644
BURDEN		248		11481			
OVERHEAD		1227		55110			
OVERTIME PREM	(21)	160		1540			
OVS./OTH. PREM	(22-29)	242		476			
TOTAL PERSONNEL COSTS		2820		109612			
TRAVEL	(55-59)			766			
SUBCONTRACT	(36)			3726			
MATERIAL	(41, 42)						
EQUIPMENT	(43)						
COMPUTER	(37, 45)						
COMMUN	(62, 63, 70, 71)	2		507			
CONSULTANT	(74, 75)						
REPORT COST	(44, 47)			99			
OTHER M&S		54		5098			
TOTAL M&S COST		56		5098			

LAST BILLING:
DATE 11-30-73
AMOUNT 11350

ACCOUNT STATUS TO DATE:
BILLED 154583
PAID 154583

TIME BALANCE % 39.4
COST BALANCE % 43.5
TIME BALANCE WKS. 41

COMMITMENTS	PTD	TO DATE	ESTIMATED	BALANCE
TOTAL LESS FEE	2876	141557	250435	108878
FEE (15.00)	158	24376	37565	13189
TOTAL	3031	165933	288000	122067

Commitment Status to Date

PO NO	DATE	OBJ	VENDOR/DESCRIPTION	TOTAL	CHARGES	BALANCE
A61289	11-21-73	41	MINNESOTA MINING	111	61	50
A61313	11-23-73	41	ALDRICH CHEMICAL	348		348
A95209	11-28-73	43	TENNECO CHEMICAL CO	5		5
A95003	11-15-73	41	UNION CARBIDE CORP	23194		23194
B95104	11-19-73	37	SCIENTIFIC PRODUCTS	600		600
B95232	11-25-73	41	VAN WATERS & ROGERS	2500		2500
018046	12-15-73	57	ROGER MD	300	150	150
		T		26847		26847

Transactions Recorded 12-15-73 - 12-22-73

LABOR

ORG	ID	W/E DATE	T/S NO	OBJ	NAME	HOURS WEEK	HOURS TO DATE
322	02345	12-22-73	363073	13	KIRK	6.0	150
322	02345	12-22-73	363073	22	KIRK	6.0	
322	03212	12-22-73	363082	13	DENSMORE	8.0	25
322	03260	12-22-73	236544	14	COOK	15.0	30
325	12110	12-08-73	C30093	15	HOWARD	15.0	82
325	12110	12-15-73	236548	15	HOWARD	36.0	
325	12110	12-22-73	376147	15	HOWARD	8.0	
325	12357	12-22-73	376149	15	SPELTZ	15.0	68
325	12369	12-22-73	376150	15	GYUIRE	15.0	17
325	12384	12-22-73	R08416	15	DILLON	40.0-	44
325	12397	12-22-73	336527	15	NAGY	31.0	31
325	12397	12-22-73	336527	21	NAGY	15.0	
652	12475	12-22-73	236548	15	KAIN	8.0	20
652	12475	12-22-73	236548	21	KAIN	15.0	

	HOURS	DOLLARS
LABOR (STRAIGHT TIME)	117.0	943
PAYROLL BURDEN		248
OVERHEAD RECOVERY		1227
OVERTIME PREMIUM LABOR	30.0	160
OTHER PREMIUM LABOR	6.0	242
TOTAL PERSONNEL COSTS		2820 S

MATERIALS & SERVICES

PO NO	REF NO	OBJ	DESCRIPTION	REQUESTOR	DOLLARS
61289	54065	48	438 REA EXPRESS	KIRK	42
17234	87413	48	456 GED SUPPLY CO	COOK	10
04461		71	448 P.T.&T. 326-6200	NAGY	2
TOTAL M&S COSTS					56
FEE					158 S
TRANSACTION TOTAL					3034 T

Exhibit 2. Northeast Research Laboratory (B) weekly project status report.

Kenney was most dissatisfied that NRL had not complied with all the provisions of the proposal, particularly those that required full screening of all materials and the completion of the theoretical work.

Lacy wondered why Denby's changes of the proposal had not been documented by the NRL team. Why hadn't he heard more of the problems of the Exco project before? Lacy requested a technical evaluation of the project from the economics process director and asked Davidson for *his* evaluation of the project. These reports are given in Exhibits 3 and 4. When he reviewed these reports, Lacy wondered what, if any, additional information he should submit to NRL top management.

Exhibit 3   Northeast Research Laboratory (B) TECHNICAL EVALUATION
by Ronald M. Benton,
Director, Process Economics Program.

Principal Conclusions

1. The original approach to the investigation as presented in the proposal is technically sound. The accomplishments could have been greater had this been followed throughout the course of the project, but the altered character of the investigation did not prevent accomplishment of fruitful research.

2. The technical conduct of this project on NRL's part was good, despite the handicaps under which the work was carried out. Fundamental and theoretical considerations were employed in suggesting the course of research and in interpreting the data. There is no evidence to indicate that the experimental work itself was badly executed.

3. Significant accomplishments of this project were as follows:

   a. *Extraction of vertile from iron ore by several alternative processes.* Conception of these processes was based on fundamental considerations and demonstrated considerable imagination. As far as the work was carried out at NRL, one or more of these processes offers promise of commercial feasibility.

   b. *Nitrogen fixation.* This development resulted from a laboratory observation. The work was not carried far enough to ascertain whether or not the process offers any commercial significance. It was, however, shown that the yield of nitrogen oxides was substantially greater than has previously been achieved by either thermal or plasma processes.

   c. *Reduction of nickel oxide and probably also garnerite to nickel.* These findings were never carried beyond very preliminary

Exhibit   **229**

stages and the ultimate commercial significance cannot be assessed at this time.

d. *Discovery that microwave plasmas can be generated at atmospheric pressure.* Again the commercial significance of this finding cannot be appraised at present. However, it opens the possibility that many processes can be conducted economically that would be too costly at the reduced pressures previously thought to be necessary.

4. The proposal specifically stated that the selection of processes for scale-up and economic studies would be the responsibility of the client. I interpret this to mean that NRL was not excluded from making recommendations based on economic considerations. Throughout the course of the investigation, NRL did take economic factors into account in its recommendations.

5. Actual and effective decisions of significance were not documented by NRL and only to a limited extent by the client. There was no attempt on NRL's part to convey the nature or consequences of such decisions to the client's management.

6. The NRL reports were not well prepared even considering the circumstances under which they were written.

7. It is possible that maximum advantage was not taken of the technical capabilities of personnel in the Electromagnetic Sciences Laboratory. Furthermore, they appeared to have been incompletely informed as to the overall approach to the investigation.

8. There was excessive involvement of the client in the details of experimental work. Moreover, there were frequent changes of direction dictated by the client. Undoubtedly these conditions hampered progress and adequate consideration of major objectives and accomplishments.

9. In the later stages of the project, the client rejected a number of processes and equipment types proposed by NRL for investigation of their commercial feasibility. From the information available to me, I believe that these judgments were based on arbitrary opinions as to technical feasibility and superficial extrapolations from other experience as to economic feasibility that are probably not valid.

Evaluation of Client's Complaints

Following are the comments responding to the points raised by the client management during your conversation:

1. *Client anticipated a "full research capability." He had hoped for participation by engineers, chemists, economists and particularly*

counted on the provision of an "analytical capability." It was this combination of talents that brought him to NRL rather than [a competitor]. He feels that the project was dominated almost exclusively by chemists.

This complaint is completely unfounded. All the disciplines appropriate to the investigation (as called for in the proposal) were engaged on the project to some degree. In addition, men of exceptional capabilities devoted an unusually large amount of time to the project. The client never officially altered the conditions of the proposal stating that no economic studies should be performed by NRL and there was no explicit expression of this desire on the part of the client until near the project termination.

2. *The analytical services were poor. They were sometimes erroneous and there were frequent "deviations." Data was given to the client too hastily, without further experiment and careful analysis, and as a result a significant amount of the data was not reproducible. NRL was inclined to be overly optimistic. "Glowing reports" would be made only to be cancelled or seriously modified later.*

There is no way of determining whether the analytical services were good or bad, but one can never expect all analytical work to be correct or accurate. Because the client insisted on obtaining raw data they would certainly receive some analyses that were erroneous. With respect to the allegation that NRL was overly optimistic, there were no recommendations or opinions expressed in the NRL reports or included in the client's notes that can be placed in this category. Whether or not there were verbal statements of this kind cannot of course be ascertained.

3. *There were "errors in the equations and the client was not informed of the changes." This refers to the case of a computer program that had not been "de-bugged." It was the client who discovered the errors and informed NRL of the discrepancies. (The program was eventually straightened out by the Math Sciences Department.)*

The client's complaint that they were given a computer program which had not been "de-bugged" is valid, but it is not certain that the project leadership gave them the program without exercising normal precautions for its accuracy. The program was developed by a person not presently with NRL and for another project. He transmitted it without any warning that "de-bugging" had not been conducted. It is even possible that the existence and source of error could not have been determined in his usage and would only appear in a different application.

4. *NRL told the client that the "vertile from iron ore" process could be handled commercially in a rotary kiln. Client prepared elaborate plans for this rotary kiln process and then was informed by his*

Exhibit   **231**

Engineering Division that this was completely infeasible. Plans were then shifted to a fluid bed process and much time and money had been wasted. Client claims that he was not warned that in the fluid bed agglomeration would probably take place. Agglomeration did take place the first time this process was tried ("open boats") and the client was greatly upset.

It is unclear whether the original suggestion that a rotary kiln be used in the vertile process came from the client or NRL. In any event, it is a logical choice of equipment and is used for the production of such low cost items as cement. Without the benefit of at least pilot plant experience that revealed highly abnormal and unfavorable conditions leading to excessive costs, no one would be in a position to state that such equipment would be uneconomic. It is true that a completely standard rotary kiln probably could not be employed, if for no other reason than to prevent the escape of toxic hydrogen sulfide gas from the equipment. At least special design would be needed and probably some mechanical development. However, it is rare that any new process can be installed without special design and development and it is naive to expect otherwise.

I do not know, of course, how much time was actually spent on the "elaborate plans" for the vertile process using a rotary kiln. I can, however, compare it with generally similar types of studies that we carry out in the Process Economics Program. For this kind of process we would expend about 45 engineering man-hours, and the design calculations would be more detailed than the client's engineer made (his cost estimates incidentally reflected inexperience in this field). I doubt, therefore, that this effort represented a serious expenditure of money and would not have been a complete waste even if the process had been based on a partially false premise.

The contention that the client was not informed of the agglomerating properties of the vertile while the reaction was taking place seems unlikely. The client's representatives were so intimately concerned with the experimental work that it would be unusual if the subject had not been raised. Moreover, it is doubtful that the client would have been deterred by NRL's warning, in view of their subsequent insistence that considerable effort be devoted to finding means by which a fluid bed could be operated.

5. *The meetings were poorly planned by NRL*

There is no way of evaluating this complaint, but certainly the extreme frequency of the meetings would not be conducive to a well-organized meeting.

6. *Experimental procedures were not well planned.*

Apparently this refers to the client's desire that experiments be planned in detail as much as three months in advance. Such an approach might conceivably be useful merely for purposes of gathering routine data. It is naive to think that research can or should be planned to this degree and certainly if NRL had acceded to the request it would have been a fruitless time-consuming exercise.

7. *Economic support was not given by NRL.*

   As mentioned above, the proposal specifically excluded NRL from economic evaluations, but NRL did make use of economic considerations in its suggestions and recommendations.

8. *NRL promised to obtain some manganese nodules but never produced them.*

   Manganese nodules were obtained by NRL but no experiments were ever run with them. Many other screening experiments originally planned were never carried out because of the changed direction of the project. It seems likely, therefore, that the failure to conduct an experiment with manganese nodules was not NRL's responsibility.

9. *The client claims that he does not criticize NRL for failing "to produce a process." He says that he never expected one, that he wanted a good screening of ores and reactions as called for in the proposal, and that he had hoped for results from the theoretical studies—Task B. This he feels he did not get. We did not do what the proposal called for.*

   The statement that a process was not expected seems entirely contrary to the course of the project. There was universal agreement among NRL personnel involved that almost immediately after the project was initiated it was converted into a crash program to find a commercial process. In fact, the whole tenor of the project suggests a degree of urgency incompatible with a systematic research program. It is quite true that the theoretical studies as a part of Task B were never carried out. According to the project leader this part of the proposal was never formally abandoned, it was merely postponed. Unfortunately, this situation was never documented by NRL, as was the case with other significant effective decisions.

Additional Comments

1. It appears that the first indication that the client expected economic studies or evaluations of commercial feasibility occurred during the summer of 1973. At this time the project leader was severely criti-

Exhibit   **233**

cized by the client's representatives for having proposed a process (hydrochloric acid pickling) that was economically infeasible. The basis for this criticism was that hydrochloric acid pickling of steel had not proved to be economically feasible. It is totally unreasonable to expect that NRL would have access to information of this kind, and such a reaction would certainly have the effect of discouraging any further contributions of an economic or commercial nature by NRL rather than encouraging them.

Actually it is patently ridiculous to directly translate economic experience of the steel industry with steel pickling to leaching a sulfided titanium ore. Nevertheless, I directed an inquiry to a responsible person in U.S. Steel as to the status of hydrochloric acid pickling. His response (based on the consensus of their experts) was diametrically opposite to the client's information. While there are situations that are more favorable to sulfuric acid pickling, hydrochloric acid pickling is generally more economic and is becoming increasingly adopted.

2. The reports written by NRL were requested by the client, but on an urgent and "not fancy" basis. If such were the case, it is understandable that the project leader would be reluctant to expend enough time and money on the report to make it representative of NRL's normal reports. However, the nature of the reports seems to indicate that they are directed toward the same individuals with whom NRL was in frequent contact, or persons with a strong interest in the purely scientific aspects. The actual accomplishments of the project were not brought out in a manner that would have been readily understandable to client's management.

Recommendations

It is recommended that consideration be given to the establishment of a simple formal procedure by which high risk projects could be identified at the proposal stage and brought to the attention of the Division Vice President. There should also be a formal procedure, operative after project acceptance, in which specific responsibilities are assigned for averting or correcting subsequent developments that would be adverse to NRL's and the client's interests.

Some of the factors that would contribute to a high risk condition are insufficient funding, insufficient time, low chance of successfully attaining the objectives, an unsophisticated client, public or private political conditions, etc. The characteristics that made this a high risk project were certainly apparent at the time the proposal was prepared.

Exhibit 4. Northeast Research Laboratory (B)

MEMORANDUM

To: Sam Lacy   Date: January 8, 1974
From: Mac Davidson
Re: The Exco Project—Conclusions

- The decision to undertake this project was made without sufficient consideration of the fact that this was a "high risk" project.

- The proposal was technically sound and within the capabilities of the groups assigned to work on the project.

- There was virtually no coordination between the working elements of Physical Sciences and Electronics in the preparation of the proposal.

- The technical conduct of this project, with few exceptions, was, considering the handicaps under which the work was carried out, good and at times outstanding. The exceptions were primarily due to lack of attention to detail.

- The NRL reports were not well prepared, even considering the circumstances under which they were written.

- The client, acting under pressure from his own management, involved himself excessively in the details of experimental work and dictated frequent changes of direction and emphasis. The proposal opened the door to this kind of interference.

- There was no documentation by NRL of the decisions made by the client which altered the character, direction and emphasis of the work.

- There was no serious attempt on the part of NRL to convey the nature or consequence of the above actions to the client.

- Less than half of the major complaints made by the client concerning NRL's performance are valid.

- The project team acquiesced too readily to the client's interference and management too easily to the client's demands.

- Management exercised insufficient supervision and gave inadequate support to the project leader in his relations with the client.

- There were no "overruns" either in time or funds.

CHAPTER **22**

Highlights

This last chapter of the book, like the last section of each chapter, consists of the most important points I've made. It provides a quick overview of everything you have read and may serve as a refresher before you start your next project.

- Projects, temporary undertakings with a specific objective that is accomplished by organized application of appropriate resources, have four distinguishing characteristics: origin, product, marketplace, and resources.

- Project management, which is the process of achieving the project objectives in any organizational framework despite countervailing pressures, consists of five steps: defining, planning, implementing, controlling, and completing.

- Five common organizational forms for project management are functional, project, matrix, venture, and task force.

- Projects are defined by the Triple Constraint: performance specification, time schedule, and money budget.

- Project specifics determine the relative importance of each dimension of the Triple Constraint.

- Proposals, which state what will be accomplished, connect the defining and planning phases of projects.

- Winning projects arise from good proposals, thoughtfully initiated to be consistent with the organization's goals.

- Writing proposals involves obtaining authorization, selecting the theme, preparing the statement of work, developing the plan, making adjustments, getting approval, submitting the proposal, and performing postsubmission follow-up.

- The proposal describes the Triple Constraint with a work breakdown structure, an activity network diagram or bar chart, and a cost estimate for each activity, which later serve as the project plan.

- Proposals should be made only if a contract is a realistic possibility.

- The contract form (fixed price, firm fixed price, cost plus fixed fee, cost plus incentive fee, and time and material, for example) determines whether the customer or the contractor will bear the financial risk.

- Both parties to the contract should be prepared to make concessions during negotiations.

- International projects introduce special problems, such as unfamiliar business practices, language, and currency and geographic distance.

- Plans, the written description of how the Triple Constraint will be satisfied, keep the project on course.

- Letting project personnel plan their own work is most likely to improve their motivation.

- Time spent planning should not exceed the time that would be spent correcting errors had there been no plan.

- The work breakdown structure identifies all work required to complete a project.

- The statement of work specifies what the customer will receive and when delivery will occur.

- Network diagrams, the most common forms of which are CPM and PERT, show activity interdependencies and clarify resource allocation.

- A network diagram, which must include every element in the work breakdown structure, should always be used to plan the schedule dimension of the Triple Constraint.

- Costs should be planned to the level of detail to which they must be reported.

- Cost estimates, usually made in dollars, can be "bottom up" or "top down," although it is best to use both, in that order.

- The elements of a project cost accounting system, a means to tally costs by project and project task, are labor, overhead burden, non-labor, and general and administrative burden.

- All project plans must contain schedule and cost contingency, which may be inserted as part of each task or by adding tasks near the end.

- Computers can be helpful in planning projects, although care must be taken to avoid entering incorrect data and making programming errors.

- Members of the project team (those who report to the project manager) may be members of the proposal team, others the organization employs, or people from outside the organization.

- It is frequently necessary to compromise by using whoever is available when making up the project team.

- Having members join and leave the project team as the work dictates and locating them near each other are two implementation techniques.

- The support team consists of those who work full- or part-time on a project for part or all of its duration but who do not report administratively to the project manager.

- Support groups should be involved as early as possible in projects and be allowed to plan their tasks.

- Every plan revision must be written out and distributed to all support and project team members who have copies of the original plan.

- Project managers need human relations skills.

- Managers plan the work; others perform it.

- Effective communication is aided by asking for feedback, issuing notices, and placing workers in close physical proximity.

- Positive reinforcement and brainstorming stimulate creativity.

- Comparison of reality with the project plan is the basis of project control.

- Project managers may exercise control over projects by requiring they approve every task or by trusting task managers, but the best approach is to check task status regularly.

- Reports, which may concern any axis of the Triple Constraint and be detailed or general, provide a means to examine the status of tasks.

- Periodic personal reviews are the best way for managers in charge of several projects to exercise control over them.

- Reviews, a project manager's most important control tool, may be periodic or topical.

- Periodic reviews should be conducted as appropriate for the project, but once a month is a good rule of thumb.

- The type of topical review used depends on the project and the customer's requirements.

- Actual project costs, which must be measured to control the cost dimension of the Triple Constraint, may also reveal schedule or performance dimension problems.

- Cost reports can show variances that result from timing, from actual work deviating from plan, or from overhead rate changes.

- Change, a project constant, may be a result of customer requests; such external events as a strike; altered environmental, health, and safety regulations; inflation; or resources being unavailable when needed.

- The seven steps to project problem solving are
  1. Identify the problem.
  2. Collect the relevant data.
  3. Find a solution.
  4. Seek several alternative solutions.
  5. Decide which is the best solution.
  6. Implement the best solution.
  7. Audit the outcome.

- Decision trees and qualitative or quantitative matrices are aids to choosing the best alternative.

- Specific meeting styles are associated with different problem-solving approaches.

- The best reason for terminating a project is satisfaction of its Triple Constraint, and the best way to do so is in an orderly and carefully planned fashion.

- Conditions of termination and acceptance must be specified in the contract.

- The project manager must understand that all personnel do not have the same stake in completion.

- Employees' perceptions of their futures will affect their performance as termination approaches.

- Projects may require postcompletion service and support, which can lead to future business.

- Careful record keeping is vital in case there is a postcompletion audit.

- Small projects are easier to understand and less likely to encounter difficulties, but they have less time and money to recover from any problems and invariably are given low priority.

- Factors that increase the odds of project success include the external (a smart and involved customer, project priority, top management support, and clear and stable objectives) and the internal (qualified, competent, experienced leadership; a team with a balance of skills; teamwork; properly sized work packages; plans; controls; plan revisions; and a well-planned termination).

- The following list summarizes the steps for successful project management:

  1. define
        project objectives
        statement of work with output specifications
        contract

  2. plan
        performance axis—work breakdown structure

schedule axis—network diagram
   initial trial
   activity times estimate
   critical path calculation
   adjustment
   contingency
cost axis—cost estimate by task and performing group
   each activity on network
   contingency

3. implement
   organization
   staffing

4. control
   inevitable problems
   reports
   reviews

5. complete
   delivery
   acceptance
   personnel reassignment
   follow-on work

Quiz Answers

1-1 _____

Something must be done.

There is a defined end result.

A person (or organization) wants it done.

It is a one-of-a-kind undertaking.

Resources are required.

Five sequential steps are taken.

There is a Triple Constraint.

(Size is not a factor.)

1-2 _____

Figure 1-4 shows SUPROMAC is organized functionally. By implication, there are other projects in SUPROMAC, so you are presumably going to operate as a project (or perhaps task force) organization.

2-1 _____

Projects are defined in three dimensions (performance specification, time schedule, and money budget), not merely in one dimension. Customer satisfaction requires an understanding of the relative emphasis to be placed on each dimension.

2-2 _____

There are several possibilities:

1. Try to convince NERESCO you are right and more materials should be studied, taking longer and costing more than they want.

2. Refuse to undertake the project.

3. Explain the risk to NERESCO in studying only a few materials

and jointly with them choose the specific (fewer) materials to be studied within their time and budget constraints.

The last is probably preferable in this case.

3-1

Avoid projects that are

> inconsistent with your organization's long-term goals
>
> inconsistent with your organization's current and near-term resources
>
> unlikely to win the proposal competition
>
> unlikely to satisfy the intended Triple Constraint
>
> insignificant or irrelevant

3-2

The following are some items for your project manager's checklist:
1. hardware engineering or study projects
> system review
> system approval
> system test criteria
> system test plan
> detailed hardware specification
> customer furnished equipment
> power requirement plan
> weight control plan
> breadboard design
> breadboard fabrication
> breadboard test
> block diagram
> schematic diagrams
> circuit diagrams
> conceptual design review
> preliminary design review
> critical design review
> final design review
> prototype design
> prototype fabrication
> prototype test
> design freeze
> drawings freeze
> functional designs

system logic design
optical design
mechanical design
electronic design
thermal design
subsystem hardware implementation
subsystem software implementation
subsystem integration
subsystem review
subsystem approval
subsystem test criteria
subsystem test plan
make/buy decisions
long lead items
special test equipment
commercial test equipment
calibration of test equipment
software tests
data reduction plan
operational software
subsystem cabling
system cabling
installation planning
experimental development plan
support plans
support instrumentation
facilities
training plans
repair facilities and requirements
inspection
preshipment review
customer inspection
customer acceptance
preparation for shipment
shipment
customer support
qualification test
flight acceptance test
launch support
mission support
personnel recruitment
personnel reassignment
documentation
   project plan
   integrated schedule
   functional requirements document

environmental requirements document
environmental test specifications
environmental test procedures
environmental test reports
interface control
safety plan
configuration control plan
failure mode and effect analysis
reliability and quality assurance plan
development test plan
acceptance test procedure
calibration plan
ground data-handling plan
experiment development plan
expendables consumption
engineering drawings and drawing list
parts list
electronic parts acquisition and screening plan
materials documentation
manufacturing release
periodic reports (for example, monthly)
special reports
final report
instruction manuals

reviews

manufacturing review
management review
critical design review
preshipment review
internal project reviews
subcontractor progress reviews
customer reviews

2. computer programming projects

applications requirements
system inputs
system outputs
design specification
program specifications
security plan
system test and acceptance specifications
feasibility studies
file and data requirements
cost and benefit analyses
program design
programming
testing

system implementation plan
turnover to operations
postimplementation reviews
documentation

3. engineering and construction projects
project work order plan
personnel assignment
client review meetings
public involvement meetings
environmental report
meetings with regulatory agencies
population projections
residential load projections
commercial load projections
industrial load projections
field checking
stream gauging records
stream gauging measurements
meteorological records
meteorological measurements
environmental baseline data
environmental sampling programs
ground surveys
photogrammetric surveys
geotechnical explorations
permits
access roads
hydrology
water quality and pollution studies
stability analysis
transient analysis
flood control studies
mathematical modeling
easement and permit drawings and descriptions
wiring diagrams
piping diagrams
construction cost estimates
estimated operation and maintenance costs
life cycle cost analysis
economic studies
value engineering
rate study
notice and instructions to bidders
bid schedules
contract documents
recommendations of award

shop drawing review
construction surveys
construction engineering
construction observation
construction record drawings

3-3

(A) The following are the steps in the proposal process:

Establish the organization's business strategy.

Understand the organization's resources.

Get the authorization (bid/no bid).

Make the preproposal effort.

Receive the RFP.

Attend the bidder's conference.

Fix the theme.

Prepare the statement of work.

Plan the job.

Adjust the proposal.

Approve the proposal.

Submit the proposal.

Present the proposal to the customer.

Negotiate the contract.

(B) The proposal contains a statement of work, which is the basic project definition. To prepare the proposal, it is necessary to do some, if not all, of the project planning. Much of this planning is commonly included in the proposal.

4-1

An FP contract is preferable when there is virtually no uncertainty about your ability to satisfy the performance specification on schedule and for, at most, your estimated costs. Such situations typically occur when you have done essentially the identical or very similar project work previously and you have the appropriate human and physical resources available.

If these conditions are not satisfied, the contract is a gamble and should be undertaken only if the risk is acceptable and the prospective reward is commensurate with it.

4-2 _____

Whenever one dimension of your proposed Triple Constraint is altered during negotiations, you must be certain compensating changes are made in the other dimensions.

5-1 _____

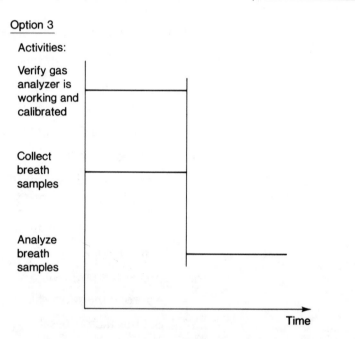

This option, with two activities being performed simultaneously (in "parallel," as it is sometimes called), requires two people (one to verify, one to collect); the other two options require only one person.

5-2 _____

Plans are used for the following purposes:

simulate how the project will be carried out

write the proposal

negotiate the contract

coordinate and communicate

motivate participants

control the project

satisfy requirements

avoid problems

record the choice between options

5-3 _____

A separate plan is required for each of the three dimensions of the Triple Constraint. These three plans must be integrated and consistent.

6-1 _____

Figure 6-1 includes the hardware for a photovoltaic solar power system, but the WBS does not list a shipping container, the installation and operation instructions, a warranty document, or a user training program, some of which might reasonably be a part of such a project.

6-2 _____

The WBS could be either of the following:

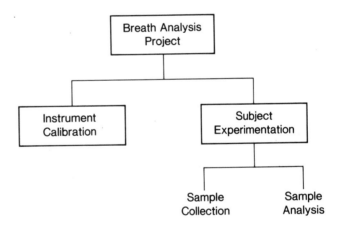

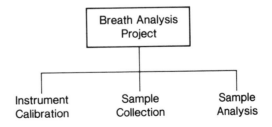

7-1 _____

Arrow Diagramming Exercise

Suggested Solution

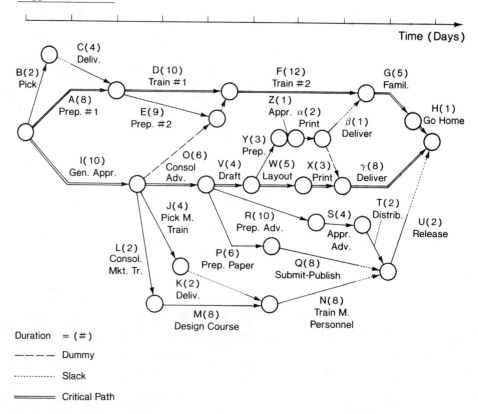

(Adaptation of Arrow Diagramming Exercise—Suggested Solution, 9-672-001, Harvard Business School. Used with permission.)

7-2 _____

Note the use of vertical dashed lines, without any dependency arrow indication, permits a node to be drawn in more than one location. This permits spatial separation of activities, thus providing additional open space in the network diagram.

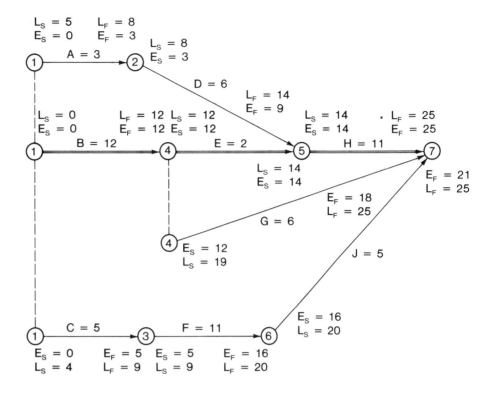

7-3

$$T_e = \left[\frac{4 + (4 \times 7) + 16}{6}\right] + \left[\frac{1 + (4 \times 7) + 25}{6}\right] + \left[\frac{2 + (4 \times 11) + 26}{6}\right]$$

$$= 8 + 9 + 12 = 29$$

$$\sigma = \left[\left(\frac{16 - 4}{6}\right)^2 + \left(\frac{25 - 1}{6}\right)^2 + \left(\frac{26 - 2}{6}\right)^2\right]^{1/2}$$

$$= [36]^{1/2} = 6$$

Two-thirds of the time this project will be completed in a duration between $(29 - 6 =)$ 23 days and $(29 + 6 =)$ 35 days. The remaining one-third of the probable completion times are shorter than 23 and greater than 35. Because these are equally likely, $(\frac{1}{2} \times \frac{1}{3} =)$ $\frac{1}{6}$ of the time it is expected completion will require more than 35 days. (Because I wished to use only small integers and obtain an easy square root extraction, the ratio of pessimistic to optimistic times has become unreasonably large in tasks 2 and 3. In general, this ratio would rarely exceed 4, with 2 or 3 being more common maxima.)

7-4 _____

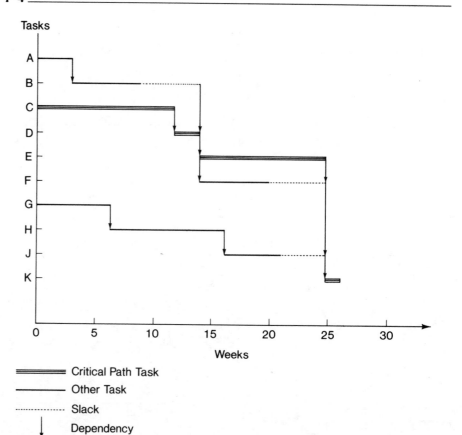

Tasks

Critical Path Task

Other Task

Slack

Dependency

8-1 _____

PROJECT _____ TASK _____ DEPARTMENT _____

COST ELEMENT		A HOURS EACH MONTH						TOTALS	
		1	B 2 C	C 3	4	5	6	HOURS	DOLLARS
LABOR	SR. PROF. $25/hr.	160	100	60				320	8,000
	JR. PROF. $20/hr.		160	80				240	4,800
	SR. TECH. $15/hr.		80					80	1,200
	JR. TECH. $10/hr.		160					160	1,600
DOLLARS EACH MONTH									
DOLLARS	LABOR COST								15,600
	OVERHEAD 100%								15,600
	DIRECT NON-LABOR	1,000	2,000						3,000
	PRIME COSTS								34,200
	G & A 15%								5,130
	TOTAL COSTS								39,330
	PROFIT 20%								
	TOTAL BILLING								

ASSUMPTIONS _____

PREPARED BY _____ DATE _____ APPROVED BY _____

9-1 _____

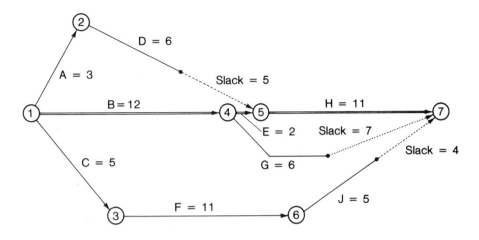

The saving of $200 / week can be obtained
for only four weeks, after which path
C-F-J also becomes a critical path.

Depending on the certainty you feel for C-F-J and B-E-H, it might be better
to shorten only activity B by three weeks, thus maintaining only one critical path.

10-1 _____

Nature of Reporting Relationship / Duration of Project Assignment	Reports to Project Manager		Works on Project but Reports to Another Manager	
	Works Only on Project	Also Has Other Assignment(s)	Works Only on Project	Also Has Other Assignment(s)
From Start to Finish				
Only a Portion of Project's Duration	A Option 1	B Option 1	A Option 2	B Option 2

Note that theoretical tasks do not run from start to finish of the entire
project.

10–2 _____

Personnel on the project team may do any of the following:

> quit (either the company or the organizational unit) to work elsewhere
>
> be sick
>
> be reassigned to other work by higher management
>
> lack interest in the project
>
> still be working to complete previously assigned tasks that have been delayed

11–1 _____

A project manager might prefer a large support team for any of the following reasons:

> He or she will not have to worry about its members when the project is completed.
>
> In the case of subcontractors, the support agreement is embodied in a legally binding instrument, namely, the subcontract or purchase agreement.
>
> The project manager has the whole world in which to find specialists or experts with the required skill.

11–2 _____

It depends. In general, it is probably best to advise subcontractors of your true need date. If you do this, you make it easier for them, and their costs to you will be lower (at least in the long run). But if subcontractors have a history of lateness, it is probably best (1) to have originally allowed time contingency for their work and (2) not to let them know of any delay you have experienced.

12–1 _____

Plan what is to be communicated beforehand rather than trying to decide while communicating. As it is sometimes stated, "Put brain in gear before opening mouth."

Use face-to-face meetings in which you can observe the other person's "body language." Allow enough time at an appropriate time of the day.

Decide which sequence and combination of telephone discussion, face-to-face meeting, and memo will be most effective.

Be consistent and follow through with actions appropriate to your message.

Use simple language.

12-2

Practice specialization and collect similar activities (dictation and telephoning, for example) so they can be done in one bloc of time. One long meeting with another person will accomplish far more than spending the same amount of time in several shorter meetings.

Delegate—that is why project personnel are assigned to the project.

Insist on quiet time for thinking—no telephone calls and no visitors. This is when you plan and think through critical issues.

Plan all meetings. Have you ever gone to a meeting for which the purpose was unclear?

Reduce paperwork. Never handle a piece of paper twice. Try to reply to memos, letters, and such by a handwritten note on the document.

13-1

There is a long period of time in the middle of the project when there are no scheduled task completions. Thus, there are no certain checkpoints available, leaving considerable uncertainty as to actual status.

14-1

The first concern would be the status on tasks H, L, and F. Does these tasks not yet being complete indicate the project is hopelessly behind schedule?

The second area of concern has to do with knowing the critical path for this particular project. In this case, the concern is whether the completed activities have already caused the project to slip hopelessly or whether the schedule variations have no significance with regard to the overall project.

14-2

As the project progresses, the participants learn more about what is involved. Also, replanning may occur, and the necessity for new tasks may become apparent.

15-1 _____

Overhead (and general and administrative burden) rates change because the actual overall business mix of the organization differs from the assumed or planned mix when the rates were initially calculated. As indicated in the text example, this can be caused by a work load mix being changed. It can also be caused by the amount of overhead expense differing from plan.

16-1 _____

Some of the changes that might occur and lead to a scope change on the material studies project are extra materials to be evaluated; a customer request to provide a duplicate experimental setup for their own use; and a formal briefing requested by the customer at the end of the job, to be supplied in addition to the written final report.

16-2 _____

Basically, you inform your customer as soon as possible after you have completed a reasonable comparison of alternative solutions to the problem. Because there is a natural reluctance to be the bearer of bad tidings and because there may always be more alternatives to consider, there is a tendency to delay.

Once the customer has been informed and has a chance to consider the issues, it is usually necessary to amend the contract in some way. Verbal redirection is not binding, although it may be acted upon (if customer relations are satisfactory) while the contract is actually being renegotiated.

17-1 _____

Formula Expression	Expression's Value					
	$n=1$	$n=2$	$n=3$	$n=4$	$n=5$	$n=6$
n	1	2	3	4	5	6
$n - (n-1)(n-2)(n-3)(n-4)$	1	2	3	4	-19	-114
$n+3(n-1)(n-2)(n-3)(n-4)(n-5)$	1	2	3	4	5	366

The point of this quiz is to show there are alternatives.

17-2

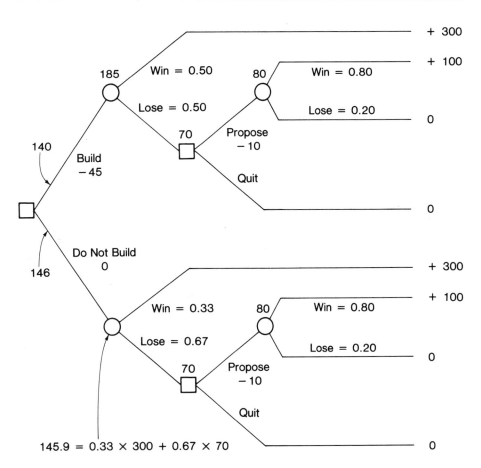

Do not build, because that has a higher value. Another way to look at this revised situation is to realize that losing the original job is less serious, having an expected value of $70,000 instead of zero.

17-3 _____

Criteria	Weighting Factor	Solution Approach 1	Solution Approach 2	Solution Approach 3
Performance Target A	0.2	60%	90%	80%
Performance Target B	0.1	90%	70%	70%
Performance Target C	0.2	90%	50%	90%
Schedule Target	0.3	70%	70%	90%
Cost Target	0.2	90%	80%	70%
Weighted Percentage Value		78%	72%	82%

In this case, solution approach 3 is now preferred. Proponents of a particular solution will manipulate this kind of matrix by arguing for high weights on factors for which their solution has a high achievement factor.

18-1 _____

As a minimum, you are going to have to participate in fact finding. At one extreme, the acceptance criteria will have been absolutely clear; the tests at your company will have been unambiguous; participation in and witnessing of these tests will have been done by qualified and responsible senior personnel; and the performance shortfall at their facility will be attributable entirely to their own actions.

More likely, questions will arise about the acceptance test, the specific equipment used to perform it (for example, accuracy, calibration procedures, or the possibility of stray magnetic fields), or what might have occurred to change the system during delivery. Regardless of contract form or your desire to obtain more business from that customer, the customer's final happiness with how well the system solves his or her problem will affect your reputation, so you may well have to engage in a lot of extra, perhaps unpaid, effort to help get the system working. In some cases, you may be able to show the fault was theirs and get them to pay you for your extra effort.

19-1 _____

The responsibility for obtaining payment usually resides with the accounts receivable department and is thus outside the normal purview of the project manager. Nevertheless, an effective project manager may be able to help persuade a slow-paying customer to pay promptly. And the project manager, in considering the possibility of obtaining more work from the customer, will be concerned with the customer's payment history because that can influence the desirability of further work. If further work is desired, the project manager does not want the accounts receivable department to take hostile action against a delinquent account. Thus, the project manager and the accounts receivable department must discuss these issues and mutually decide on the mix of persuasion, cajoling, or legal action to take.

20-1 _____

There are at least four options to consider:

1. Be late on the small project.
2. Request you spend only one-quarter time on the large project so you can spend three-quarters on the small one.
3. Request paid overtime approval for the small project.
4. Simply work unpaid overtime on the small project.

The choice among these, and any other viable options, can be aided by a qualitative matrix.

21-1 _____

At its simplest, the Northeast Research Laboratory (NRL) case is concerned with the issue of what controls are feasible to make management aware of impending difficulties. This key issue is identified in the last sentence of the second paragraph: "What should he recommend to avoid the recurrence of such a situation in the future?"

There were innumerable danger signals from the beginning that should have alerted NRL management to the problems on this project:

1. NRL was hungry, anxious for new business of any sort.
2. This project was a commercial effort, whereas NRL was accustomed to government contracts.
3. It was a multidivisional and multilaboratory project, whereas by implication NRL typically had projects within one group.

4. There was pressure from the customer to submit a proposal very quickly.

5. A letter proposal was informally prepared and submitted, rather than preparing a formal proposal with appropriate controls.

6. A scientist (North) was appointed to act as manager.

7. Ross's view of Denby was never taken into account.

8. There was the issue of the power supply.

9. Denby's interest in his salary review was self-serving.

10. Denby pressured for change of direction without formal documentation.

11. Denby criticized North.

12. Denby removed Fenton from the project.

13. Denby removed North from the project.

The purpose of the case is to have you formulate recommendations. The following recommendations are important and appropriate:

1. NRL presently has a functional organization. If more multidisciplinary projects are to be undertaken, NRL should consider instituting a matrix organization. This would provide a better focal point for multidisciplinary projects. If that is not done, the vice-president of research operations should be involved in future multidisciplinary projects.

2. NRL needs a more organized and disciplined way to conduct its business. There should be a formal proposal sign-off procedure at NRL. When a contract is received, it should be done so formally. Any later changes to it should be documented and signed off by officially designated people. If a person who is supposed to approve the proposal or contract change is absent, there should be a formalized system to vest his or her authority in another person (that is, delegation upward or downward). And all contracts should include clear measurables with regard to project completion. In this case, such measurables might be the number of ores to be tested.

3. In instances where customers exert great time pressure to start an effort, the project might be allowed to start on the basis of a letter of intent. In such a case, it should be clear that project effort cannot exceed one month duration (or some dollar limitation) to avoid the development of future problems. During this initial effort, a formal contract must be negotiated or work must then stop.

4. NRL requires a project control system. As an absolute minimum, there should be formal internal project reviews by some level of

management every month. Beyond that, it is a good idea to insist on them occasionally with the customer, externally. The 10 percent list at NRL should be changed to a problem list (suppose 15 percent of the projects are in trouble), and the criteria by which projects are designated for inclusion on the list should be clarified. There were more than enough danger signals on the Exco contract for NRL to have identified it as a problem contract. Although it is not absolutely certain from a reading of the case, it appears from Exhibit 2 that the basis for getting onto the 10 percent list is purely financial, whereas there should be other bases by which projects can get onto a problem list for management attention.

5. The entire project management function should be clarified. Regardless of organizational form, the project leader's responsibility and authority must be clarified. Beyond this, criteria for leader selection might be established and a training program made available for those scientifically trained personnel who are assuming managerial responsibilities.

6. NRL needs a better client interface policy. This might require all visitors to be escorted on NRL premises at all times.

7. Morale will need rebuilding. NRL has been storing up some people problems, especially with North and Fenton, and these will have to be dealt with promptly.

In summary, NRL failed to define, plan, implement, and control the project, so their customer did not let them complete it.

Although it is not really a part of the case, another issue is whether the project should be terminated or whether it could be resold. Lacy is a free-reign, laissez-faire type of manager and therefore might not be dynamic enough to resell the program, but a different kind of manager might well be able to do so. The basis on which this might be done would be first to institute the previously noted recommendations. Then NRL could approach Kenney at Exco, citing both the good work done on the original contract and NRL managerial changes. Such an approach might very well lead to an authorization to continue the work. Also, Kenney might ask about Denby's involvement and then replace him as the liaison representative or at least check on his involvement periodically.

Glossary

Actual cost of work performed (ACWP)   A term in the Cost/Schedule Control System Criteria (C/SCSC) system for the costs actually incurred and recorded in accomplishing the work performed within a given time period

Bar chart   A scheduling tool (also called a Gantt chart) that shows the time span of each activity as a horizontal line, the ends of which correspond to the start and finish of the activity as indicated by a date line at the bottom of the chart

Bid/no bid decision   The decision whether to submit a proposal in response to an RFP

Bottom up cost estimating   Making detailed estimates for every task in the work breakdown structure and summing them to provide a total project cost estimate or plan

Budgeted cost of work performed (BCWP)   A term in the Cost/Schedule Control System Criteria (C/SCSC) system for the sum of the budgets for completed work packages and completed portions of open work packages plus the appropriate portion of the budgets for level of effort and apportioned effort

Budgeted cost of work scheduled (BCWS)   A term in the Cost/Schedule Control System Criteria (C/SCSC) system for the sum of budgets for all work packages, planning packages, and similar items scheduled to be accomplished (including in-process work packages) plus the amount of level of effort and apportioned effort scheduled to be accomplished within a given time period

Burst node   A node in a network diagram at which two or more activities commence when the preceding activity is completed

Buy-in   A proposal cost bid that is unduly optimistic or even less than the estimated project costs made in order to win the job

Chart room   A room filled with planning documents displayed as charts, typically hung on the walls, used on large projects and usually marked to indicate current status

Commitment   An obligation to pay money at some future time, such as a purchase order or travel authorization, that represents a charge to a project budget although it is not yet actually paid

Contingency   An amount of design margin, time, or money inserted into the corresponding Triple Constraint plan as a safety factor to accommodate unexpected and presently unknown occurrences that may arise during the project

Cost plus fixed fee (CPFF) contract   A contractual arrangement in which the customer agrees to reimburse the contractor's actual costs, regardless of amount, and pay a negotiated fee independent of them

Cost plus incentive fee (CPIF) contract   A contractual arrangement similar to CPFF except the fee depends on some specified result, such as timely delivery

Cost/Schedule Control System Criteria (C/SCSC)   A U.S. Department of Defense planning and control reporting system intended to foster greater uniformity and provide early warning of impending schedule or budget overruns

Costed work breakdown structure   A work breakdown structure showing costs corresponding to its major elements

Critical path   In a network diagram, the longest path from start to finish or the path without any slack, thus the path corresponding to the shortest time in which the project can be completed

Critical Path Method (CPM)   A network diagram with the activities labeled on the arrows

Customer furnished equipment (CFE)   Equipment the customer provides to the contractor for the project that is typically specified in the contract

Documentation   Any kind of written report, including such items as final reports, spare parts lists, instruction manuals, and test plans

Dummy activity   An activity in a network diagram that requires no work, signifying a precedence condition only

Earliest finish   In a network diagram schedule, the earliest time an activity can be completed

Earliest start   In a network diagram schedule, the earliest time an activity can be started

Firm fixed price (FFP) contract   A contractual form in which the price and fee are predetermined and not dependent on cost

Fixed price (FP) contract   Same as FFP

Functional organization   An organizational form that groups all people with a particular kind of skill (such as engineering) in one department, reporting to a single manager for that functional speciality

Government furnished equipment (GFE)   The same as CFE in projects where the customer is a governmental entity

Hardware project   A project in which the principal deliverable item is a product or functioning device

Latest finish   In a network diagram schedule, the latest time an activity can be finished

Latest start   In a network diagram schedule, the latest time an activity can be started

Matrix organization   An organization with a project management functional speciality and other functional specialities where the project management function has responsibility for accomplishing the project work by drawing upon the other functional specialities as required

Merge node A node in a network diagram at which two or more activities precede the start of the subsequent activity

Milestone A major event in a project that typically requires the customer to approve further work

Network diagram A scheduling tool displaying activities or events as arrows and nodes that show the logical precedence conditions between them

Periodic review Any kind of project review conducted on a periodic basis, most commonly a monthly project review

"The Plan" A document or group of documents that constitutes all project plans, frequently contained in a notebook or series of notebooks

Planning matrix A matrix listing planned activities on one side (usually the left) and involved people or groups across a perpendicular side (usually the top) and showing involvement of an individual or group in a particular activity by a tic mark where the row and column intersect

Program Evaluation and Review Technique (PERT) A network diagram that displays events as nodes and precedence constraints as connecting arrows

Progress payments Payments made to the contractor by the customer during the course of the project rather than at the end, the terms of which are specified in the contract

Project An organized undertaking utilizing human and physical resources, done once, to accomplish a specific goal, which is normally defined by a Triple Constraint

Project cost accounting system A cost accounting system that accumulates actual costs for projects in such a way that total costs for all work in an organization can be allocated to the appropriate projects, normally providing monthly cost summaries; also used in cost planning to summarize the detailed task cost estimates

Project organization The form of organization in which all or nearly all the people working on a project report to the project manager

Project plan The entire plan for a project, consisting of the WBS, network diagram, and task budgets; sometimes taken to mean only the network diagram

Project team A term used in this book to designate the personnel working on a project who report to the project manager administratively, not merely for the work on the project

Proposal A document (sometimes accompanied by models) submitted to a prospective customer that describes work being offered

Request for proposal (RFP) A document one organization issues to another organization (or to several other organizations) describing work the issuer wishes the recipient(s) to undertake and inviting the recipient(s) to respond with a proposal

Request for quotation (RFQ)   Similar to an RFP except the desired items are stock or catalog items and only price and delivery time need be proposed

Slack time   The amount of time on any path in a network diagram other than the critical path that is the difference between the time to a common node on the critical path and the other path

Software project   A project in which the principal deliverable item is a report or other form of documentation, such as a computer program

Statement of work (SOW)   That portion of a proposal or the resulting contract that states exactly what will be delivered and when

Subcontractor   An organization, usually a company, working for another organization on some aspect of the project for which the other organization is under contract

Support team   A term used in this book to designate the personnel working on a project who do not report to the project manager administratively

Task force   An ad hoc group designated to cope with a project, similar to a project organization although frequently staffed with personnel on part-time assignment, usually adopted by a functional organization having only one project or at most a few projects at any given time

Time and material (T and M) contract   A contractual form in which the customer agrees to pay the contractor for all time and material used on the project, including a fee as a percentage of all project costs

Time compression   Reducing the planned time for an activity, accomplished perhaps by adding unplanned staff or using overtime

Top down cost estimating   Making a cost estimate or plan by using judgment and experience to arrive at an overall amount; usually done by an experienced manager making a subjective comparison of the project to similar previous projects

Topical review   Any kind of project review devoted to a single topic, such as a final design or manufacturing review

Triple Constraint   The term used in this book to describe the three key project objectives that must be simultaneously accomplished, namely, the performance specification, the time schedule, and the monetary budget

Work breakdown structure (WBS)   A family tree, usually product oriented, that organizes, defines, and graphically displays the hardware, software, services, and other work tasks necessary to accomplish the project objectives

Venture organization   The form used in some large organizations where a three- or four-person team, itself functionally organized, is established within the larger organization to develop and commercialize a new product

Index